THE COMPANY TOWN

The *Company* TOWN

The Industrial Edens and
Satanic Mills That Shaped
the American Economy

HARDY GREEN

BASIC BOOKS
A Member of the Perseus Books Group
New York

Books published by Basic Books are available at special discounts for bulk
purchases in the United States by corporations, institutions, and other
organizations. For more information, please contact the Special Markets
Department at the Perseus Books Group, 2300 Chestnut Street,
Suite 200, Philadelphia, PA 19103, or call (800) 810-4145, ext. 5000,
or e-mail special.markets@perseusbooks.com.

Designed by Brent Wilcox
Type set in 11.75 point Adobe Garamond

Library of Congress Cataloging-in-Publication Data
Green, Hardy.
    The company town : the industrial Edens and satanic mills that
shaped the American economy / Hardy Green.
        p.   cm.
    Includes bibliographical references and index.
    ISBN 978-0-465-01826-0 (alk. paper)
    1. Company towns—United States—History.   2. Industries—
United States—History.   3. Industrial relations—United
States—History.   I. Title.
    HT123.G723 2010
    307.76'70973—dc22
                                                    2010013434

10 9 8 7 6 5 4 3 2 1

For Maruja

CONTENTS

Introduction

In 1917 the Pinkerton Detective Agency sent twenty-three-year-old Dashiell Hammett to help break a miners' strike against the Anaconda Copper Co. in Butte, Montana. Hammett—who would later gain fame for his hardboiled detective fiction, such as *The Maltese Falcon*—had worked for two years for Pinkerton, tracking stolen property, transporting prisoners, and shadowing suspects. He later said he'd had no political consciousness when he was sent to Butte. But he did discover that he didn't like strikebreaking.

The Butte strike was sparked by a mine fire that killed 178 miners. It was led by the radical, syndicalist union, the Industrial Workers of the World (IWW)—the romantic organizer of down-and-outs, miners, lumberjacks, oil-field roustabouts, and immigrant textile workers. The union's slogan was "One Big Union" in a day when most union "brotherhoods" defined themselves along craft lines and seemed more like fraternities than the embodiment of the cooperative commonwealth. The IWW's symbol was an arched-back black cat, yowling at the viewer—an image associated with sabotage and machine-breaking in the name of militancy and worker solidarity.

In Butte, the IWW's man was Frank Little, a one-eyed, part-Indian whirlwind of an organizer. Known as the "hobo agitator," he had been at the center of worker struggles in Fresno, San Diego, Duluth, and most of the major IWW conflicts. An Anaconda executive offered Hammett $5,000 to shoot Little—or so Hammett later said—but the young Pinkerton agent declined. No matter. In short order, vigilantes apprehended Little and lynched him at a railroad crossing along with three other perceived troublemakers.

1

Hammett decided he'd had enough, quit the detective agency, and joined the U.S. Army.[1] But he never forgot Butte, which he later immortalized as "Personville" (nicknamed "Poisonville") in his first novel, *Red Harvest*, a crime fiction classic. "The city wasn't pretty," he wrote. "The smelters whose brick stacks stuck up tall against a gloomy mountain to the south had yellow-smoked everything into uniform dinginess. The result was an ugly city of forty thousand people, set in an ugly notch between two ugly mountains that had been all dirtied up by mining."[2] But the biggest stain on Butte, in Hammett's eyes, may well have been the Anaconda Copper Co. itself.

Created at the turn of the twentieth century by a charismatic Irishman named Marcus Daly, Anaconda was soon involved in suspect dealings. Standard Oil directors James Stillman, William Rockefeller, and Henry H. Rogers bought the company with borrowed money, renamed it, and quickly resold it to gullible investors, pocketing a profit of $36 million.[3] Another early owner was George Hearst, father of newspaper magnate William Randolph Hearst. The company passed through various corporate hands and by the 1920s held a virtual monopoly over the mines in and around Butte. The town, once known for gold and silver mining, grew prosperous thanks to the area's abundant copper, which was increasingly in demand for electrical wiring. Butte attracted workers from around the world—and became known as a wide-open Sin City. Its red-light district, "The Line," featured hundreds of saloons and houses of prostitution.

But contrary to this image of freedom and licentiousness, Butte was in fact locked down—totally under Anaconda's thumb. In *Red Harvest*, Hammett captures the spirit of the town: "For forty years old Elihu Willsson . . . had owned Personville, heart, soul, skin, and guts. He was president and majority stockholder of the Personville Mining Corporation, ditto of the First National Bank, owner of *The Morning Herald* and *Evening Herald*, the city's only newspapers, and at least part owner of nearly every other enterprise of any importance. Along with these pieces of property he owned a United States senator, a couple of representatives, the governor, the mayor, and most of the state legislature. Elihu Willsson was Personville, and he was almost the whole state."

Hammett's Willsson was likely a fictional amalgam of many rough-hewn executives of the day. But it's possible that the author had in mind

John D. Ryan, a former department store clerk who succeeded Daly and ran Anaconda until his own death in 1933.

Anaconda remained hugely powerful not only in the town but across Montana, so much so that in 1946, when reporter John Gunther published his celebrated panorama of American life, *Inside U.S.A.*, he observed, "For years the company dominated both parties, and controlled almost all elections, if necessary by dragging in the 'cemetery vote.'" Gunther painted a picture of Anaconda as greedy and stingy—keeping other industry out of the area so labor remained cheap, removing far more riches from Montana than it ever put in. "Aside from one threadbare little park . . . it has never given the city of Butte, from which it has extracted a roaring Golconda of wealth, anything," he wrote.[4]

It is companies like Anaconda and the experience of towns like Butte that have tainted a term familiar to us all: company town. To those who like to think of the United States as a sweet land of liberty, the very words sound un-American. A company town seems necessarily to be a place where one business exerts a Big Brother–like grip over the population—controlling or even taking the place of government, collecting rents on company-owned housing, dictating buying habits (possibly at the company store), even administering where people worship and how they may spend their leisure time.

It's true: Company towns are un-American—and they are the essence of America.

The United States has a unique experience with company towns. With its vast expanse of virgin land and a government that has generally taken a laissez-faire attitude toward business, the United States has provided a greater opportunity for developing such settlements than other countries. The United States also has a tradition of social experimentation: If the Pilgrims could construct their ideal City on a Hill, so too could American businessmen create their own communities, from Lowell, Massachusetts, to Pullman, Illinois; Morris Run, Pennsylvania; and Valsetz, Oregon. By one estimate, more than 2,500 single-enterprise towns once dotted the country.

Trace America's economic evolution, and you get a tour of company towns—from early textile sites such as Lawrence, Massachusetts, and Manchester, New Hampshire, to today's company campuses in New York state and California. Along the way, you'll have to take note of coal towns in Pennsylvania, Ohio, Colorado, and Appalachia; steel towns in the Monongahela River valley and Illinois; Texas and Oklahoma oil camps; shipbuilding centers in Connecticut and California; meatpacking burgs in Iowa, South Dakota, and Minnesota; and the government company town of Oak Ridge, Tennessee.

Some of America's seminal industries have faded from the scene—and along with them, the towns they were associated with have fallen into decrepitude or even disappeared. Hard times are irrevocably associated today with Lowell; Gary, Indiana; the former textile villages of North and South Carolina; and such once-proud meatpacking towns as Ottumwa, Iowa.

But company towns are not simply a phenomenon of the past: In an age of transnational corporations and exurban sprawl, company towns remain a basic part of American life. They are as near as Corning, New York, and Hershey, Pennsylvania, their products as familiar as Tabasco Sauce, Spam, and Kohler bathroom fixtures.

And maybe even as familiar as Google. For in a remote part of Oregon along the banks of the Columbia River, that company recently built a large industrial complex mostly in secret. The facility, known as Project 02, stretches over several acres, with electric-power equipment much in evidence. Given Google's business, it can hardly be surprising that the prime residents of the campus's three large buildings are computer servers—perhaps tens of thousands of inexpensive processors and disks—necessary to keep Google's search engines and Web services humming. But a few humans are needed, too, if the effort is to be completed and maintained. "The project has created hundreds of construction jobs, caused local real estate prices to jump 40 percent, and is expected to create 60 to 200 permanent jobs in a town of 12,000 people," wrote the *New York Times* in 2006.[5] That means that fundamentally, what may be coming together in The Dalles, Oregon, is a contemporary—and low-employment—version of the company town.

Such towns generally tend toward one of two models, although many fall in between. In this account, I will refer to the Butte model as "exploitationville." Perhaps the apotheosis of such towns may be found in Appalachian coal country, home of the likes of Lynch, Wheelwright, and Coal Run, Kentucky. The logic behind such places is simple and familiar. It rests on the thinking of every bean counter: Business exists to make a profit, not to coddle employees. Society as a whole benefits most when enterprises are cost-effective, productive, and profitable. The very ruthlessness that surfaced in these places seems less like an inevitable outgrowth of such logic than a willful expression of malicious personalities.

But another model regularly shows up in the United States, recurring across the decades: ideal communities backed by companies that promise to share their bounty with workers and their families. These utopian towns were and are characterized by modern public buildings, libraries and facilities for leisure, education, and cultural enrichment, and comfortable dwellings for managers and workers. A paternalistic attitude may be present as well—sometimes resulting in a watchfulness toward the citizenry on the part of the company overlords: Such guardians have tended to favor tidiness in housekeeping, sobriety, and oftentimes regular religious observance.

Although one might expect idealistic experiments to fade as industrial society matured, instead the utopian model has resurfaced again and again. For example, in Pullman, Illinois, the eponymous railroad-car maker in the 1880s erected a model town where "advanced secular Gothic buildings" lined tree-shaded streets. Scotia, California, founded by Pacific Lumber as a rustic forest camp in the 1880s, evolved into a pin-neat, saloon-free Shangri-La amid redwood forests; workers got low rent, full medical benefits, college scholarships for their kids, and more. Hershey, Pennsylvania, built by chocolate man Milton S. Hershey in the early 1900s, featured electrified, centrally heated homes, a free playground and zoo, and a model school for orphan boys supported by a foundation that held a majority of his company's stock.

At around the same time, companies began erecting such "industrial satellite towns" as Firestone Park, Ohio (Firestone Tire & Rubber Co.), Alcoa, Tennessee (aluminum producer Alcoa), and Kohler Village, Wisconsin (plumbing-fixture maker Kohler Co.). Such eminent figures as planner Frederick Law Olmsted Jr. and architect Irving Gill promoted modernist aesthetics in Torrance, California. But ultimately, the successful model would emulate Britain's carefully planned garden cities, with their wide, attractive boulevards and balance of space devoted to park-land, residences, and industry. Evoking preindustrial villages, such set-tlements were very different from the grimly functional early company towns with their strict gridiron of streets and rows of cookie-cutter hous-ing. In general, corporations in this period made a major effort to house their employees: By 1916, a thousand companies were providing housing for 60,000 employees—roughly 3 percent of the U.S. population.[6]

In the 1930s, government began to play an ever greater role in hous-ing development, and New Deal figures questioned the propriety of com-pany towns, particularly in the southern textile belt, running from North Carolina down into Georgia. Nevertheless, company-built utopias con-tinued to sprout—notably during the 1940s, when wartime demand led Henry J. Kaiser to transform the bayside village of Richmond, California, into a major shipbuilding area. Kaiser became a pioneer in providing in-expensive, universal health care to his workers with a program that was the forerunner of today's vast Kaiser Permanente health plan.

Today, the ideal lives on in such model communities as Columbus, Indiana—home of Cummins Engine and "a veritable museum of mod-ern architecture," according to *Smithsonian Magazine*—and Corning, New York—home base of the global high-tech corporation Corning Inc. Such companies openly argue for doing well by doing good—and while a bit of this is intended as public relations and corporate branding, it's hard to deny that there is also an element of genuine good-spiritedness.

Most recently, the utopian company town has taken a new form—that of the corporate campus. Both Pepsico's Purchase, New York, campus and the Googleplex in Mountain View, California, are company town–like in that most all human needs are provided for: gourmet food, barber shops, laundry service, exercise facilities, and even nap rooms at Google. This velvet-glove approach is not without its downside, captured in Dou-glas Coupland's 1995 novel, *Microserfs*, in which snack-addicted, servile geeks willingly labor as twenty-four-hour-a-day vassals of Microsoft seigneur Bill Gates. (One worker rhapsodizes: "Bill is wise. Bill is kind. Bill is benevolent. Bill, Be My Friend . . . Please!") Employees need never leave such a cosseting environment—or ever truly end a working day.

CHAPTER 1

A City on a Hill

Unfitted to some extent for the purposes of commerce by the sand-bar at its mouth, see how this river was devoted from the first to the service of manufactures. . . . It falls over a succession of natural dams, where it has been offering its privileges in vain for ages, until at last the Yankee race came to improve them. Standing here at its mouth, look up its sparkling stream to its source . . . and behold a city on each successive plateau, a busy colony of human beaver around every fall. Not to mention Newburyport and Haverhill, see Lawrence, and Lowell, and Nashua, and Manchester, and Concord, gleaming one above the other. When at length it has escaped from under the last of the factories it has a level and unmolested passage to the sea, a mere waste water, as it were, bearing little with it but its fame.

—HENRY DAVID THOREAU,
"A Week on the Concord and Merrimack Rivers"[1]

"Whoever says Industrial Revolution says cotton," observed British historian E. J. Hobsbawm.[2] And in the United States, at least in the early going, whoever said cotton mills said water power.

Postrevolutionary America had no shortage of rivers ripe for industrial exploitation. The first to be utilized for textile production were in Rhode Island, beginning in the 1790s. One observer found: "The manufacturing operations of the United States are carried out in little hamlets, which often appear to spring up in the bosom of some forest, around the water fall which serves to turn the mill wheel."[3]

Americans were determined to go their own way in creating models for industry and society, just as they had created their own political system. But there were two powerful British influences.

First, the Rhode Island mills employed technology appropriated from the Brits by this country's most famous intellectual-property pirate, Samuel Slater. Apprenticed as a lad in England to the firm of Arkwright and Strutt and rising to the rank of overseer, Slater made a careful study of that company's innovative equipment. Then, in 1789, he boarded a ship for America—he concealed his textile experience from the ever-watchful British port officials and traveled in the guise of a simple country fellow. Once in the United States, Slater gained employment at the mercantile firm of Almy and Brown, where he and his assistant built a working water frame, similar to the one that spun yarn in the Arkwright factory. Establishing the template for Rhode Island mills, Slater's first operation was on a small scale, a factory in a rented building next to the Blackstone River at Pawtucket. His workforce: seven boys and two girls, ages seven to twelve.[4]

Another key British influence was negative. The creators of the U.S. industry repeatedly invoked images of the foreign city that embodied all they wished to avoid: Manchester, England.

Francis Cabot Lowell, a wealthy Boston merchant visiting Britain in 1811, wrote to a friend that "we found the manufacturing towns very dirty" and later remarked on "the great corruption of the highest and lowest classes, and the great number of beggars and thieves."[5] Manchester drew numerous visitors, some perhaps seeking a squalor-induced frisson like what draws today's tourists to New York and Mumbai. Others, such as Friedrich Engels—whose descriptions written a few years after Lowell's still have the power to startle and repel—had reform in mind. To Engels, the city seemed to be "an outgrowth of accident" rather than the result of any plan. Amid the "knotted chaos of houses," he found himself repeatedly subjected to "filth, ruin, and uninhabitableness, the defiance of all considerations of cleanliness, ventilation, and health." Engels provides his readers with a tour of various working-class neighborhoods in the city. His conclusion: "In such dwellings, only a physically degenerate race, robbed of all humanity, degraded, reduced morally and physically to bestiality, could feel comfortable and at home."[6]

Manchester's size multiplied tenfold between 1760 and 1830, by which time it housed 180,000 citizens. Aside from the slums, few could help noting the "hundreds of five- and six-storied factories, each with a towering chimney by its side, which exhales black coal vapour."[7] Another report described "an inky canopy which seemed to embrace and involve the whole place."[8]

None of this was right for the New World, concluded the founders of America's textile industry.

New England workers, its magnates decreed, would be youth drawn from rural soil—borrowed for a short time from their pastoral lives, not destined to become a permanent and degraded proletariat. By 1815 there were 170 small-scale factories in Providence alone. Hundreds more would sprout in the 1820s and '30s. The typical southern New England mill village—Slatersville (Rhode Island), Phoenixville (Connecticut), or Ware Village (Massachusetts), for example—contained only one mill employing one hundred or fewer workers, primarily children, and these hands and their managers probably supplemented their factory work with agricultural labor.[9]

But more ambitious capitalists saw that larger scale enterprise could mean greater profits—without requiring the immiseration of the worker. Unlike Manchester, larger developments could be bright and airy, marked by stately brick factories and dormitories built alongside sturdy and inspiring churches. Nor would the skies be dark—America, which had an ample supply of coal, as yet lacked the transportation network necessary to bring it to the East Coast. Of necessity, New England's mills would run on the ultimate renewable resource: kinetic energy from falling water.

Even a less-than-torrential river might do. The group of Boston capitalists who became known as the Boston Associates demonstrated this by building a fully integrated factory at Waltham, Massachusetts, its water wheel and machinery driven by the gently rolling Charles River. All steps of production, from "bale to bolt," could be carried out at the Boston Manufacturing Co.'s facility, avoiding the inefficiencies of the Rhode Island "putting out system," in which storekeepers arranged "outwork" on cottage industry handlooms. Waltham's labor force consisted of young women fresh from the farm, housed in company boardinghouses, and the superintendent's mansion was close by.

Despite these differences in scale and organization, the Waltham mill-works shared one striking similarity with Rhode Island: intellectual piracy. It was with an eye to constructing an American textile industry that Lowell made his pilgrimage to Manchester, where he studied the machinery. Britain prohibited the export of its manufacturing technology and kept a sharp lookout for any sketches or representations of it. Twice the authorities searched Lowell's luggage—but he had strong powers of memorization. By 1814, he and Massachusetts mechanic Paul Moody had produced a version of the Manchester power looms for Waltham.[10]

The three Boston capitalists behind the Waltham development were Lowell, Nathan Appleton, another wealthy merchant, and Appleton's brother-in-law, Patrick Tracy Jackson, who would become the on-site su-perintendent. In contrast to many other mills, which were owned by in-dividuals, this and the later enterprises of the Boston Associates were structured as limited-liability corporations. Lowell and Jackson put up the greater part of the outfit's initial capitalization of $400,000. Accord-ing to Appleton, Lowell (who died in 1817) was "the informing soul, which gave direction to the whole proceeding."[11]

Although U.S. textiles prospered during the War of 1812 embargo, the peace of 1815 saw the return of foreign products to the U.S. market, proving ruinous to many Rhode Island manufacturers. But the Waltham operation prospered, thanks to the productivity of its power looms. By 1820, three mills were operating at Waltham, producing a half-million yards of cloth. Within its first seven years—by 1819—the operation earned back its initial capitalization. Dividends averaged over 19 percent a year between 1817 and 1821 and rose to more than 27 percent in 1822.

The third mill exhausted the water power available at Waltham. In search of another place where a similar operation could be erected, Ap-pleton traveled to New Hampshire, where he inspected a falls on the Souhegan River. Shortly thereafter, he learned through Moody of a site at East Chelmsford, Massachusetts, with a falls of thirty feet on the Merri-mack River.

In November 1821, with a light snow covering the ground, Apple-ton, Jackson, Moody, and three others traveled to that sparsely settled location, where no more than a dozen houses stood. But there was some infrastructure development, particularly two canals: the Pawtucket, which circumvented the falls to make the river navigable, and the Middlesex, through which horse-drawn barges pulled freight down to the Mystic River and Boston beyond. The visitors "perambulated the grounds and scanned the capabilities of the place," as Appleton recalled. They quickly arranged for a quiet purchase of the available, surrounding lands and of the company that owned the canals, the Proprietors of the Locks and Canals. They also immediately petitioned the Massachusetts legislature for an act of incorporation in the name of the Merrimack Manufacturing Co., with shares held by Appleton, Jackson, Moody (rewarded for "his agency in the discovery" but also key to the enterprise due to his proven mechanical ability), and John Boott and his brother Kirk, who was appointed treasurer, the title the Associates gave those who functioned as chief executive officers, with an annual salary of $3,000. The company's initial capitalization of $600,000 eclipsed that of Waltham.[12]

Such was the beginning of America's first large-scale planned industrial community: Lowell, Massachusetts.

The America in which Appleton, Jackson, and the others lived was, of course, only a few decades removed from revolution and the invention of a new political culture and set of political institutions. Questions of economics and development were very much on the national agenda as Americans grappled with just what sort of society they hoped to construct.

As foreign as the idea of founding a town in addition to a business may sound today, to the generations of early Americans, such a notion did not seem so outlandish. In 1791, for example, the nation's first Treasury secretary, Alexander Hamilton, was among the founding members of what would now be called a startup backed by venture capital: the Society for Establishing Useful Manufactures (SEUM). Hamilton and his colleague Tench Coxe believed that a purely agrarian America, as championed by Thomas Jefferson and others, would always remain subordinate to Europe, easy prey for Continental bullying and manipulation. Spawning manufacturing in America, Hamilton believed, would require various tactics, including pilfering Britain's technological advances. Another key ingredient: the construction of a manufacturing hub—a town

where goods from sailcloth to stockings, blankets, and beer might be produced. Investors in the town's enterprises would benefit from both the
sale of such goods and the rising value of the town's real estate. Looking
for a site that combined affordable land, water power, and proximity to
existing urban centers, the Treasury secretary and his colleagues decided
upon an area near the Great Falls of the Passaic River in New Jersey. It
would be named Paterson, in honor of that state's governor.

In little over a year, Paterson had begun to take shape, with the
SEUM's directors giving the go-ahead to construction of a textile mill
and textile-printing plant, spinning and weaving operations, and worker
housing. The founders retained Pierre Charles L'Enfant, the architect
who had just laid out the plans for the nation's new capital, to compose
a similar plan for Paterson. But the stars were not favorably aligned: The
spinning, weaving, and printing operations commenced, but L'Enfant's
plan proved both too ambitious and somewhat misguided, and soon he
withdrew from the field. By 1796, the New Jersey project had been
abandoned. But it was a workable idea—as the revival of the development in the 1840s would prove, after which Paterson became an industrious mill town.[13]

The period was also rife with technical and engineering marvels that
seemed to encourage the most high-flown visions of what was possible. The stream of inventions ranged from Eli Whitney's cotton gin
and weapons made with interchangeable parts to Oliver Evans's high-
pressure steam engine and Robert Fulton's steamboat. The Erie Canal,
completed in 1825 and linking the Great Lakes with the Hudson River,
seemed to demonstrate that no geographic hurdle was too great to defeat
modern engineering prowess.

On the frontier, land developers appealed to investors, offering to let
them in on the ground floor of what were certain to be metropolises in
years to come. Many who were drawn into these schemes got skinned, as
they discovered that their newly purchased plots of ground were in fact
plots of swamp. But urban centers from Detroit to Cincinnati and Indianapolis did demonstrate astonishing growth. St. Louis, home to 3,500
souls in 1818, ballooned to 6,000 in 1830. Over the same period,
Louisville, Kentucky, doubled in size, while Cincinnati's population almost quadrupled, from 6,493 to 24,831.

In 1820, the country contained only five cities of note: New York, Philadelphia, Baltimore, Boston, and New Orleans. By 1870, these would be joined by St. Louis and Chicago, while forty-five other cities with populations between 25,000 and 250,000—including San Francisco, Buffalo, Pittsburgh, Cleveland, and others—grew up in their shadow.[14]

With the nation exhibiting that sort of urban growth, who was to say that entrepreneurs shouldn't build their own towns along with their factories?

It took two years to get the new Merrimack River textile center up and running. Kirk Boott became the primary architect of the project. An unusual character, in one existing portrait now at Lowell's city hall, the handsome, dark-haired oligarch appears half-smiling, as if privy to some secret between him and the painter—at his ease but also eager to tackle the bundle of documents that lie on a table near his right hand. Harriet Robinson, a millworker who later compiled a memoir of her time in Lowell, recalled: "Boott . . . was a great potentate in the early history of Lowell, and exercised almost absolute power over the mill-people. He was not popular, and the boys were so afraid of him that they would not go near him willingly, for many of them had known what it was to have his riding-whip come down on their backs."[15]

Haughty and dictatorial, Boott was born in the United States but went to Britain to attend school at Rugby and military college at Sandhurst. He bought a commission in the British army, served under Wellington in the Peninsular Campaign against Napoleon, and returned to the United States only when his unit was about to be sent to America to fight in the War of 1812. He was unemployed when he was hired by Appleton and the others to become treasurer of the nascent project.

Boott applied his engineering skills: laying out streets and designing the mills and boardinghouses, recruiting thirty Irish laborers for construction, and overseeing the building. It was determined that the Merrimack mills would be situated so as to benefit from the whole of the thirty-foot falls. The Pawtucket canal, not much used for years, was enlarged to become a feeder for yet-to-be-built power canals, and a new canal connecting it to the river was built. Thus the area where mills were built was bounded on one side by the Merrimack River and by a series of canals on another.

Legal provision was made allowing the Merrimack Co. to utilize the patented machinery of the Boston Manufacturing Co. Another early consideration for the town: a church for the mill employees and other citizens, since the new village's residents could not be allowed to become as heathenish as Europe's degraded proletariat. Jackson and Boott were appointed to erect a suitable house of worship "built of stone and not to exceed $9,000 in cost." As Boott was an Episcopalian, he deemed that St. Anne's Church would be of that denomination, regardless of the preferences of any who might attend. An additional $500 was dedicated to establish a circulating library.

The Merrimack Co.'s first water wheel was set in motion in September 1823. The moment prompted in the generally unsentimental Boott something akin to a worshipful response. "After breakfast, went to the factory and found the wheel moving round his course, majestically and with comparative stillness," he wrote in his diary. Honoring the spirit of the enterprise, the founders felt the settlement needed a new name. The Anglophile Boott wanted it to be Derby. Appleton—the proper gentleman, respectful of his elders—overruled him: It would be Lowell, Appleton dictated, in honor of the Boston Manufacturing Co.'s founder.[16]

Waltham had manufactured cheap cloth that competed well against imported British fabric. The Merrimack Co. focused on a more expensive fabric, printed calicoes. The product was an immediate success, and the Boston Associates followed up by further expanding the town. All of the land and water power not being used by Merrimack was sold to the Locks and Canals Co. in 1824—a company that was owned by virtually the same group of capitalists, the Boston Associates. But the Locks and Canals Co. would serve as the town-development mechanism, selling land, leasing water power rights, and constructing mills, boardinghouses, and textile machinery for new firms.

Shortly, multiple new firms emerged and built mills on the Lowell site: the Hamilton Corp. (1825), the Appleton and Lowell corporations (1828), the Suffolk, Tremont, and Lawrence corporations (1830), the

Middlesex Corp. (1831), the Boott Corp. (1835), and the Massachusetts Corp. (1839). The Lowell Machine Shop, headed up by Moody and incorporated as an independent entity in 1845, designed and constructed machinery for the plants, and ultimately locomotives, turbines, and steam engines. Although the corporations' boards consisted mostly of the same men, creating new companies allowed fresh capitalization and a slow expansion of the circle of key players. Meanwhile, interlocking directorates ensured concentrated power and allowed policies to be coordinated: The companies would pay identical wages (and simultaneously announce wage cuts) and have identical working hours and regulations for their operatives. Their management structures—with the treasurer as chief officer, the agent as the on-site chief (Boott assumed both of these roles for Merrimack, but thereafter they were filled by two persons), a superintendent overseeing production in the various departments, and a clerk who managed accounts—were identical. And they marketed their cloth via the same Boston commission houses.

The textile firms were hugely profitable, as was the Locks and Canals Co., which averaged annual profits of 24 percent from 1824 to 1845. The mills built in the 1830s were redbrick affairs, four to six stories high with regular rows of windows, each "capped with a little white belfry," in the words of visitor Michel Chevalier. There was plenty of light inside but little circulation of air, since companies nailed the windows shut to maintain the humidity the fabric needed. Like college dormitories, the mills were grouped around landscaped quadrangles, and as anyone who visits Lowell today realizes, they were built to last. Like America's political Founding Fathers, Lowell's builders seemed to feel they were setting up institutions that would last many lifetimes.

Different operations occupied different floors of the mill buildings, with the most basic tasks (carding and spinning, whereby the raw cotton was cleaned and drawn into yarn) near the bottom and the most skilled operations (dressing, or preparing the yarn for the weaving process, and weaving on power looms) occupying the top floors. By 1850, forty mill buildings lined the river for almost a mile, powered by six miles of canals and a system of gates and flow-measuring devices that regulated the water flow and diverted excess water back into the Merrimack. English-born engineer James Francis was a primary architect of the complex hydraulics—

valuable intellectual property that was in time marketed to the builders of other mill towns.

As the factories got ever larger over the course of the 1830s, the workforce soared to more than 10,000. Most workers lived in the boardinghouses, which stood close to the mills. Initially made of wood, in time they became imposing brick edifices that conveyed the solidity and benevolence of the enterprise, thus serving as a draw to workers and a reassurance to their families. Boott's imposing mansion stood, like the man, somewhat aloof yet nearby enough to allow him to keep watch. Less important executives lived in smaller but equally dignified dwellings.

The town's population ballooned from 2,500 at the town's incorporation in 1826 to 18,000 in 1836 and then to 33,000 in 1850, by which point it had become the second largest city in the state. A middle class appeared, occupied chiefly in supplying the needs and wants of the workforce. For these, separate zones arose in the town—areas of shops and middle-class housing the companies never sought to control. By the middle '20s, against the wishes of the class-conscious Boott, who felt that education was a frivolous indulgence for the working rabble, five schoolhouses had been completed. Twenty-six churches appeared in three waves of construction, with most completed by the mid-1840s. The poorest part of town was "New Dublin" or "the Acre," home to hundreds of little shanties that housed the Irish construction workers who'd built the place.[17]

There were two distinct groups of employees in nineteenth-century Lowell. From the 1820s into the 1850s, workers came from the pool originally targeted by the Boston Associates: young Yankee women just off of farms in the surrounding area. But for various reasons, this labor pool was soon exhausted, and Lowell employers turned more and more to immigrant labor, first from Ireland and then from French Canada and elsewhere.

The early group of female workers drew a great deal of publicity and favorable attention to Lowell. In Appleton's words: "The contrast in the character of our manufacturing population compared with that of Europe has been the admiration of the most intelligent strangers who have visited us." And the visitors were not only intelligent, but they were celebrated and well-connected as well. Michel Chevalier, sent by the French government in 1834 to inspect U.S. public works but staying on to observe and write about the New World more generally, found the girls well-paid and a far cry from the European industrial workers who were afflicted by drunkenness and prostitution. Charles Dickens, after an 1840 visit, contrasted the place with Britain's "great haunts of desperate misery" and reported that he could not recall "one young face that gave me a painful impression, not one young girl whom . . . I would have removed from those works if I had the power." The mill girls, he went on to say, had access not only to pianos and circulating libraries, but they also produced their own literary periodical, the *Lowell Offering*, filled with poems, essays, and stories of the mills and those who worked in them.

Today the poetry and many of the tales in the *Offering* seem formulaic, derivative, and sentimental, but a glimmer of journalistic truth peeks through in the reflections on life in the factory and boardinghouses. An 1845 piece by Josephine L. Baker titled "A Second Peep at Factory Life" complains about pay cuts and "the practice of sending agents through the country to decoy girls away from their homes with the promise of high wages, when the market is already stocked to overflowing." In "Almira's" 1841 "The Spirit of Discontent," two mill girls debate the virtues of life in Lowell versus that in the country—one asserts "I won't stay here and be a white slave"—before agreeing that "since we must work for a living, the mill, all things considered, is the most pleasant, and best calculated to promote our welfare."

That magazine, which Dickens said "will compare advantageously with a great many English Annuals," was the subject of favorable reviews in the *Times* of London and the *Edinburgh Review*. It also drew comment from Harriet Martineau, another English visitor and chronicler of 1830s American life, who effused about the boardinghouse arrangements and the operatives' ample earnings, and noted that "all look like well-dressed young ladies. The health is good."[18]

The paternalistic Waltham/Lowell system that drew such praise contained several key ingredients. Since workers were to be recruited from a wide area, few would be able to live at home and most would have to stay in boardinghouses, as at Waltham. But Lowell's hundreds of boardinghouses had to provide more than shelter: After all, families needed to know that the young women—most of whom started work as mere teenagers—would not only be safe and well-looked-after, but that they would reside in an atmosphere of civility.

The older women who served as boardinghouse keepers provided supervision and made sure the girls were in by 10 p.m. The presence of such cultural totems as pianos and libraries reassured families that, as management often stated, they were not surrendering their daughters to a lifetime of toil. No, whatever time elapsed in Lowell was more akin to a period of preparation for later life, perhaps even for marriage. Lowell would not threaten middle-class aspirations: The girls could read and discuss the latest literature and poetry, even write their own compositions, continue their musical studies, and come of age in refined surroundings. Circulars that survive suggest a lively intellectual and cultural scene, with elevated amusements including lectures by such luminaries as Ralph Waldo Emerson. In a society given over to the headlong pursuit of wealth, nineteenth-century American women were required to become counterbalancing agents of culture and moral sensitivity. Lowell would help them fulfill those roles.

Operatives were required to attend church (paying a "pew fee" to support the institutions), and their morals were the object of close scrutiny by a "moral police" system in which the boardinghouse keepers and even the other operatives played a key part. Companies had the power to fire anyone charged with immoral conduct, including consuming alcoholic beverages or even attending dancing classes. Operatives' contracts required them to commit to one year of service and to give two weeks' notice before quitting. Anyone who fell afoul of the moral policing or failed to serve out her term of work would be denied an "honorable discharge" upon leaving—and would be blacklisted from employment in the area. (The corporations, of course, offered no guarantee regarding the length of employment or steadiness of wages.) Such in loco parentis, observed historian Norman Ware, was capable of "being turned into a very effective and harmful despotism."[19]

And despotism there was, in the form of still more regimentation: Bells, bells, bells rang all day. The factory bell woke workers at 4:30 a.m. and another summoned them to work at 4:50. A bell announced when it was time to begin and end each meal, and another rang at 7 p.m. to signal the close of the workday. Finally, a 10 p.m. bell announced the curfew. The tocsin governed a twelve-hour working day, six days a week, with only three annual holidays.

Then there were the incentives: Unlike the Rhode Island system, where companies paid operatives with credit at company stores, in Lowell the operatives received their wages in cash. Workers there had no say over their wages or hours of work. But the pay—$12 to $14 a month in the 1830s—compared well with other alternatives, especially farm labor or domestic service, and it was six or seven times the average teacher's salary. Although some operatives doubtless sent money home, many saw Lowell as a way out—a means of escape from family dependency—and in time used their savings as a dowry or for college tuition. For older daughters, possibly encouraged to leave home to ease the burden on their fathers, emigration to Lowell was akin to the westward migration chosen by many young men.

Most of the operatives—75 percent in the 1830s—did live in boardinghouses. The food seems to have been plentiful and pretty good, with meat served twice a day and such treats as apple pie and plum cake regularly featured. But ventilation was poor and the places were crowded, with twenty-five women per house and as many as six per bedroom, two per bed. Privacy was unknown. Familiarity must have bred at least some discontent, with the women working and living together every hour of the day. Still, Lowell offered a lot that was unknown back on the farm, including the lectures, library books, and stylish clothing from the town's stores.[20]

The system had its critics: Some intellectuals likened factory labor to slavery, concentrating their fire on Waltham/Lowell rather than Rhode Island's laissez-faire system, which offered little care for its workers, including the "little half-clothed children" who made up a large part of that state's textile labor force. The Boston *Daily Times*—aligned with the Democratic Party as opposed to the factory-owner Whigs—staked out a position of opposing the entire factory system, which it saw as robbing operatives of their dignity and independence. The 1841 pamphlet *Corporations and Operatives*, written by a "Citizen of Lowell," charged that workers had only fifteen minutes for meals, were made to live in vermin-infested housing, were subjected to regular wage cuts, and even experienced outright theft of their time, as factories added more minutes to the working day each year. (Charges that management cheated workers of their free time arose regularly: Writing to the reformist *Voice of Labor* in 1846, one Lowell mechanic alleged that the mill clock was "fixed," slowing down to add minutes to the working day, then speeding up at night to summon the operatives earlier. In Pawtucket, citizens raised $500 to purchase a town clock that would not be subject to the manipulation suspected of the factory clock.)[21]

But Lowell operatives demonstrated that they were hardly slaves by engaging in two dramatic work stoppages, in 1834 and 1836. In the first of these, falling prices for textile products prompted management to announce a wage cut. In response, the workers circulated a petition "pledging not to enter the factory" on the day of the wage reduction, and eight hundred stayed out. One-sixth of the workforce paraded through the Lowell streets, expressing their independence as "daughters of freemen." They saw the wage cuts as an attack on the independence of spirit that lay behind their very decisions to migrate to Lowell. Although shocked, the Boston directors refused to yield, and the walkout came to a quick end.

The 1836 actions were even more pronounced and, coming at a time of high demand for textiles and labor shortages, disrupted production considerably. When the companies raised the room and boarding fees, about 2,000 operatives, or one-third of the total workforce, "turned out." Many may have left the city, as several mills were forced to run at less than full capacity for months. Some of the boardinghouse increases, at least, were revoked.[22]

In general, the late '30s and early '40s were hard times. As new mills in other towns ramped up production, oversupply followed. Lowell mills ran part time and hundreds were laid off. In an attempt to restore profits, the corporations sped up the machinery, assigned workers once responsible for two machines to as many as four machines, lengthened the workday to thirteen hours from eleven, and cut piecework rates. Moreover, supervisors who got the greatest production out of their workers got cash bonuses. Once again, the Yankee mill girls' bid for self-sufficiency and independence was threatened, and in response they pressured the Massachusetts legislature to enact statutes limiting the workday to ten hours. Yearly petitions from Lowell received thousands of signatures from operatives. The *Voice of Industry*, a pro-worker Lowell newspaper whose editorial committee included former operative and *Offering* contributor Sarah Bagley, was a leading voice favoring reform. In contrast, the *Lowell Offering*, which had come into existence with the intent of bettering factory conditions, became a corporate defender, opposing reform and steering clear of criticizing the companies.[23]

In the 1850s, the Whig Party, strongly supported by the Boston Associates and hewing to management's side in the ten-hour agitation, lost electoral control of the statehouse to a coalition of Democrats and Free Soil Party members. While this may have seemed a positive sign for reform, dark clouds loomed on Lowell's horizon.

The companies' original paternalistic orientation was waning, reflecting a broader ownership of company stock and a generational shift in top management. And the labor force was changing. The Yankee girls had never stayed for long in Lowell: the average period of employment was around three years. Now, despite the best efforts of labor recruiting agents who patrolled Vermont and New Hampshire, such women increasingly were turning elsewhere—to westward migration and to other professions that offered better pay and more independence. Meanwhile, beginning with the potato-famine-inspired migration of the 1840s, immigrants, primarily from Ireland, were eager for mill employment and disinclined toward militancy despite three cuts in piece wages during the 1850s. Increasingly, Lowell was moving toward a family-labor system like that of old Rhode Island, employing adults and children alike. By 1850, the companies had abandoned requirements that workers live in company-owned housing and attend church. Ever more employees lived in private housing, especially since the construction of company housing had not kept pace with the expansion of mill capacity.[24]

The days of enormous profits were also coming slowly to an end. The Lowell companies tended to pay out much of their profits in the form of dividends to investors; during the 1820s, these generally ran around 10 percent of investment, increasing to nearly 15 percent in the 1830s. But in that decade, the cost of erecting new mills fell sharply, resulting in the appearance of more and more competitors—even as the Boston Associates expanded. Most new outfits were small. The Boston Associates themselves built new factories in Chicopee, Massachusetts, Manchester, New Hampshire, and Saco, Maine. Then in 1845, they decided upon an ambitious new development at Lawrence, Massachusetts, making the Essex Mills the first to rival the scale at Lowell. In 1847, a similarly ambitious plan was announced for what became Holyoke, Massachusetts.

Even with the U.S. market growing in the West and South, there was too much production. By the late '40s, the country entered an economic depression. In 1857, five of the Associates' now numerous companies failed, including the Middlesex Co. And with the outbreak of the Civil War, the supply of cotton from the American South was cut off and most of the Lowell mills shut down. (The exception was Middlesex Mills, which produced woolen cloth used in Union troops' uniforms.) Ten thousand Lowell workers lost their jobs.

Nathan Appleton, a president or director of twenty-two textile companies, was active in management until his death in 1861. But much of the founding generation was long gone—Kirk Boott had died in 1837—and a third generation of management was in charge. Critics charged these new managers with nepotism and incompetence, even callousness toward the workers. In general, the later generations of the Associates were preoccupied with a wide range of businesses, including railroads, banking, and insurance. Philanthropic missions, including the Boston Athenaeum, Massachusetts General Hospital, the McLean Asylum, and educational foundation the Lowell Institute, also occupied their attention. It is fair to say that the idea of Lowell as a model town no longer held its original fascination for the businessmen.[25]

The original experiment was all but dead, even though Lowell mills continued to operate well into the twentieth century.

Enormous changes were apparent when the mills reopened after the Civil War. For one thing, steam power was slowly replacing hydraulics, and by 1880 the city of canals relied more on steam than on water power. This shift, which was being made all across the U.S. textile industry, benefited other textile centers more than Lowell, particularly Fall River and New Bedford, Massachusetts, which were located on the coast and could get their coal shipments via oceangoing transport. Another profound change in Lowell: The transition to immigrant labor, begun in the 1850s, was now complete. No longer needed to house the Yankee mill girls, the companies gradually sold off their boardinghouses to private owners, who turned them into tenements.

With the arrival of the Irish beginning in the mid-1840s, immigrants came to Lowell in waves, precipitating a political struggle that reflected changes in the town's composition. Slowly the political dominance of the mill managers gave way, with the first Irish Catholic mayor being elected in 1882. After the turn of the century, middle-class reformers, agitating against ward-heeler machine politics, got the city charter rewritten to provide for citywide elections. But it wasn't long before Irish Catholic politicians regained control of the city.

Following waves of immigrants included French Canadians in the 1860s and '70s, then Greeks, Poles, and forty other national groups in the 1890s and 1900s. Neighborhoods tended to be segregated by nationality, and each one established its own separate institutions, including churches. And as would be common elsewhere, the companies pitted one group against another, using the more desperate newcomers to undermine efforts to limit the working day legislatively and to serve as strikebreakers.

Numerous strikes occurred in the late nineteenth century. In 1867, skilled mule spinners struck three mills in an unsuccessful attempt to limit the workday to ten hours. The same group again struck in 1875, this time in protest of a wage cut. They were locked out and fired. Three years later, female operatives struck over another wage cut, and they too were fired.

The first citywide strike came in 1903, when skilled operatives walked out in pursuit of a 10 percent wage raise. All the mills but one immediately closed down, reopening two months later with Portuguese, Polish, and Greek workers taking the place of the strikers. Then in 1912, several unions united in a walkout as they sought a 15 percent pay increase. (The companies agreed to a rise of 6 percent to 8 percent.) This militant effort was led by the radical Industrial Workers of the World, fresh from their legendary victory at Lawrence, where they had overcome national divisions by reaching out to workers in various languages and where a highly publicized campaign for strikers' children had drawn emotional public support across the eastern seaboard. Manufacturers in other cities had already granted more than the Lowell companies were offering—and after a few weeks, the New England Association of Textile Manufacturers criticized Lowell for not offering 10 percent. The Lowell companies capitulated, and the unions accepted the offer.

But Lowell's very slow decline continued. Prosperity during World War I gave way to numerous mill closings thereafter. Among the disappearances: Middlesex, Bigelow Carpet (formerly Lowell Manufacturing Co.), Hamilton, Tremont, and Massachusetts. Appleton mills moved to South Carolina, and the Lowell Machine Shop, now called the Saco-Lowell Shops, relocated to Maine.[26]

The late 1920s and the 1930s were a very difficult time in the city. The New England textile industry was already depressed when the Great Depression hit, and shortly 40 percent of the town's population depended on government relief. Reporting for *Harper's Magazine*, left-leaning writer Louis Adamic visited Lowell along with other New England mill towns in 1930. He found that two-thirds of Lowell's population was either unemployed or employed only part time. The town's devastated streets were dominated by eight enormous mills with tall unsmoking chimneys, "all idle for years," and in the main business district, only the five-and-ten stores seemed to be doing any trade. Butchers told him they sold only the cheapest cuts of meat; doctors, that their patients couldn't pay their bills; and dentists, that they conducted a disproportionate number of extractions instead of preventive care. Charity, he reported, was the biggest industry in Lowell. Rather than applauding his findings, the Lowell city fathers trashed Adamic: He was denounced in scores of editorials and condemned in city council resolutions.[27]

Of the original mills, by 1940 only three were still in operation—Merrimack, Boott, and Lawrence—and the first two would close in the 1950s. There was a brief rise in textile production during World War II, but soon thereafter millwork all but disappeared in the city that had pioneered it.

There was a twofold spur behind the closings and exodus: wages and technology. First, while management perceived labor in Lowell and elsewhere in the East as relatively costly, these same managers had allowed the town's mills to become technologically obsolete. The South had cheap labor, and its mills, which didn't really get going till late in the nineteenth century, featured modern high-speed machinery.[28]

Bear in mind, though, that there was another side to Lowell—one independent of the mills. As in any other city, there were professionals and middle-class citizens who must have known about the plight of industry, but whose lives weren't wholly shaped by it. For example, Beat writer Jack Kerouac was born and reared in Lowell as part of a middle-class French Canadian community. Kerouac's portrayal of the local scene in his 1950 first novel, *The Town and the City*, makes Lowell (fictionalized as "Galloway") seem much like any other New England small town—and life for young people there seem focused on the usual run of school, sports, romance, and nature. "She lived in the southern part of Galloway," he writes of one character, "in an old ramshackle farmhouse on the banks of the Concord River there . . . with its vines over the porch and its drooping trees, with the dark river beyond, and the aura of pastoral simplicity all around, it never failed to cast a spell of fearful enchantment."[29]

The town has recovered somewhat in recent decades, with the slow population decline reversing. In the early 1970s, local government and business labored to transform the former mill district—or at least what remained of it after some demolition—into what became the first urban national park in 1978. Hundreds of thousands of visitors tour the site each year. Moreover, the local branch of the University of Massachusetts has tried to attract high-technology enterprise. But that sector has shown itself to be as vulnerable as any other: Computer maker Wang Laboratories expanded into Lowell in the 1970s, but by 1990, that company was extinct.

A very great deal has been written on Lowell, much of it emphasizing the specialness and impermanence of the town's early years. For example, historian John Coolidge has written, "Nothing of Francis Cabot Lowell's utopia has stood the test of time." He asserts that the textile cities of central New England, including Lawrence and Manchester, were "sports in the general line of American industrial evolution, transitory as ideal communities, unimportant as models."[30]

Coolidge is one of the most insightful of Lowell's chroniclers, and his *Mill and Mansion* stands as a model of architectural history and social and economic analysis. But these statements are not altogether accurate. Certainly, further Lowell-like major industrial hubs arose later, including Gary, Indiana, founded by U.S. Steel in 1906 on Lake Michigan swampland, and Ford Motor Co.'s giant River Rouge facility in Dearborn, Michigan.

If Coolidge has in mind simply the use of workers drawn from the countryside and housed in dormitories, where they became the object of a watchful paternalism, he is largely right: That part of the Lowell experience was driven by a labor shortage that became less pressing after 1850, when waves of immigrant laborers started coming to the United States. Still, neither corporate paternalism nor the capitalist utopian impulse disappeared. These would remain themes throughout following decades and even into the twenty-first century.

One thing is certain, though. There can be no such utopias without prosperity. Once the New England textile industry entered a period of decline, and its corporate masters began seeking ways of squeezing the labor force, they abandoned utopian ideals. It would not be long before they resurfaced elsewhere.

CHAPTER 2

Utopia

At my feet lay a great city. Miles of broad streets, shaded by trees and lined with fine buildings. . . . Public buildings of a colossal size and architectural grandeur unparalleled in my day raised their stately piles on every side. Surely I had never seen this city nor one comparable to it before.

—EDWARD BELLAMY, *Looking Backward* (1888)

By the late nineteenth century, American cities were growing at a vertigo-inducing pace. In 1850, around 30,000 people lived in Chicago; by 1870, there were 300,000. New York's 1875 population of just under 1 million made it the world's third-largest city; over the next twenty-five years, that population would double.[1] Civic activists grew concerned, not merely due to this population explosion but also because of the accompanying, very visible division of society into extremes of wealth and poverty. "The rich are richer, and the poor are poorer in the city than elsewhere," wrote Reverend Josiah Strong in *Our Country: Its Possible Future and Its Present Crisis*, an 1885 pamphlet that sold 130,000 copies among concerned churchgoers. "Is it strange that such conditions arouse a blind and bitter hatred of our social system?" he asked. In *The City: Hope of Democracy*, urban reformer Frederick C. Howe observed: "The humanizing forces of to-day are almost all proceeding from the city." Yet, he continued, "along with the gain there is . . . a terrible lost account. The city has replaced simplicity, industrial freedom, and equality of future with complexity, dependence, poverty and misery close beside a barbaric luxury like unto that of Ancient Rome."[2] The confluence of such factors might lead to the degradation of the populace, if not to social revolution.

For many social reformers, the new class of Gilded Age capitalists was composed of prime villains. So it is a surprise to find that many industrialists shared the concerns of Strong and Howe and were themselves moved to take action.

The first whiff of social revolution came in 1877, as a massive railroad walk-out turned into a national conflict. When the Baltimore & Ohio Railroad cut wages for the second time in a year, a strike of company workers broke out in West Virginia and, after federal troops intervened, the insurrection spread. Within days, crowds of workers were fighting state militias in the cities of Maryland, Pennsylvania, and Ohio, with at least forty-five people killed in Pittsburgh. Soon 100,000 men from numerous industries were on strike as far away as Chicago; St. Louis; Kansas City; Galveston, Texas; and San Francisco. It took federal troops armed with Gatling guns two weeks to quell the uprising. The upper classes were deeply alarmed. "Any hour the mob chooses it can destroy any city in the country—that is the simple truth," wrote Assistant Secretary of State John Hay to his father-in-law.[3]

Chicago newspapers reported events in articles headlined "Horrid Social Convulsion" and "Red War." Department store mogul Marshall Field suggested that the danger of further riots required a large standing army to be permanently on guard. Field and his friend, railroad sleeping-car magnate George Pullman, felt the squalor that underlay the working-class uprising was due to workers' own profligacy and intemperance.[4] Within a few years, Pullman would take steps to change things.

Pullman was a prototypically American self-made man. Born on a farm in western New York state in 1831, he took his first job, in a country store, at age fourteen. By seventeen, he was a cabinetmaker's apprentice, and it was there he gained an appreciation for elaborately carved wood and woven fabric. Three years later, he was helping to move buildings out of the path of the expanding Erie Canal. These house-moving skills would prove essential to his first business success as an adult, when in the late 1850s he led the way in showing how Chicago buildings might be raised above the water level and thus avoid having their cellars flooded with Lake Michigan water. Of average height and possessed of a youthful appearance accentuated by his round face and bright eyes, Pullman was simultaneously bold and cautious in business matters—striking the perfect balance of capitalist instincts.[5]

In 1853, a punishing overnight train trip between Buffalo and Westfield, New York, made clear to Pullman that there was much room for improvement. He determined to enhance sleeping cars by installing actual beds in them. And by the 1860s, the project of transforming cross-country train travel from a dirty, jolting misery into a pleasurable, middle-class outing had made him a rich man. Both ornate and comfortable, the Pullman Palace Car Co.'s sleeping cars contained plush carpet, brocaded fabrics, carved and polished wood, and hinged berths that could be folded away during daylight hours. The "Pioneer," first built in 1864, came with shock-absorbing coiled springs and cost five times the price of an ordinary railcar.

Many railroads resisted what seemed like an extravagance. They also resented that Pullman refused to sell the cars to the railroads. Instead, he leased them, providing them with separate crews and maintenance, while collecting 50 cents from every fare. In a brilliant if cynical marketing flourish, Pullman arranged for his car's debut to occur on the last leg of Abraham Lincoln's funeral-train procession, which was met by crowds everywhere as it made its way from Washington, D.C., to Springfield, Illinois.[6] Test runs on the Michigan Central Railroad proved hugely successful as passengers jammed the Pullman cars on every trip. Generous profits followed, allowing the Pullman Co. to pay its shareholders a dividend of 8 percent from its first year of operation.

The sleeping cars weren't Pullman's only product. He also constructed dining, passenger, freight, and refrigerator cars, along with streetcars, but the company was primarily identified with the opulent sleepers. Pullman believed that not only would his luxurious vehicles command higher fares from the public, but also that their beauty would have a civilizing influence upon even the roughest of customers. And as experience seemed to bear this out, he came to believe that civilized surroundings would also have an "ennobling and refining" effect on his workers.[7]

To that end—and because land prices within Chicago were becoming prohibitive—in 1880, Pullman decided to build a model factory town fourteen miles out of the city in an area free of "all baneful influences."

He began secretly buying up 4,000 acres along Lake Calumet's west bank. In four years' time, he transformed the swampland into the site of a giant production works with a population of 8,000, about half of them employees. Working with architect Solon Spencer Beman and landscape designer Nathan F. Barrett, he designed an "all-brick city" that would become a showpiece for the company and a must-see curiosity for visitors to the area. The company's office and production facilities—including a foundry, wood shop, engine room, lumber storehouses, and more—sprawled over thirty acres and were able to turn out forty Pullman cars per day.

Across a major boulevard from the manufacturing works lay the residential area, consisting of a dozen detached homes, block upon block of two- to five-family row houses, and ten large tenements. All houses came with natural gas and running water, and the larger homes had bathrooms. Near the residential area was a large market complex, with a public hall and stalls selling meats and vegetables. Also close by was the most spectacular of Pullman's edifices—the Arcade Building, which housed thirty retail shops, a bank, a Moorish-style theater of 1,000 seats, and a library with 6,000 volumes donated by Pullman himself. Completing the picture were a handsome hotel—which contained the otherwise-dry town's only bar—a school, parks, and playing fields. Altogether, there were more than 1,500 buildings in Pullman, all owned by the company, with an estimated worth of $8 million.

What passed for government was firmly in company hands—a theme common in other company towns. The town clerk and treasurer were both officers of the Pullman company, as were most members of the board of education.[8] There was no elected government and no newspaper.

Visitors taking the 30-minute train ride out to Pullman could not resist commenting on the town's appearance. Economist Richard T. Ely, writing in *Harper's Monthly*, found "the newness of things" to be "a little distressing, as is also the mechanical regularity of the town." Yet, with its "advanced secular gothic" public buildings and "Queen Ann-style" hotel, the development was as attractive as any "wealthy suburban town," he concluded.[9]

No one should imagine, though, that Pullman was a do-gooder where his workers were concerned. Instead, the town was "a business venture pure and simple," as explained by a later officer of the Pullman Co.:

"Stockholders would get a return, fortunate employees would work harder, and the company would be the beneficiary. Pleasant working conditions would draw out the workers' qualities of loyalty, honesty, and perseverance." In Pullman's words, the employees would work out "valuable and well-rounded lives in proportion to their opportunities."[10]

In taking this approach, Pullman was echoing the business community's prevailing wisdom that due to "natural law," it did no good to offer men charity—that morality and business must be held separate, and that the best philanthropy was the payroll and incentives that encouraged people to help themselves.[11]

Pullman wasn't alone in announcing that the model town was creating a new type of dependable worker. But already by the mid-1880s, there were critics. Although the living quarters were desirable, residents were unable to buy their homes, only to rent. (Rents varied from $4.50 per month for the cheapest flats to $100 per month for the largest private houses.) Every organization, including churches, was compelled to rent rather than to own its building, and any tenant could be evicted with a notice of only ten days. Others questioned the atmosphere in town, especially the use of "company inspectors," who day and night kept an eye on Pullman resident-workers to make sure that both their opinions and their habits were acceptable. Some like Ely challenged the total control of the company and the absence of elections and representative government, concluding that the very "idea of Pullman is un-American. . . .It is benevolent, well-wishing feudalism."[12]

By 1893, the Pullman Co. had experienced years of a near-monopoly over sleeping-car transportation. With 14,000 employees across the United States, it had record earnings of $11 million. But as the country entered a serious economic depression, layoffs followed wage reductions. Within a year, the average wage at Pullman fell by 28 percent. (The average wage reduction across the country was closer to 12 percent.) Meanwhile, the company refused to lower its rents in the town, which were generally higher than rents paid by working people elsewhere. As the company told the *Chicago Herald* in 1894, it could not cut rents because profits on housing had already dipped under 4 percent, which was "a manifestly inadequate return upon the investment."[13] However, once rent was deducted from workers' paychecks, some were left with only pennies.

In the spring of 1894, Pullman workers organized. They affiliated with the American Railway Union (ARU), led by Eugene Debs, who would in time become the preeminent advocate of socialism in the United States. The company refused demands for either a return to earlier wage levels or a reduction in rents, so the workers went on strike. And when after two months the company still refused to negotiate, ARU's national convention called for a nationwide boycott of Pullman. The action spread rapidly, as trainmen refused to work on any trains from which Pullman cars had not been detached—and the boycott turned into a great strike involving 50,000 men, with mobs barricading and sabotaging tracks and attacking trains.

The disruption of U.S. mail delivery allowed an antilabor President Grover Cleveland to intercede. Attorney General Richard Olney obtained a federal injunction prohibiting strike leaders from organizing the boycott and sent in federal troops to clear the tracks. Striker casualties mounted: In a Fourth of July confrontation in Chicago, thirteen strikers died and fifty were wounded. The general strike was broken, and its leaders, including Debs, were prosecuted for civil contempt and jailed.

By July, the strike in Pullman itself was at an end. Forced to resign from the ARU, 1,900 Pullman workers returned alongside 800 "replacements." Many of Pullman's prestrike workers had left the area, but 1,000 remained unemployed.[14]

The model town that had seemed to stand for progressive labor relations had become notorious, associated worldwide with industrial strife, blacklists, and managerial repression. One often-overlooked irony: Out of the failed utopian experiment of one man, George Pullman, came a very different utopian perspective—the scientific socialism of Eugene Debs. Celebrating his fortieth birthday in the Woodstock, Illinois, jail, Debs read Karl Marx's *Das Kapital* and works by German socialist Karl Kautsky. He emerged from imprisonment disillusioned with the possibilities of trade unionism but hopeful about overthrowing the capitalist system via the ballot box. Debs was also now a celebrity, who would garner millions of votes in five subsequent presidential campaigns.[15]

Pullman died in 1897, and eulogists largely repudiated the idea behind his personal utopia. A year after his death, the Illinois Supreme Court ruled that the Pullman Co. charter did not permit the holding of real estate beyond what was required for its manufacturing business. The town entered a period of slow decline, with the city of Chicago assuming municipal functions in 1899 and the company gradually selling off its town properties beginning in 1904.[16]

After the events at Pullman—which were widely reported and commented upon throughout the United States—one might expect that the day of industrial utopianism was done in America. But the impulse toward social perfectionism was strong in the late nineteenth century. The greatest manifestation of that urge was the reception given to a novel written by Edward Bellamy, *Looking Backward: 2000–1887*. Published in Boston in 1888, the book follows a Rip Van Winkle scenario: Julian West, a man of the late nineteenth century, awakens after a 113-year sleep to find society entirely transformed. That millenarian vision proved so compelling that *Looking Backward* sold nearly a half-million copies over the next few years, became an international best seller translated into several other languages, and inspired some fifty imitative works over a few decades. Even more immediately, the book became the manifesto of a national movement, the Bellamy Clubs, which had chapters in twenty-seven states.

Of course, Bellamy's vision was hardly a celebration of company towns, even in their most ideal form. In fact, when the author wrote that, in industry, "feudalism still survives in its pristine vigor," his reference point was his own hometown of Chicopee Falls, Massachusetts, a settlement filled with textile mills and plants making everything from bicycles to agricultural implements.

Chicopee's factory workers lived in row after row of dreary tenements, not far from the white-clapboard, middle-class house where Bellamy, the son of a Baptist minister, grew up. The young man settled on a career as a writer after attending college in New York state and traveling in Europe—and after a very brief career as a lawyer, which he termed "the dirty trade of a local pettifogger." Among his early literary efforts were editorials penned for the newspaper of Chicopee's neighboring town, the *Springfield Union*. In one of these, he inveighed against the miserable living conditions of Chicopee's immigrant poor. Particularly worrisome, he thought, were the "ragged and meager" children who worked in the mills. "The mere sight of them; so old and worn and miserable to look at, yet so young, is proof enough that a great wrong exists somewhere among us," he wrote in an 1873 *Union* editorial. "Civilization does not deserve the name in any land, if it cannot run its business enterprises of whatever kind . . . without such a sacrifice of human rights and well being." Since the Boston Associates owned one of the Chicopee mills, Bellamy's words read as an indictment of Francis Cabot Lowell's own utopia gone wrong.

In contrast to such a hell, *Looking Backward* envisions a coming golden age, realized by the year 2000, in which all individual companies are replaced by a socialist government that operates all enterprise—in which the nation becomes "the one capitalist in the place of all the other capitalists." As part of an all-encompassing industrial army, every citizen does the work he or she is best at (women, now liberated, play a significant role), and all receive identical remuneration. There are no rich and no poor, but everyone benefits from efficiencies in production and distribution and the elimination of war and criminality. In the words of Dr. Leete, the character who explains everything to Julian West, "The brotherhood of man, which to you were but fine phrases, are, to our thinking and feeling, ties as real and as vital as physical fraternity."[17]

Bellamy's novel often strikes us now as mechanical and dull—a social blueprint masquerading as literature. But Bellamy, who had written four previous novels and numerous short stories for such top literary magazines as *Scribner's* and the *Atlantic Monthly*, knew how to engage readers of his day. For the romantic-minded, *Looking Backward* contained a love story with a heartwarming conclusion; for fans of progress and technical gadgetry, he supplied telephones that, radiolike, delivered music to homes and an apparatus to shield sidewalks from inclement weather.

And the true brilliance of *Looking Backward* lay in its ability to persuade the reader that its ideal society is also the ultimate in practicality. Nineteenth-century captains of industry may have said they favored efficiency, but Bellamy judged that their society was built on waste and fraud. "Their system of unorganized and antagonistic industries was as absurd economically as it was morally abominable. Selfishness was their only science. . . . Combination is the secret of efficient production," Leete instructs. But Bellamy was not altogether consistent on this point.

Where might nineteenth-century readers have caught a glimpse of this level of efficiency? Leete observes: "You used to have some pretty large textile manufacturing establishments, even in your day, although not comparable with ours. No doubt you have visited these great mills in your time, covering acres of ground, employing thousands of hands, and combining under one roof, under one control, the hundred distinct processes between, say, the cotton bale and the bale of glossy calicoes."[18]

The picture could hardly be clearer: Through Leete, Bellamy is describing the Waltham/Lowell manufacturing scheme. Although Bellamy denounced contemporary capitalist civilization and the Boston Associates' contribution to it, at the same time he recognized the utopian elements inherent in Francis Cabot Lowell's manufacturing scheme. Indeed, Bellamy had difficulty describing his own utopia without referring to Lowell-like manufactories.

With the success of *Looking Backward*, Bellamy made himself into a public speaker for the Nationalists and an activist for the People's Party, as the Populist organization of the 1890s was known. But his health was poor, and he died in 1898 at age forty-eight, a victim of tuberculosis. Nevertheless, he was far from alone in his attempt to translate his feelings for the brotherhood of man into a real-world community.[19]

Like both Pullman and Bellamy, Milton Hershey was a man with major reservations about contemporary urban life. In the 1880s, as a wavy-haired, mustachioed twenty-six-year-old proprietor of a New York City candy store, he came into frequent contact with the criminal gangs and appalling squalor of the Hell's Kitchen area. "Cities never seemed natural to me," he reflected later, "and I never learned to like them."[20]

Although his New York store failed, within a decade Hershey had become a successful candymaker and wholesaler as head of the Lancaster Caramel Co.—the country's number-one caramel maker—based in Lancaster, Pennsylvania. Then, on a trip to the World's Columbian Exposition, held in Chicago in early 1893, he paid several visits to an exhibition of chocolate-producing machines owned by the J. M. Lehmann Co. of Dresden, Germany. At the time, few Americans had even heard of chocolate, and those who had knew it as an expensive European delicacy. Nevertheless, Hershey shortly decided that public demand for caramels would soon fade and that he should become a chocolatier. He bought the Lehmann machines, imported skilled chocolate workers from as far away as Switzerland, and began producing cocoa powder, baking chocolate, and chocolate coatings for candy. He also began years of experimentation aimed at creating his own unique recipe for milk chocolate. In 1900, he sold his lucrative caramel business for $1 million to concentrate on chocolate, and shortly thereafter he introduced a line of five-cent Hershey's Milk Chocolate Bars. By 1901, his chocolate enterprise had more than $620,000 in annual receipts, and profits grew steadily thereafter.[21]

The Chicago trip, along with later journeys to England, had another major impact on Hershey. By 1903, he was laying the plans for construction of his own model town, somewhat in the mode of Pullman, which he may have seen, and of Bourneville, the English model town erected by British chocolate company Cadbury.[22] First he obtained 1,200 acres of real-estate options in Derry Church, Pennsylvania, near his birthplace. Then he hired surveyors to create landscape maps and arranged for an architect to design the factory and public buildings to come. When newspapers began to report on Hershey's intentions to build a town in the area, some expressed wonder that he would choose such a remote, amenity-bereft place. But Hershey saw in the site one major virtue: dairy farms that would supply the milk needed for his milk chocolate. There was also no shortage of clean water, and the local industrious folk would provide a reliable workforce.

Like Pullman in the early days, Hershey was widely described in the press as a philanthropic, morally superior person—quite unlike the "malefactors of great wealth" President Theodore Roosevelt would shortly excoriate. How could such a welcome food's producer—the Chocolate Man—be otherwise? Although Hershey himself offered few reflections on his motivations for building the town, the inspiration appears to have come from several sources in addition to Pullman and Bourneville. First, there were his mother's religious principles—she was a fervent Mennonite, a member of a sect similar to the Amish that emphasized Bible study, community service, and abstemious living in pastoral surroundings. Hershey's planned village, with its clean-living, prosperous workforce, nicely echoed Mennonite values.

Perhaps more important, creating the town was something of an adventure. And Hershey had always been drawn to the audacious ways of his profligate father, a man who was ever ready to take a flyer on bold enterprises, from berry farming to the invention of a perpetual-motion machine. Finally, Hershey disliked urban squalor and the labor unrest that it bred. He could hardly have been unaware of the nationwide railroad strike connected with Pullman or of a bitter 1897 strike in nearby Lattimer, Pennsylvania. There, in an altercation with sheriff's deputies, scores of strikers were killed or wounded. In contrast, he would build a city—echoing Bellamy—where, as he declared, there would be "no poverty, no nuisances, no evil."

Such a place would serve as a standing advertisement for the Hershey Co., its wholesome values, and its products. In short order, thousands of visitors would arrive via trains and trolleys to admire Milton Hershey's community.

The houses that began appearing in Derry Church in 1904 were modern affairs equipped with indoor plumbing, central heating, even electricity. Hershey decreed that his town should be free of any industrial atmosphere: Consequently, he demolished an initial group of residences he thought were too uniform, and the ones that followed had landscaped yards. Unlike those in the town of Pullman, these homes could be bought for between $1,200 and $1,500. There were also one hundred lots available to those who wanted to build their own houses, although these came with detailed restrictions both on the construction and future use of any buildings.

As for chocolate making, Hershey's new factory was spread over eighteen buildings, including a two-story executive wing and a power plant with two giant boilers that made electricity for the plant and for the town. Cocoa beans arrived at the plant by rail and then moved through the facility to be cleaned, roasted, shelled, ground, and turned into the liquid that became candy, cocoa powder, and cocoa butter. Milk from the region was condensed and mixed with cocoa, and the combination was dried and molded into bars. The factory, which was graced by two enormous brick smokestacks inscribed with the word HERSHEY, tripled in size within a few years, supporting 1,700 workers by 1911.

Hershey and his admirers wasted less rhetoric than Pullman on the civilizing impact of his town upon its workers. Moreover, the Pennsylvania town—which was nameless in the beginning and won its appellation via a contest in which the public suggested various ideas—was slow in development. Financed with the company's considerable profits, there were soon parks and a zoo, numerous public buildings, a public library, a swimming pool and golf course, an extensive trolley system, a medical clinic, free schools, and athletic teams. There was abundant greenery, including the ornamental shrubbery that spelled out the words HERSHEY COCOA in ten-foot letters.

For himself, Hershey built a twenty-two-room colonial mansion, dubbed High Point, that sat on a hill overlooking the factory.

The trade-offs for town residents followed what would become a familiar pattern in model company towns. Workers got a cornucopia of benefits, including insurance, medical coverage, and a retirement plan. There were no local taxes, jobs were abundant, and services such as garbage pickup and snow removal were a given. The company donated property and buildings for local schools, including a junior college with free tuition for town residents. Each of five local churches received a $20,000 endowment. But the town remained unincorporated and had no elected officials. Milton Hershey served as its mayor, constable, and fire chief. Moreover, he was his own "moral police," riding around town and taking notes as to which homes were not being maintained and receiving reports from private detectives as to which employees were too fond of alcoholic refreshment.

Milton Hershey's paternalism came to include one very unusual feature, though: Beginning in 1909, one of the town's most significant sites was the Hershey Industrial School, a residential institution for orphan boys that was thought up by Milton's wife, Kitty. It was but one of dozens of such institutions founded during this period, but Hershey's school was unrivaled in its gifts. After Kitty's early death in 1915, the chocolate magnate donated his entire estate to the institution in her memory. All of his company stock, which was valued at $60 million, would be held by a trust that supported the place. Although this latter provision was certainly charitable, it also offered a means of keeping Hershey stock closely held by a party unlikely to disagree with Milton Hershey about the direction of his company.

The Hershey Industrial School was, and in some ways remains, a study in contrasts. The childless and poorly educated Milton Hershey lavished his fortune on the institution, setting up a well-appointed library, auditorium, and gymnasium. The students received a splendid education—Milton wanted them to have everything he had missed—and after graduation each got $100, a wardrobe, and help finding a job or a full college scholarship. But the students were housed on nearby farms, where they had to perform chores—planting, milking cows, and harvesting grain—all of which were thought to be wholesome and character-building. Students were never left in doubt about the identity of their benefactor, who frequently dropped by the institution and once a year invited the students to his mansion for a special breakfast. (The school is still in operation today, with standards and facilities that rival the likes of Choate; 80 percent of its graduates, who no longer perform farm work, go on to college.)

In the town harmony reigned. As seems fitting in a Never-Never-Landish spot where Chocolate Avenue intersects with Cocoa Avenue, neither a funeral home nor a cemetery was allowed within Hershey, Pennsylvania. A precursor to Disneyland, Hershey Park was drawing 100,000 visitors a year by 1913. Tourists came to see and smell the chocolate-scented town, to ride on its miniature electric train and merry-go-round, and to listen to popular orchestras in the Hershey dance hall. The village had become such a sensation that little other marketing was needed—and the company ceased its print advertising.

That same year, the company staged a vast tenth-anniversary celebration of its move to the area, complete with parades, bands, fireworks, and an air show with James B. "Birdman" McCalley exhibiting his biplane. And there was oratory: In a pretelevision age, stemwinders from politicians such as William Jennings Bryan or evangelists such as Aimee Semple McPherson provided enlightenment and bombastic entertainment. (Abraham Lincoln once observed, "When I hear a man preach, I like to see him act as if he were fighting bees.") Thus Hershey's celebration required a keynote address, here delivered by Omar Hershey, a famous orator unrelated to Milton. "If Big Business adopted the Hershey idea" there would be less labor unrest, he noted. "Where simple justice and plain, ordinary common sense prevails, some of the problems quickly adjust themselves," he concluded. The company founder was presented with a silver cup, inscribed to the town's "beneficent Jove."[23]

The company and the town prospered: Within a decade, sales of the candy bars and such new products as the Hershey's Kiss rose to almost $8 million. By the 1930s, Hershey, Pennsylvania, had reached maturity, with the construction of sports venues, a community center, a theater, and a monumental, 170-room hotel helping to build a tourist trade. Built atop a hill overlooking downtown, the community center and Hotel Hershey were traditional Italianate and Spanish rococo structures. Much more daring was the new modern office building downtown—constructed without windows and with a uniform controlled environment.

But while the new construction was intended partly as a Depression-era make-work project, hard times inevitably led to layoffs and reduced work hours in the chocolate factory. Meanwhile, from 1930 to 1936, the Hershey Chocolate Co. made more than $37 million in after-tax profits— or ten times its annual payroll. A more sophisticated, ethnically diverse workforce also resented company efforts to control off-the-job behavior, ranging from marital infidelity to carpooling, and there were accusations of favoritism in promotions.

In 1937, a whirlwind organizing campaign by a new union federation, the Congress of Industrial Organizations (CIO), resulted in recruitment of 80 percent of the company's 3,000-odd production workers. Initial talks between the CIO's United Chocolate Workers and management seemed to augur well, with the company agreeing to raise wages. But then came layoffs of several union militants and production speed-ups. The result was a sit-down strike that paralyzed the factory.

A startling outburst of violence followed. Four days after the strike began, several thousand local farmers who depended upon selling their milk to Hershey attended a parade in support of the company. They delivered an ultimatum to the strikers: Leave the plant or be forcibly ejected. After an exchange of taunts with the strikers, the army of farmers and pro-company employees armed with rocks and pitchforks stormed the facility. Outnumbered four to one, the strikers were bloodied— several were brutally beaten—and evicted.[24]

The incident left a suddenly divided town and a mark on Hershey's reputation. Within two years, federally conducted union elections resulted in recognition of the conservative, craft-oriented Bakery and Confectionary Workers Union as a bargaining representative for the workers. Union contracts meant that, going forward, it would not be up to one man to make every decision about life in Hershey, Pennsylvania. The town was becoming a more mature—and more complicated—place to live.

Milton died in 1945, and his company drifted for several decades. Generations of his successors were punishingly slow to act, seemingly frozen by the question of "What would Milton do?" It was years before Hershey Chocolate Co. took on such modern corporate functions as marketing and research and development. There was no Hershey advertising until 1970.

But beginning in the late 1970s, the enterprise instituted many changes. Having become Hershey Foods Corp., with such noncandy products as pasta and Friendly Ice Cream, management placed all operations on more of a business footing. Most significant, Hershey was redefining its relations with the town.

Among the first changes was the appearance of a new Pennsylvania State University medical center, founded in 1963 with a $50 million donation from the company. As that institution matured, it brought a new element into the community: a large number of medical personnel.

The park, which began as a free recreational facility for the townsfolk, had long been evolving toward something else. A simple merry-go-round was replaced in 1912 by an elaborate carousel with fifty-three carved animals. In the '20s, more rides including a Ferris wheel and airplane swing were added, and in the '30s came a penny arcade, a "mill chute" ride, and more, so that by the late '40s the park contained more than two dozen rides. But in 1970, it was closed—and reopened as Hersheypark, a Disney-style theme park with daily admission charges.[25]

Finally, many of the town's historic buildings were repurposed. In 1977, Milton Hershey's High Point mansion was turned into a suite of offices for top corporate officials. In 1980, the company closed the community center and transformed it too into offices.[26] Like Lowell before it, Hershey, Pennsylvania, was surrendering many of its quirks—and perhaps its unique identity.

In the West, the exploitation-minded, smash-and-grab side of the American personality reached its fullest expression. The area's very bounty seemed to prompt a rapacious stripping of resources and only a tenuous relationship with any given place. As early as 1871, Mark Twain observed of the gold-mining territory around Sacramento, California: "You may still see, in places, its grassy slopes and levels torn and guttered and disfigured by the avaricious spoilers of fifteen and twenty years ago. You may see such disfigurements far and wide over California."[27]

The lush forests of the Northwest encouraged just such an approach. Logging camps arose in Oregon, California, Washington state, Idaho, and Montana to cut stands of spruce, cedar, fir, and redwoods. Crews were ever on the move to virgin woods, so these camps were never more than temporary homes. Some featured barracks to which wheels could be easily attached for relocating, and in others cabins were constructed as barges for easy flotation down rivers.

Timber-mill towns were more permanent affairs. The first such community was likely Port Gamble, established in 1853 by the Puget Mill Co. on Washington Territory's Kitsap Peninsula. With a second mill constructed five years later, the town had a workforce of 175. Like many of the mill men who built the Northwest's timber industry, Port Gamble's founders were transplants from the Northeast, primarily from Maine. With its growing number of small frame houses, the town looked every bit a New England village. To be sure, not all the workers were considered members of the family: Port Gamble employed many American Indians whom it segregated into a separate outpost, a town called Little Boston on the other side of Gamble Bay from Port Gamble.

Operations in Port Gamble continued into the twentieth century, as did production at such places as Valsetz, Oregon; Sappho, Washington; and McCloud and Samoa, California. But many mill towns were short-lived. Wanton cutting was followed by abandonment of the settlements. The Manley-Moore Lumber Co. town of Montezuma, Washington, for instance, was left deserted after that company shuttered its mill in the early twentieth century. As giant corporations took over other companies and their towns, owners showed little interest in maintaining the towns or in maintaining family-like relations with workers.[28]

The clearest example to the contrary—and, perhaps, of utopian promise on the West Coast—was Scotia, California, the Pacific Lumber town in the Northern California redwood forests that was established in 1882 as Forestville.

Up to that time, the prospect of harvesting the mammoth redwood forests had seemed daunting. Some redwoods were as much as a thousand years old, hundreds of feet tall, and fifteen feet in diameter. Moreover, in pre-automobile days, it was difficult simply to get access to such trees. But with America's eastern forests and their stands of smaller trees increasingly logged out, there were few alternatives.

By the late 1880s, Pacific Lumber founders A. W. McPherson and Henry Wetherbee had three hundred employees living in Forestville. The settlement contained little more than a church, post office, and telegraph station. Reflecting the presence of many emigrants from Canada's eastern coast, the town's name was changed to Scotia. Pacific Lumber had become the largest producer of lumber in Humboldt County.

In the early 1890s, the company was purchased by Simon Jones Murphy, who'd made a fortune lumbering in Maine and in Michigan real estate, mining, and timber. It was the beginning of a long Murphy family association with Pacific Lumber. Although an 1895 fire destroyed the town and all of the company's facilities, Pacific Lumber quickly rebuilt and expanded. By 1920, the company had 1,500 workers and owned 65,000 acres of forest.

If left to its own devices, Pacific Lumber might not have become an environmentally progressive company. Both tax benefits and pressure from San Francisco conservationists encouraged the tendency. But for whatever reason, Pacific Lumber became a trailblazer in forest conservation: In the 1920s, it sold the largest remaining contiguous holding of old-growth redwoods—over 9,000 acres—to the Save the Redwoods League, becoming part of Humboldt Redwoods State Park. Moreover, in the following decade the company announced it was abandoning the industry standard of clear-cutting—or taking down everything in a given area—in favor of "selective cutting." No more than 70 percent of the mature trees in a stand would be felled, with younger trees left to hold the soil and reseed. Finally, the company began harvesting on what it called a "perpetual sustained-yield basis": Never would it cut more trees than its forests could regrow in a year. Hiring some of the industry's first foresters, Pacific Lumber began its own nursery that would plant up to a million seedlings a year.[29]

More to the point, Pacific Lumber became renowned for its humane employment practices. "We're a paternalistic company," president Stanwood Murphy told a journalist in 1971. "I know that's a dirty word," continued the red-haired, craggy-featured executive, "but it's accurate." Tiny, picturesque Scotia included attractive wood-frame bungalows, with low rent, free water and garbage removal, and regular maintenance by the company. The town also included a range of stores, a school, a forty-bed hospital, a skating rink, a Catholic and a Protestant church, an administration building, a fancy directors' cottage (for overnight use by corporate directors), and the ornate, all-redwood Winema Theater. Pacific Lumber gave its workers pensions, free life insurance, and bonuses, and their children got college scholarships. Every Labor Day, everyone in town gathered at the bank of the Eel River for a holiday blowout.

Labor at Pacific Lumber was difficult, sometimes dirty, and frequently deafening. Out in the woods, loggers felled the huge trees, then trucked them into Scotia and either stacked them at the "cold deck" or plunked them into the ten-acre millpond. In Scotia's three huge mills, men operated cranes, conveyor belts, rollers, and a variety of saws. Seventy-ton logs would be stripped of their bark, then sliced into a variety of lengths and widths. Then the lumber was sorted by grade and size, stored in warehouses for a lengthy drying period, and perhaps even kiln-dried.

Generation after generation of workers found the package to be a good deal. There were trade-offs, of course. Although Pacific Lumber paid better benefits and higher wages than rivals, it fought hard to keep unions out. Up until World War I, Scotia featured a "safety valve" called the Green Goose—a combination brothel, saloon, and gambling parlor. But with Prohibition, Scotia became a dry town—and it stayed that way. Afterward, social life in town centered on the volunteer fire department and a little-used, YMCA-like Scotia Men's Club, where card-playing was allowed but no gambling. (To be sure, gambling and drinking continued in establishments right across the Eel River, in the town originally known as Wildwood and later as Rio Dell.)[30] All in all, life in Scotia was pretty calm—at least until the 1980s.

In that decade, with Scotia seemingly frozen in time and Pacific Lumber holding 70 percent of the remaining privately owned old-growth redwoods, corporate raider Charles Hurwitz moved to take over the company. The company's physical property—including a new headquarters building in downtown San Francisco—its cash position, and its absence of debt made it an appealing target. Hurwitz's Maxxam Inc. quietly obtained just under 5 percent of company stock. Then in October 1985, after an initial offer of $797 million, or $38.50 per share, Maxxam persuaded initially resistant Murphy family members to give in. The final purchase price was $868 million.

But the buyout, organized by Wall Street takeover specialists Drexel Burnham Lambert, meant taking on lots of debt. To pay this down, Pacific Lumber's new owners announced they would be ending the company's pension plan, absorbing $60 million in "overfunding," and selling off the company's non-forest assets. They also announced a doubling of their redwood harvest. For a short time, Scotia's workers were raking in the overtime pay, and its mills were running extra shifts. But the aggressive new tree-cutting inflamed California's environmental activists, prompting almost two decades of struggle that featured protest marches, confrontations with pepper-spray-brandishing police, "tree sits"—in which protesters actually lived for months in the high branches of threatened redwoods—and a car bombing that nearly killed two activists from the Earth First! organization.

Moreover, within three years of the buyout, the insider trading scandal broke, in which it came out that Drexel junk-bond kingpin Michael Milken and trader Ivan Boesky had engaged in a series of bets on corporate takeovers based on inside information. Among the deals on which they wagered and Milken helped finance: Maxxam's buyout of Pacific Lumber. The Milken-Boesky activities violated federal law, and when their shenanigans were revealed, both men were sentenced to prison terms. Boesky was fined $100 million and barred from the securities industry. Moreover, Los Angeles stockbroker Boyd Jefferies was accused of having "parked," or clandestinely purchased, 539,600 shares of Pacific Lumber stock on Hurwitz's behalf. The shares were key to Maxxam's Pacific Lumber takeover effort.

What had happened to the idealistic company, its sheltered workers, and the model town? Buyouts such as Maxxam's were then—and are today—justified on the grounds that new owners streamline operations and maximize a company's value. But in the case of Pacific Lumber, to all appearances the new owners brought little other than a fresh rapaciousness, and their very aggressive pursuit of profit, not to mention the Drexel scandals, damaged Pacific Lumber's reputation. Despite a 1988 announcement of a voluntary moratorium on clear-cutting of virgin redwood forests, Pacific Lumber regularly fell afoul of California forestry regulations and faced court injunctions issued to stop its logging. As if in divine judgment against the turn of events, in April 1992, three major earthquakes struck the Scotia area within eighteen hours. Sawmills and homes were badly damaged, and the local shopping center was destroyed.[31]

It took seven more years to negotiate, but in 1999 Pacific Lumber sold to the U.S. Interior Department what remained of the old-growth-rich Headwaters Forest—about 7,500 acres—for $480 million in federal and state funds. Then in 2007 Maxxam filed for bankruptcy. Pacific Lumber was taken over in June 2008 by yet another group of outsiders, the Donald Fisher family, owners of The Gap, Banana Republic, and the Mendocino Redwood Co. They reorganized Pacific Lumber's mill-and-forest holdings as Humboldt Redwood Co. Mendocino partner and former PALCO creditor the Marathon Structured Finance Fund now owned the town and all of its buildings. Pacific Lumber—the company and the all-embracing way of life—ceased to exist.

Humboldt's owners have pledged to take a conservative approach to logging, letting the forest regenerate at twice the rate it harvests. Environmentalists, who point to Mendocino Redwood's Forest Stewardship Council–awarded green seal, say the new owners are credible.

Scotia is now home to what the company calls a "state-of-the-art sawmill," where computers position logs for cuts that command the best prices and that match consumer demand. The cut lumber is also graded and sorted by computer. Some of Pacific Lumber's paternalistic policies, including its college scholarships, are still in place. But as of 2009, there are only a few hundred workers—more than one round of layoffs has hit the workforce—and Marathon's attempts to sell parts of the town are a source of unease. The grand Scotia Inn, with its wood-relief carvings and twenty-two cozy rooms, has been assigned a price tag of $2.5 million. A major obstacle to the sale of Scotia real estate: The entire four hundred–

acre town exists as one tax parcel and must undergo various zoning and environmental hurdles before it can be subdivided.

With all of that, many locals are relieved to see the back of Maxxam and are hopeful about the future. The company's new owners "may put the town back to where it used to be, honoring its roots," butcher Mel Berti told the *Santa Rosa Press Democrat*. "People here are concerned about the roots."[32]

In Pullman, the defining characteristic proved to be its restrictions. For Hershey, it was a benevolent one-man rule joined with an increasingly quaint philanthropy. And at Scotia, a paternalistic legacy gave way to a ruthless late-twentieth-century capitalism defined on Wall Street. All three—and Lowell, for that matter—shared one thing: an initial vision and daily existence articulated and elaborated by a capitalist father figure. Each place outgrew that plan. Today, Pullman is a down-at-the-heels urban area, Hershey features a diverse service economy that includes a Disneyland-like theme park, and Scotia is an isolated but lovely town in the woods struggling to maintain its legacy.

No discussion of ideal company towns would be complete if it failed to include a singular type: the domicile of the high-tech company. Such places include Schenectady, New York, long associated with General Electric; Redmond, Washington, home to Microsoft—and Corning, New York, home base for Corning Inc. Neither a purpose-built model town like Pullman and Hershey nor a single-enterprise village like Scotia, Corning developed as a country crossroads and railroad town, with a growing concentration of glassmaking enterprises. As Corning Inc. became the area's preeminent glass concern, it emerged as the town's benefactor—and savior. Its philosophy was also different from those of the three other enterprises in this chapter—a modern "corporate welfarism" that, executives said, in no way conflicted with the company's primary goal of making money.

Like most high-tech outfits, Corning Inc. came of age in the 1940s and 1950s. The specialty-glass maker has experienced an unsteady, boom-and-bust-prone life ever since. Perhaps its happiest period began in 1959, with the release of Corning Ware, the Sputnik-age cooking products made from a material also used in rocket nose cones. The decade that followed would be an unusual period of prosperity and self-assurance for Corning Glass Works, as it was known until 1989, since the company enjoyed near-monopoly control of the highly lucrative television-tube market. Further high-tech glass products such as fiber-optic cable would follow. During the 1960s and 1970s, the company made its most pronounced commitment to the town of Corning, New York.

Corning Inc. traces its existence back to the mid-nineteenth century, and especially to 1868, when the proprietor of the Brooklyn Flint Glass Works, Amory Houghton Sr., arranged to relocate his operation to Corning, an agricultural town of 7,000 souls on the Chemung River in upstate New York. He moved his furnaces, pots, molds, and other equipment up the Hudson River and on to Corning via canal. Two years later, the company came close to folding, but a bank bailout led to its revival. Thereafter, focusing on such items as railroad signal lenses, thermometer tubes, and lamp chimneys, the glassware company grew slowly along with the town whose name it adopted. It also long maintained a dynastic organizational structure: Except for a few intervals, a member of the Houghton family was at the company's helm through the late twentieth century. Common stock was not sold to the public until 1945.

A signal event was the decision by Thomas Alva Edison to purchase glass globes for his lightbulbs from Corning Glass Works, beginning in 1880 and continuing with the organization of General Electric Co. in 1892, ensuring the ongoing health of the glassworks. The development also indicated the company's future course—electronics and scientific applications of glass, as opposed to, say, the making of bottles or window glass.

During this period, the town of Corning was evolving from an agricultural trading center into a manufacturing burg that included glass-making operations, several foundries, stove makers, farm-implements factories, and more. Companies such as T. G. Hawkes & Co. and J. Hoare & Co. produced intricate and popular cut-glass wares. Even more significant, the town was becoming a railroad hub through which passed the Erie Railroad; the Blossburg, Corning, and Tioga Railroad; and the Delaware, Lackawanna, and Western Railroad. In 1891, 12,000 trains passed through Corning. Hundreds of local men worked on these railroad lines, while Corning Glass Works employed between

270 and 780 workers, variously. With a population approaching 10,000 in 1890—the year in which Corning, New York, was incorporated—the town supported seven churches, fourteen hotels, thirty-four saloons, eighteen barbers, fifteen boardinghouses, twenty-seven dressmakers, ten tailors, and an opera house that hosted touring theater companies, meetings, and minstrel shows. The village was also home to two daily newspapers of opposing political viewpoints, the *Corning Democrat* and the *Corning Journal*.[33]

In 1908, the town built a large park with pavilions, a wading pool for children, a bronze fountain, and a ball field. It was named Denison Park for the businessman who contributed most of the land. Only several years later, in 1916, did the glassworks contribute to public facilities, when the Houghton family conveyed to the town a plot of land north of the Chemung River, which became Pyrex Park, named for the company's popular glassware.[34]

However, Corning Glass Works was becoming an ever more important employer and physical presence. By 1913, it had three large plants in town, arrayed along the river and marked by what would become a town landmark: a 187-foot tower in which molten glass was stretched for thermometer tubing. Stenciled on the outside of the tower was the blue-on-white silhouette of "Little Joe" the lightbulb blower.

The company's two notable products after the turn of the twentieth century included the clear glass kitchenware Pyrex—adapted from battery jars—and lightbulbs. (Corning was also responsible for the art-glass productions of Steuben, an independent company it absorbed in 1918.) A round of department-store demonstrations in 1915 kicked off a Pyrex marketing campaign, and by 1917, the product had annual sales of $460,000. Lightbulbs were hand-blown, as if they were art glass, into the twentieth century: Corning demonstrated no urgency about developing a mechanical electric-bulb-making machine, but by 1913 it operated five such devices. During World War I, Corning increased its production of scientific glassware, a product once supplied largely by Germany. Although mechanization led to some layoffs and deskilling of workers, the glassworks had 2,000 workers by 1916, a year in which bulb sales reached $1.7 million. The area's second-largest employer, compressor-maker Ingersoll Rand, employed around 800.

Like many other corporations, Corning Glass Works adopted a number of so-called corporate welfare programs in the 1920s, intended to build loyalty among employees and to enhance the company reputation among the general public. Innovations included a company hospital and clinic, health and accident insurance for all workers, and a factory upgrade to reduce chemical hazards, which had killed four workers in 1910. There was also a Corning band, a baseball club, and service awards handed out to longtime employees. At the same time, the glassworks was openly antiunion: In the 1910s, when the American Flint Glass Workers Union attempted to organize a local, the company dismissed two hundred of its five hundred glassblowers.[35]

The Great Depression initially resulted in a large number of layoffs and wage cuts, along with price cuts in such key products as Pyrex glassware. But the company's fortunes turned around quickly, and the new joint venture with Owens-Illinois Co., Owens-Corning Fiberglass, brought sizable revenues. Corning initiated a so-called company union (discussed at great length in later chapters) in 1933, called the Industrial Council; its joint labor/management committees discussed a variety of workplace issues and announced reforms that included paid vacations and guaranteed minimum wages. And in the larger community of Corning, New York, the company formed the Corning Realty Co. to expedite home-building and to construct a centrally located apartment complex.[36]

A growing, mature sense of community within the company led to a changed relationship with workers, stakeholders, and with the town on the Chemung beginning during World War II. In 1944, the company acknowledged the inevitability of unionization and facilitated a union election that was won by the Flint Glass Workers over the more militant United Electrical Workers. (The latter would shortly become the bargaining agent for employees at Ingersoll Rand.) In 1945, as the war approached its end, management realized that it would need new capital for postwar expansion—and that a public offering of shares could serve as an incentive to employees as well as allow a market for the holdings of the increasingly numerous Houghton heirs. As a result, the company put up for sale 412,340 shares, representing 15 percent of its equity. Finally, the company backed various development schemes in the town, ranging from new apartments and houses, donation of land on which the War

Memorial Stadium would be constructed, and, in 1951, opening the Mies van der Rohe–designed Corning Glass Center (later renamed the Corning Museum of Glass). Constructed in only a year and embellished with a panoply of glass surfaces, the center housed a historical collection of glass objects, a science hall, a factory for Steuben art glass, and a large auditorium that would become the venue for touring theatrical presentations including that year's *Happy Birthday*, starring Hollywood actress and Academy Award nominee Joan Blondell.[37]

Corning Glass Works was now anything but a one-town company: As early as 1917, it had begun moving production out of its cramped hometown. Over the years, its operations were increasingly far-flung, from Pennsylvania to Ontario. In 1954 it completed a five-year plan of plant construction running to $48 million. Altogether, it had 12,250 employees. Such joint ventures as Owens-Corning also multiplied to include a glass-block enterprise with Pittsburgh Plate Glass Co. and a silicone-products venture with Dow Chemical that became Dow Corning Corp. But Corning Glass Works did not neglect the town of Corning, where it had more than 3,000 employees by 1959: In an area north of the Chemung River, it built a new complex known as Houghton Park that included a nine-story office building, and it purchased four hundred acres in the nearby town of Erwin, where it constructed a research-and-development center, Sullivan Park, named for the company's longtime research chief. In 1960, the Corning Foundation offered a $4.5 million grant to jumpstart construction of Corning Community College, where in time employees would be able to take courses for which the company largely footed the bill.

And in that decade, company management seemed to realize that if the town of Corning were to avoid the fate of other, increasingly down-at-the-heels upstate burgs, Corning Glass Works would have to be a prime mover. At the urging of Amory Houghton Sr., who had retired as company president in 1941 but remained much involved, the company began a community projects department to oversee its efforts in the town, contributing $9 million to the $39 million needed for various buildings including a new library, a two hundred–unit apartment complex, new recreation facilities, and more. It also became a vocal champion of revitalizing the eight-block downtown core.

Much of this was made possible by two hugely successful products: Corning Ware and television tubes. Known to generations of yard-sale aficionados as the indestructible casserole dishes embellished with a blue-cornflower pattern, Corning Ware was invented by accident when a scientist inadvertently jacked up the temperature of a laboratory oven. While the company did sell the resulting Pyroceran to the Defense Department for missile nose cones, the glass was far more profitable when made into cookware that could go from the freezer to the oven without breaking. Memorable magazine advertisements showed a Corning Ware casserole dish half immersed in a block of ice—and half sticking out into the flames of a blowtorch. In 1959, its first year on the market, consumers snapped up $15 million worth of Corning Ware.

The product was also advertised via Corning's favorite medium: television, on such popular programs as *Cheyenne* and *The Lineup*. As the exclusive supplier of bulbs for U.S. television-set manufacturers, Corning Glass Works was responsible for the guts of over 11 million sets sold in 1965, both black-and-white and color. Not that these were Corning's only wares: According to its annual report, that year the company produced 43,000 different products in thirty-seven manufacturing plants. By 1970, it would have international sales of $166.7 million.[38]

The Glass Works' community-development efforts would escalate even further following a 1972 flood that left four feet of water standing in the downtown area and 6,000 townsfolk homeless. Amid rumors that the disaster could prompt the company to leave Corning, Amory Houghton Jr., who'd become company chairman in 1964, went on local radio to assure employees that their jobs were secure and that the company intended not only to rebuild but to expand operations in town. With major help from the company and its foundation, the business district and its central thoroughfare, Market Street, got a complete facelift and became home to a new city hall, an open-air skating rink, a shiny new Hilton Hotel (now a Radisson), and a new office building for the Flint Glass Workers local. Other additions would include a spiffy new corporate headquarters, built on the site of the original plant, and the Glass Innovation Center.[39]

These developments, however, coincided with a violent swing in company fortunes. With its sale of television tubes in decline—the Japanese were eclipsing U.S. television makers—Corning in 1975 closed five domestic plants, ended the manufacture of black-and-white bulbs, and reduced employment by 40 percent. In the early 1980s, it sold its remaining lightbulb plants.

Then an unexpected savior appeared in the form of the Reagan Justice Department: In 1982, the feds announced the breakup of AT&T. That company would be forced to divest its Baby Bell companies and to accept the end of its monopoly over long-distance telephone service. This was Corning's opportunity to deploy a new technology.

Since the 1960s, Corning scientists had been working on a new kind of cable to carry voice transmission—thin strands of optical glass that could transmit higher-quality voice signals than the much-used copper cable. Although Corning felt its years of unremunerated effort and an investment of $100 million had resulted in a technological breakthrough by 1970, AT&T never supported the Corning efforts, being engaged in its own fiber-optic research. The ill winds that buffeted AT&T in 1982 resulted in a windfall for Corning: Later that year, MCI, backed by junk-bond money from Wall Street, placed an order for 100,000 kilometers of Corning's cable—a $90 million purchase. Sprint Communications followed with a similar order the following year.[40]

Such good fortune seldom lasts—and at times it presages ruin. To meet these orders, Corning had to make its biggest investments in company history: $94 million in new plants and equipment. By 1986, this meant profitable growth with more than $220 million in sales. But by the following year, there was a glut in fiber optics, with new competitors entering the field and the major trunk lines complete. Sales rebounded a bit with orders from local phone companies—and in 2000, the company had $7 billion in sales and a market value of $100 billion. But by 2001, after the company took on huge debt to build more capacity, fiber-optic sales tanked for good. Sales fell by half, and company stock plummeted 95 percent. Corning, which had a workforce of 40,000 in 2000, laid off 19,000 workers, including 3,500 in its hometown. CEO James Houghton, who'd retired in 1996 after thirteen years at the helm, was drafted to return and help revive the company. His personal stockholdings, once worth $129 million, had plunged to $1 million in value.

After a rousing speech at the company's annual meeting, Houghton sold the company's precision lens business, exited telecom photonics—which expedite the movement of light through fiber via lasers and amplifiers—and closed four of the company's five fiber-optic plants. By 2004, Corning Inc. announced it had cut its debt in half, to $2.7 billion and, rather than losing money, had earned $163 million in the first half of that year. It has been in the black ever since.[41]

By 2009, Corning had placed a new major bet—on liquid-crystal display glass for an ever-growing list of consumer products including laptops, digital cameras, navigation systems, video games, and personal digital assistants. It is still involved with fiber optics, along with materials used in emissions- and pollution control and more than 150 other materials. Company employment in the town as of 2009 stands at just under 5,000, with almost 3,000 spread between Corning headquarters and its research center, and the rest in production of materials for auto and truck catalytic converters. Corning Inc. is still much involved in downtown renovation, helping develop deteriorated buildings into retail and residential properties. Its community development wing, Corning Enterprises, and the foundation also participate in local school district programs and spend $2 million a year on child-care facilities, where half of the six hundred–odd slots go to kids of employees.

No one claims that such initiatives are purely philanthropic—clearly having a pleasant, resource-rich downtown and good schools helps Corning Inc. attract and retain employees. Its startlingly modern headquarters buildings, sited next to the picturesque Chemung River, also serve notice that this is a cutting-edge operation. In the eyes of professionals such as Corning's research-and-development scientists, the town with its amenities and low cost of living even compares favorably with places like the San Francisco Bay Area, observes former chairman James Houghton. "What we're doing in Corning is totally in our self-interest," he told me. "It's smart business." The business-district rejuvenation and the glass museum—support for which runs to $20 million each year—help build Corning's brand name and public goodwill. Some might say these efforts qualify for that dirty term "gentrification." But one only has to compare Corning's business district with that of atrophied upstate burgs to see that gentrification isn't always something to sneeze at.[42]

Another group of company towns emerged in the early twentieth century, defined by a different sort of idealism—once again motivated by corporations' desire to escape from urban wilderness and often the necessity of locating close to natural resources. These "industrial satellite" towns, however, were different from earlier company utopias in one key way: They were the province—and experimental playthings—of architects rather than of visionary capitalists. It is an approach that seems much more modern today, as we are accustomed to the notion of the architect as visionary (thank you, Ayn Rand). At the same time, the architectural style exhibited in most of these towns was anything but avant-garde.

One of the first of these was U.S. Steel's Fairfield, Alabama, located close to the iron ore, limestone, and coal needed for production in the Fairfield Works steel plant. (The town, first called Corey, was originally owned by Tennessee Coal and Iron, a company the J. P. Morgan interests dramatically absorbed in 1907 largely to stave off a stock market panic.)[43] Fairfield was part of a group of company towns that seemed to deny their industrial purpose. Here, planner George Miller and architect William Leslie Walton erected a series of craftsman-style homes in a sylvan setting. Like several British company towns inspired by England's "garden city" movement, the reigning aesthetic was preindustrial.[44]

Indian Hill, a suburb of Worcester, Massachusetts, built for the Norton Co., resembled a colonial New England village, complete with cottages, leafy streets, steepled churches, and a town square. In Tyrone, New Mexico, one of several company towns built for copper-mining company Phelps Dodge, architect Bertram Goodhue adopted a rococo motif, with mansions, a school, and a hospital reminiscent of buildings in coastal Spain.[45] The streets of Atco, Georgia, built by the American Textile Co., were lined with modest clapboard bungalows evocative of nineteenth-century Southern country villages.[46] Aluminum maker Alcoa built settlements with similar structures in both Alcoa, Tennessee, and Massena, New York.[47] Lynch, Kentucky, built in 1917 in Harlan County by the U.S. Steel subsidiary U.S. Coal and Coke Co., featured a sandstone-block commissary, post office, theater, hotel, hospital, churches, and schools; workers lived in single and double houses with asphalt shingles.[48]

Altogether, around forty new industrial towns were constructed from 1900 to 1920, in which single-family homes came in numerous varieties—

but in which the repetitive looks and gridiron pattern of earlier company towns were "obsessively avoided," in the words of architectural historian Margaret Crawford. The factory, mill, or mine was consistently out of sight of the residences.[49]

It was in this same period that American modernist architecture began to make its mark. By the final years of the nineteenth century, celebrated Chicago architect Louis Sullivan was already developing the modern skyscraper with such edifices as the Carson Pirie Scott department store in the Windy City and the Guaranty Building in Buffalo, New York. By 1900, thirty-three-year-old Frank Lloyd Wright was recognized as the chief practitioner of the Prairie School of modern homes, marked by flowing lines, open space, and a functionalist absence of fussiness. Observers celebrated Wright's Larkin Soap Co. administration building in Buffalo for its radical use of plate-glass windows, built-in furniture, and air conditioning. But in the midst of such developments, the new company towns seemed to draw aesthetic cues from another place—possibly from Agatha Christie or the New England novels of Harriet Beecher Stowe. Modernist touches were rare: Torrance, California, was virtually alone in making such aesthetic choices. In that oil-refining center, working-class residents were turned off by architect Irving Gill's spare, streamlined houses, which seemed only to connote austerity and poverty. Instead, they opted for California bungalows, with their gardens, privacy, and associations with the British Empire and rural life. From the late twentieth century on, many model company towns would face daily life in disguise, pretending to be something other than what they truly were.

But for a number of companies, aesthetics—and the comfort of the workers housed—was a matter of little concern. Such companies focused only on the bottom line and saw their employees strictly as a means to the end of profit, perhaps as something less than full-fledged members of the human race. They seemed almost to take delight in exploiting their workers, to the point of justifying the most extreme claims of political radicals. These were the enterprises that flourished in the kingdom of coal.

CHAPTER 3

Exploitationville

Straight Creek is a narrow zigzag valley that runs up into the mountains from Pineville. . . . The houses are low shacks set up on stilts, scattered in disorderly rows up and down the valley floor. . . . The A.P. man and the gentleman from the Courier-Journal *. . . keep looking around behind things as if they felt the houses had been put up to hoax them. They refuse to believe that people can be so badly off as that.*

—JOHN DOS PASSOS
in *Harlan Miners Speak* (1931)

Some American phenomena cannot be exaggerated: The rhetoric and guile of a Louisiana politician. The head-snapping recklessness of a New York City taxi driver. And the near-totalitarian, super-exploitative conditions of life in a coal-mining company town.

The basic formula for coal towns was as follows: Companies built their settlements, sometimes little more than camps, close to the mines. To recoup this investment, they made it a condition of employment that workers live in rental housing there—employees were not allowed to buy. The owners, or "coal operators," as they were known, barred outsiders including peddlers or businesses not affiliated with the company, and any such persons daring to enter risked arrest for trespass. Operators paid workers in cash or scrip—company-issued money, denominated like U.S. currency but redeemable chiefly at the company store—at the end of the month, with deductions for rent and utilities and sometimes for school fees and taxes. And when workers ran out of money between paydays, as they often did, they had little choice but to turn to the company store, where they could get credit in the form of scrip for time already worked but not yet paid. Potentially, then, they were always living on credit. Prices at the store were noticeably higher than elsewhere, but outside merchants tended to discount scrip by 10 percent to 25 percent. Should a miner become injured and unable to work, the company evicted him and his family from its housing with as little as ten days' notice. Eviction also occurred if the miner went on strike, and if he died in a mine accident, his family had to leave.

This template was in place as early as the 1870s in the semi-bituminous coal districts of eastern Pennsylvania and was widely copied. Although not every mining town adhered to every part of the formula—"open" towns in Colorado, for example, included primitive housing built by the miners themselves—it remained the standard for the next half-century.[1]

The living quarters in mining camps were among the worst in the country, according to a 1925 report of the U.S. Coal Commission. Most houses were the cheapest kind of wooden structures, with roofs made of tar paper rather than shingles. Each boxlike, three- or four-room building drew its heat from open fireplaces or a single potbellied, coal-fired stove. Only 14 percent of coal town houses in Virginia, West Virginia, and Kentucky had running water, and most had privies out back that emptied directly into a nearby creek. Few towns had any sort of recreation facilities—other than the ubiquitous saloons or occasional bordellos and gambling halls. Twenty-two years after the Coal Commission report, a different U.S. government study found things had changed little. The average camp, it said, consisted of "monotonous rows of houses and privies, all in the same faded hues, standing alongside the railroad tracks close to a foul creek; or camps like ones farther up the valley, with their scattered houses on stilts, perilously perching, with their privies behind them, on steep hillsides." Even in somewhat nicer towns, such as Export, Pennsylvania, there was a dull sameness: That burg's "Red Row" consisted of forty identical barn-red two-family dwellings, and its "White Row" of identical single-family houses.[2]

Law enforcement was strictly in the hands of the coal operators. "To use the expression of the Middle Ages," one owner bragged, "I was the high justice, the middle, and the low." The primary aim of such justice:

keeping unions out. Few other American businessmen were as antiunion as the coal operators. The industry spread blacklists of suspected union sympathizers and employed private guards, often from the Baldwin-Felts strikebreaking and security firm out of Bluefield, West Virginia. Such security could be costly: Pittsburgh Coal employed more than three hundred police, spending more than $670,000 during one two-year period. Local sheriffs were assigned deputies, generally paid directly by the companies, and these would arrest and jail any suspected union organizers. In Logan County, West Virginia, in the 1910s and '20s, Sheriff Don Chafin received tribute from all the mine owners and named three hundred mine guards as his deputies. Chafin met every train that came into the area, grilled strangers as to the purpose of their visit, beat up union sympathizers and drove them from the county, and arrested and jailed political opponents. In other towns, voters were told whom to vote for, and these preferences were driven home by deputies who handed out printed slates of favored candidates at the polls. In Harlan County, Kentucky, miners weren't even allowed to serve on juries—since they lived in company housing and paid no taxes—which left coal company officials, farmers, and merchants to dominate juries.[3]

In places, coal miners and actual prisoners were interchangeable. In 1871, miners at Tennessee Coal & Mining Co.'s Coal Creek mines went on strike against harsh company demands—which included getting paid in scrip only and signing a "yellow dog contract" in which they pledged not to join a union—at which point the company shut down its mines. Shortly thereafter, it announced it would reopen the mines using convict labor rented from the state of Tennessee. Several pitched battles resulted, finally involving 5,000 Tennessee National Guard troops. Rebel miners were hunted down and arrested. The conflict continued until, after the governor lost a reelection bid, the legislature outlawed the convict-lease system.[4] But other states continued the practice far longer: Alabama did not end the practice until 1928.[5] In that state, the coal mining–convict association was particularly strong. From 1890 to 1905, Docena, Alabama—on the outskirts of Birmingham—was a prison camp. Then, TCI, formerly Tennessee Coal, Iron, and Railroad Co., turned it into a coal-mining company town with a labor force of former sharecroppers.[6]

It would be a wonder if coal miners hadn't rebelled. The history of the industry is one of clandestine union organization and retributive violence. Two spectacular examples suffice for now. In January 1875, Pennsylvania anthracite-region miners led by a union called the Workingmen's Benevolent Association (WBA) struck in protest of wage cuts of as much as 20 percent mandated by the Philadelphia & Reading Railroad, which had come to dominate coal mining in the region. The WBA had emerged only seven years before and had won several agreements with the area's Anthracite Board of Trade, in the process helping to impose order on a chaotic industry. But railroad chief Franklin Gowen favored a different arrangement. First, he drove most of Schuylkill County's small coal operators out of business by buying up tens of thousands of acres of coal land. Then he set out to break the union with pay demands that seemed designed to provoke a strike. After four months, the union members were suffering, and by June the strike had failed totally. The union collapsed.

Violence marked every step of the proceedings: Management engaged vigilantes and the private Coal and Iron Police to selectively assassinate union activists, sometimes firing into miners' meetings. Twenty-six union officials were charged with conspiracy and imprisoned. For their part, some coal miners engaged in brutality, too, though the WBA repeatedly forswore violence. The months following the union defeat saw acts of sabotage and at least six assassinations of mine superintendents and public officials. Anonymous letters, some signed "Molly," threatened reprisals for management misdeeds. Was this part of a union conspiracy or perhaps a secret Irish organization, the Molly Maguires, that had committed a series of assaults and killings dating to the 1860s?

The Mollys now seem to have been less of an organization and more of an informal pattern of threats and violence: Night riders often engaged in personal vendettas following a tradition that grew out of rural Ireland. But during the strike, railroad chief Gowen vowed to get to the bottom of the Molly Maguire phenomenon and hired detectives from the Pinkerton agency to infiltrate labor ranks. In the aftermath, management announced that a terrorist conspiracy had been at work—involving not only the union but also an Irish fraternity named the Ancient Order of Hibernians (AOH) and its alleged alter ego, the Molly Maguires. Virtually the entire leadership of the anthracite region's AOH—in reality only a fraternity something like the Odd Fellows—was indicted and put on trial for murder and conspiracy. Arrested by the private Coal and Iron Police force, they were tried with evidence given primarily by a Pinkerton detective/agent provocateur and union turncoats, and prosecuted by attorneys who worked for the railroad and mining companies—including Gowen himself. Mere membership in the AOH was offered as proof of guilt. Some testimony intended to conflate the two organizations and to play up spooky practices referred to secret identifying AOH hand signals and verbal greetings: "The nights are very dark," one member might say, and another must answer, "I hope they will soon mend." (The melodramatic sign language and verbiage so impressed Sir Arthur Conan Doyle that he included some of it in his Molly Maguires–inspired Sherlock Holmes tale *The Valley of Fear.*) In the end, twenty alleged Mollys were convicted and hanged.[7]

In coal, violence often rose to the level of military confrontation. In the summer of 1921, for example, an army of miners variously estimated at 5,000 to 13,000 marched on Sheriff Chafin's nonunion Logan County in an attempt to free jailed labor activists. Chafin and an army of 2,000 deputies, mine guards, and volunteers under the command of a West Virginia National Guard colonel fortified positions on Blair Mountain overlooking the town of Logan. Attempts to disperse the miners—including threats by President Warren G. Harding to send in federal troops and bomber aircraft—were to no avail, and a battle began on August 29. Aircraft, including some Army bombers and private planes hired by Chafin, did drop World War I surplus explosive and gas bombs on the miners. Amid sporadic gun battles, thirty of Chapin's men were killed along with perhaps fifty to one hundred miners. Federal troops arrived on September 2, and the miners scattered. In the aftermath, 985 miners were indicted on charges ranging from murder to treason against the state of West Virginia, and many served prison terms.[8]

Despite these abuses, unions caught on slowly in many coal-mining areas. In the words of Jim Garland, an Appalachian folksinger and brother of the more famous Sarah Ogan Gunning: "The mountain people thought that if your employer did not treat you right, you should quit or try to give him a good whipping."[9]

The demand for coal far outstripped its supply, though there was plenty of the stuff west of the Appalachians. By 1816, the iron- and glassworks of the burgeoning industrial town of Pittsburgh, Pennsylvania, were burning copious amounts of it. One observer reported "a cloud which amounts to night and overspreads Pittsburgh with the appearance of gloom and melancholy." But it was difficult to ship coal economically over the mountains and on to the factories in Massachusetts and other parts of the eastern seaboard. In the 1830s, the cost of running a coal-fired steam engine on America's East Coast was double the cost in England.

Initially, much of the coal used by American industry was anthracite—a hard, clean-burning ore mined from deposits east of the Appalachians. In 1825, the Schuylkill Canal opened, making the Schuylkill River navigable between the coalfields near Port Carbon and Philadelphia. Mules and men pulled barges loaded with anthracite down the hundred-mile route. Soon other canals cut across New Jersey, connecting the Delaware River with the Atlantic Ocean. But rising demand for coal soon put the canals out of business, as companies built railroads right along the canal route. The Philadelphia & Reading Railroad—one of the main actors in the Molly Maguires affair—was carrying 2.5 million tons of coal by 1859.[10]

Consumption of coal by America's growing industries and its burgeoning cities doubled every decade between 1850 and 1890. In the latter decade, the United States produced 243 million tons, bypassing production in then-second-place England by 43 million tons. North America held the world's richest coal deposits, including plentiful bituminous, or soft-coal, deposits in Illinois, Indiana, Ohio, and western Pennsylvania that supplied much of the U.S. market until the late nineteenth century. In southern Colorado, three great bituminous fields were discovered, and mining began there in the 1870s when railroads moved into the region from Kansas City, Denver, and New Mexico. Finally, a vast field—50 million acres of coal reserves—stretched across Appalachia down to Alabama.[11] Problem was, much of the Appalachian land remained heavily forested and dominated by towering mountain ranges. Moreover, prior to the late nineteenth century, no railroads or other transport extended there.

Reports of the southern coalfields set off a stampede of land speculation after the Civil War. Speculators were often backed by northern or

European capital—a fact that later led to charges of carpetbagging and plundering—but several of the most active land-grabbers were sons of Dixie. George L. Carter, for example, the son of a Confederate Army officer, was the key organizer of the Tom's Creek Coal Co. and became one of the leading coal operators of southwestern Virginia. John C. Calhoun Mayo, a former math teacher and lawyer who married into the Old South aristocracy, acquired options on thousands of acres of eastern Kentucky land and by the turn of the twentieth century was a chief stockholder in Consolidation Coal Co. Mayo and figures like him showed the way for the absentee owners who bought up millions of acres of Appalachian land for as little as 25 cents to $3 per acre.

Major Jedediah Hotchkiss, one of the primary cartographers for General Robert E. Lee's Army of Northern Virginia at Gettysburg, became the scout for a very different invader: the Norfolk and Western Railway (N&W).[12] Railroad building accompanied and furthered the Appalachian land boom beginning in the 1880s, with four railroads playing key roles. The N&W pushed into southwestern Virginia, drawn by the vast deposits around Flat Top Mountain. The Chesapeake & Ohio Railroad (C&O) made tracks for southern West Virginia; the Louisville & Nashville (L&N) forged into eastern Kentucky and Tennessee; and the Southern Railroad pioneered development of western North Carolina. Generally the railroads came first, followed closely by would-be mine operators, but sometimes the developers just couldn't wait. When N&W railroad builders reached the Tazewell County, Virginia, settlement of Pocahontas in 1883, they found it was already a thriving boom town with fifty houses, a company store, shops ranging from a butcher to a milliner, a newspaper, two saloons, and coal operations already in progress. A pile of 40,000 tons of coal awaited, along with one hundred ovens for the manufacture of coke, the porous, low-sulfur fuel used in iron smelting.[13]

Appalachian coal production tripled in the 1890s, then increased fivefold up to 1930, at which point it constituted 80 percent of U.S. production. More than five hundred coal-company towns existed there by the 1920s, housing more than two-thirds of the area's miners (80 percent in West Virginia).[14] Hundreds of independent coal operators employing from ten to thirty miners joined the coal rush, leasing land from the big landholders. Operators could get a mine off the ground with as little as $20,000 or $30,000 in seed money. "All that was required was to build houses for the miners, a store to supply them, and a tipple structure to dump the coal into railway cars," observed one operator. A coal camp might begin with little more than the mine, a company office, and a commissary or grocery store. Within a year or so, miners who'd been living in tents would be able to move into rudimentary housing, and if things went well, in time more family dwellings would appear along with schools and maybe churches. (Miners were never particularly keen on churchgoing.)[15]

The bituminous seams were too widely dispersed to allow monopoly control, and mines were fiercely competitive. Even so, big operators dominated coal production in Appalachia, among them the U.S. Coal and Oil Co., predecessor of the Island Creek Coal Co., whose beachhead was Logan County, West Virginia. By 1910, mines there were producing more than 2 million tons of coal each year. The Pennsylvania Railroad and its ally, U.S. Steel, controlled the Flat Top–Pocahontas region of Virginia. U.S. Steel subsidiary U.S. Coal and Coke Co. extracted 5 million tons of coal annually from West Virginia mines, and Consolidation Coal Co. of Maryland led the way in the Elkhorn field area of Kentucky, with its operations center located in the model company town of Jenkins.[16]

Model towns with such amenities as comfortable housing, recreation facilities, and well-laid-out streets and parks composed only 2 percent of Appalachia's company towns. As might be expected, many of these were the properties of the biggest companies, which could afford generosity toward their employees. Jenkins, Kentucky, for example, provided garbage collection and sewers. Holden, West Virginia, owned by the Island Creek Coal Co., had a theater, a library, two bowling alleys, and a clubhouse with showers. Widen, West Virginia, owned by the Elk River Coal & Lumber Co., featured well-run schools, a swimming pool, a hospital, and a YMCA that included a bowling alley, a basketball court, and a theater.[17]

But big operators didn't necessarily take more care with their towns. Wheelwright, Kentucky, for instance, was at various periods the property of Consolidation Coal affiliate Elkhorn Coal Corp., Inland Steel, and Island Creek Coal Co. Elkhorn, which operated the community between 1916 and 1930, offered the least in the way of development, with streets left unpaved and garbage simply dumped in a nearby hollow. White children attended a four-room schoolhouse, while black children had no school at all. Inland Steel, the proprietor of Wheelwright between 1930 and 1963, saw improvements as good for business. That company reconditioned four hundred houses, installing flush toilets among other things; built a water-filtration plant for the town; equipped the mines with better ventilation; and constructed a bathhouse with showers for miners. In 1965, Island Creek took over, and it showed no interest in Wheelwright, auctioning off much of its housing.[18]

In Colorado, model towns were built specifically to undercut worker militancy and labor organization. In 1894, with the United Mine Workers of America (UMWA) having called for a strike that led 125,000 workers in the East and Midwest to put down tools, coal miners in Colorado voted for a one-week sympathy strike. An unusual feature of the Colorado walkout were cross-country marches in which some 1,200 miners trekked across perhaps one hundred miles of countryside, from Fremont County down to Las Animas County. With flags flying and brass bands leading the way, they traveled from town to town urging miners to stop work. They often succeeded, as at Walsenburg, where 115 walked out and joined the marchers. The mining giant of the area, Colorado Fuel and Iron (CFI), had over 7,000 employees and nearly 72,000 acres of coal land—so it had much at stake. It fought back with injunctions and path-blocking deputy sheriffs. But the most effective mechanism, the area's coal operators discovered, was the closed company town.

Often the Colorado mine companies had allowed and even encouraged workers to build their own homes on company land. Open camps such as Coal Creek, Colorado, consisted mostly of such worker-owned housing, ranging from log cabins to Mexican adobes. Other towns, including Rouse and Sopris, were "closed," resembling the coal towns in Pennsylvania and Appalachia. The 1894 marches generally stalled at the borders of such closed camps. In the 1900s, companies in Colorado began expanding the number of such places and upgrading their housing. At Redstone, for instance, architect Theodore Davis Boal built

eighty-five arts-and-crafts-inspired cottages for CFI. The town also featured hydroelectric power, clean water, a modern school and clubhouse,
a theater, a well-stocked store, and more. CFI magnate John Osgood figured that such benevolent gestures would be the undoing of unionism,
and his company continued the model-town movement with settlements
at Primero, Segundo, Tercio, Cuarto, Quinto, and Sexto. American
Smelting and Refining Co.'s Cokedale featured electric streetlights and
other modern amenities. Such towns offered kindergarten and adult-ed-
ucation classes, social clubs, and lectures on topics ranging from European art to germ theory.

But the iron fist inside the velvet glove was not hard to find: Colorado's model towns were generally surrounded by barbed-wire fences
and patrolled by camp marshals and mine guards. There was surveillance
in every town and saloon. Undesirables, from peddlers to state labor officials, were kept out. UMWA organizers were followed and harassed:
"There was never a time that I wasn't followed constantly by one to three
guards," testified District 15 president John McLennan. The companies
bribed voters to control local elections, and as in Logan County, West
Virginia, local sheriffs did their bidding.[19]

Kentucky's coalfields—among the most famous nationally perhaps due to
the frightening level of conflict in Harlan County—were among the last to
be developed. The L&N, the Lexington & Eastern Railroad, and the Baltimore & Ohio made their way into eleven counties in the eastern part of
the state on the eve of World War I. The L&N's extension to the head of
the Cumberland River in Harlan County signified the final opening of the
area, and by 1914, miners were hauling over a million tons of coal.

Thousands of miners moved in, tripling the area's population by 1920
and doubling it again by 1930. Harlan (confusingly, the name of both
the county and the town formerly known as Mt. Pleasant) became the
leading coal-producing area in the state, with the largest operations near
the town of Benham, which was under the control of Wisconsin Steel
Co., a subsidiary of International Harvester Co. Two miles from Benham, U.S. Steel subsidiary U.S. Coal & Coke Co. built the community

of Lynch, ultimately constructing 2,000 buildings and, by 1919, housing a population of 10,000. All the coal from Lynch was sent to another company town—Gary, Indiana, home of giant steel mills run by U.S. Steel.[20]

Harry M. Caudill, a lawyer, Kentucky state legislator, and lifelong resident of Letcher County, chronicled developments in Kentucky. He felt the coal companies took far more than they gave to the Appalachian region—if indeed they gave it anything at all. Caudill's *Night Comes to the Cumberlands* (1963), one of eight books he wrote about Kentucky and what he considered its sad fate, is a Kennedy-era classic that, like Michael Harrington's *The Other America*, helped U.S. progressives "rediscover" poverty and build a movement that shook the country's middle-class complacency.

Caudill took note of the smaller coal towns, which "copied in the most shabby fashion" the pattern laid down by the likes of Lynch and Benham. In places with "a variety of startling names—such as Neon, Blackey, Cumberland, Hellier, Hi-Hat, Garrett, Whitaker, Chevrolet, and Jeff," houses were built for miners on which "not a dollar was spent . . . beyond the barest necessity" and which "were slums as soon as they were occupied." He excoriated those he called "the Big Bosses," who he said "exercised absolute dominion over the towns they had built," whether these were the so-called model communities or "a cluster of thirty or forty grimy shacks centering about a rickety commissary and tipple." In such locations, Caudill wrote,

> The miner came to be almost wholly insulated against the world outside his coal camp. In return for his labor, his employers clothed his back, filled his belly, sheltered and lighted his household, and provided his family with medical treatment, fuel and water. The thoughtful operators even organized burial associations, withholding a couple of dollars each month from the workman's wages for payment to a favored undertaker, so that when death came the mortician's bill had been paid in advance. Needless to say, the company realized a profit on each of these endeavors. The miner found himself on a treadmill from which he lacked the knowledge and self-discipline to escape.[21]

Daily life in these communities was unremittingly grim, according to Caudill, plagued by the "monstrous coaldust genie" that hovered in the air above the tipple and "crept into every nook and cranny in the town." Then there were the huge slate dumps—mountains of unwanted rock and low-grade coal that arose near every tipple and that tended to spontaneously burst into flames, with accompanying clouds of sulfurous, oily smoke. In the polluted atmosphere, paint peeled from the walls of houses, eyes and throats ached, and "communities gradually took on that sickly hue which miners called 'coal-camp gray.'"[22]

With their solid grip on the state's politicians, the companies ensured that taxes stayed low—with the effect that infrastructure was little developed and state governments were mired in debt, he wrote. Caudill traced the coal industry's history, including its World War I boom, Depression-era bust, World War II revival, and ultimate collapse. But perhaps the author's most adamant and angry prose focuses on the area's environmental devastation. "Nowhere in the [Cumberland] plateau does a single tract of virgin forest remain," he wrote. "Hundreds of worked-out mines have become subterranean lakes. . . . The valleys are sprinkled with hideous car dumps where Fords, Chevrolets, Cadillacs and once magnificent limousines lie piled in rusty array. As eyesores they are second only to the ghastly trash dumps . . . [that] abound on roadside and stream-bank." For all of this, Caudill left little doubt, it was the Big Bosses who deserved the blame—the corporations that siphoned off hundreds of millions of dollars' worth of resources and treated the Appalachian region as "a colonial appendage of the industrial East and Middle West."[23]

Caudill remained an outspoken rebel until his self-inflicted death in 1990. (Parkinson's, it seemed, had sapped his will to live.) In a 1975 interview with *Mother Earth News*, he contrasted the fate of Switzerland, one of the world's richest countries despite its natural handicaps, and that of West Virginia, one of the poorest areas in the United States despite its natural wealth. His bête noire had become the strip miners, who he felt had taken up where the previous generation of coal operators had left off. The impoverishment of the Appalachian region could have been avoided, he insisted, had the states simply collected a very small tax, as little as 10 cents per ton, on the coal moving out of the area and used it to finance public education. "We've got everything in the world here in these mountains that's required to build anything we want to build except the willpower and the mind," he concluded.[24]

———

The legendary "company store" owes its infamy largely to practices in coal-company towns. Who doesn't know the phrase "I owe my soul to the company store"—and perhaps other lyrics of the song "Sixteen Tons"? We owe that to the repeated airplay of a recording by 1950s television personality Tennessee Ernie Ford, but the song was in fact penned by Merle Travis, a hillbilly musician and the son of a coal miner, born in Muhlenberg County, Kentucky, in 1917.

Travis attended classes through the eighth grade at a one-room school-house in Ebenezer, near the digs of Beech Creek Coal Co. At age sixteen, he enlisted in the Civilian Conservation Corps, a New Deal–era make-work agency, and thereafter became an entertainer. After appearing on radio shows in Evansville, Indiana, and in Cincinnati—and with a break for World War II service in the Marines—he moved to Hollywood and signed with Capitol Records.

In his album-cover photos, his broad forehead, sleepy eyes, and toothy grin make him seem the very picture of an unaffected country boy. Capitol Records encouraged Travis to record some coal-country songs (at first he said he didn't know any), so he wrote and recorded several such tunes on a 1946 album, *Folk Songs of the Hills*. "Dark as a Dungeon" ponders the coal miner's attraction for work in pits "where the sun never shines," noting that "it will form as a habit and seep in your soul" and that "a man will have lust for the lure of the mines." (Curiously enough, Travis penned that miner's lament just after a musical appearance in sunny Re-dondo Beach, California.) Meanwhile, in a spoken aside recorded along with "Sixteen Tons," Travis reflected,

> Yessir, there's a-many a Kentucky coal miner that pretty near owes his soul to the company store. He gets so far in debt to the coal company he's a-workin' for that he goes on fer years without being paid one red cent in real honest-to-goodness money. But he can

always go to the company store and draw flickers or scrip—you know, that's little brass coins that you can't spend nowhere, only at the company store. So they add that to his account and every day he gets a little farther in debt.[25]

The song became a hit for Ford in 1955, thanks to the power of television and, in significant part, to the public's growing ability to relate to the condition of permanent indebtedness. But were coal miners of Travis's father's generation really living in a condition of debt peonage? Historians have disagreed about the charge, with some saying that the existence of railroad networks meant that miners were far from isolated and hardly dependent on their town's store.[26] Caudill believed that "most miners got into the habit of living almost entirely by scrip," which they spent at the company store. His analysis is supported by one study conducted by New Deal agency the National Recovery Administration (NRA), which found some workers who had received no cash payments for fifteen years. Moreover, Caudill asserted that "an increasing harshness" among Depression-era Big Bosses led them to insist that miners make all their purchases at the company store, where prices were often twice as much as elsewhere. (The NRA study found the disparity to be lower, from 2.1 percent to 10.4 percent higher than at neighboring independent stores.) John Brophy, a second-generation miner from age twelve who in time became an official of the UMWA, wrote in his autobiography that prices in the Urey, Pennsylvania, company store were much higher than at private stores and a miner's chances of saving anything were worse than slim. "Only my mother's rigidly economical management of what income we received saved us from getting into debt slavery," he recalled. By avoiding debt, Brophy's family was able to move regularly, living what he called "a gypsy life."[27]

The actual company stores varied greatly. Some were little more than small-town groceries, but those in the larger communities sold a variety of goods, from food to furniture, clothing, window screens, nails, pharmaceuticals, refrigerators, and garden tools. They might offer services such as haircutting and dry cleaning, and the buildings might house meeting rooms, a post office, a payroll window, and administrative offices for the company.

If some stores were little more than shacks, others were substantial: Photographs of the company store (now demolished) in Lynch, Kentucky, show an appreciable, three-story modern stone building with large plate-glass windows. Colorado Fuel and Iron's Colorado Supply Co. operated large, well-stocked emporia featuring branded consumer goods, meat departments, furniture, Indian handicrafts including Navajo blankets and Zuni bows and arrows, and more. It isn't difficult to imagine that in such a place miners might while away hours of free time, jawing and smoking. Many stores served as a meeting place and a center of town social life.[28]

Company stores, scrip, and indebtedness were hardly the subject of every coal-miner ballad. There were a great many songs, of course, given that making old-timey music was a regular Appalachian pastime. Other subjects included romance, honky-tonks, moonshine whisky, work (the traditional folk ballad "Nine-Pound Hammer" also appeared on Travis's 1947 record), migration to distant cities, dramatic weather events, bloody car crashes, favored pets and livestock, religion, and, inevitably, union-management conflict. Of these, some of the most well-known include the traditional "Only a Miner," on death due to a mine collapse; Florence Reece's "Which Side Are You On?" which grew out of a 1930s Harlan County labor battle and urges listeners not to scab; and Sarah Ogan Gunning's "Dreadful Memories," which relates her experiences with the Communist-led National Miners Union in the 1930s.

The coal industry boom lasted from the 1880s into the late 1920s, during which time there was ever a shortage of willing workers. Gangs of laborers, many of whom were black, built the railroads, and some companies prevailed upon these men to stay and dig coal. Construction gangs from such cities as Baltimore, Cincinnati, and Louisville built the mushrooming towns, but few of these construction workers changed occupations. Although large companies brought supervisory personnel, clerks, executives, and the necessary engineers into Appalachia from coalfields in Pennsylvania and elsewhere, the actual miners were always in short supply.

Company labor agents scoured the countryside, and many poor whites—some pushed off the land by the big companies' land grab or by hard times—gave up farming to mine coal. But, particularly in the early years, Appalachian hillbillies proved unreliable: They were willing to go into the mines during the harsh winter months but gravitated back to the farms during planting and harvesting seasons. During the first three decades of the twentieth century, only a quarter of West Virginia mining families stayed in one place for longer than five years.

While some mine operators turned to convict labor, there was hardly enough to go around. There were reports, too, of Deep South states freeing black convicts so long as they agreed to migrate and take up coal mining.

Finally, labor agents began recruiting workers from Europe, particularly Italy, Hungary, Poland, Albania, and Greece. Sometimes recruiters went to these countries, but mostly they haunted the docks and ethnic neighborhoods of New York, Philadelphia, and Baltimore. Recruits were hastily loaded onto train cars, the doors of which were sometimes sealed to prevent escape. "These penniless 'transportation men' stepped from their cars at Jenkins, McRoberts, Benham, Lynch, Middlesboro, Wayland, Wheelwright and numerous other wild coal towns to jeers and hoots from crowds of mountaineers," reported Caudill. Shunted off to separate-but-not-always-equal housing in "Woptowns" and "Hunkytowns," or crammed into ten- to twenty-five-room boardinghouses for single men, the recruits discovered that their train tickets were not gratis: The men were already in debt for their "transportation."

This massive influx of people swelled the Appalachian population: The Harlan County population rose almost threefold, from 10,564 in 1910 to 31,546 in 1920. The work was hard and dirty—and labor recruiters worked for other employers, too, notably those in Detroit and other Midwestern cities. In Stonega, Virginia, about a quarter of the Europeans fled before they'd worked off their transportation. World War I interrupted the flow of foreign workers, and some immigrants returned to Europe. Restrictive immigration laws of the early 1920s ended such practices altogether.[29]

The immigrants worked side-by-side with southern whites. Blacks were generally given the worst, hottest, heaviest labor, such as "pulling," or extracting, the heavy coke from blistering coke ovens. The others worked below ground in the mines. Most Appalachian digs were "drift mines" dug into hillsides above the valley, meaning workers entered laterally rather than via the long, vertical shafts that were common elsewhere in the United States.[30]

Here's how coal mining was done: The miner awoke early, perhaps at 3 or 4 a.m., and, as "Sixteen Tons" suggests, he picked up his gear and walked to the mine, which after all was close by his house. That equipment consisted of a manually operated augur or drill, a pick, a shovel, a lamp, and his dinner pail. Some electric machinery appeared as early as 1915 but wasn't widespread until the 1930s. He walked down to his "room" at the mine—a tunnel cut through the coal seam that might be anywhere from three to eight feet in height and twenty-four feet wide. Surrounded by solid walls of coal left standing to support the roof, he and his workmate (it was common for two men to work a room) went to the front wall, or "coal face," at the bottom of which they chiseled out a wedge-shaped section. Given the low ceiling, a miner usually lay on his side and swung his pick in the confined space. Then, using the drill, he and his workmate bored holes several feet above that wedge and filled these with black powder and a fuse. "Fire in the hole!" they would yell to alert those in other nearby "rooms" as they lit the fuse. The subsequent explosion would dislodge a layer of coal that they would then shovel into a railcar and push to the entryway to be hauled off. This set of tasks called for "an unusual blend of a craftsman and a laborer," according to labor historian David Montgomery, since "to bring down that coal so it could be loaded required artistry, judgment, and self-reliance." Not to mention plain ol' guts.

Though there were "day men" who received straight-time, hourly wages for such work as pumping water or doing carpentry, most miners were paid by the ton. That meant that time spent laying more railway track into a room or cross-cutting tunnels to other rooms—needed for ventilation and communication—was time wasted in terms of pay. On the positive side, miners worked at their own speed and faced few hassles from supervisors, since there was only one such straw boss for every ten to twenty men. It was not unusual for miners to knock off for the day whenever they felt they had met whatever expectations they'd set for themselves.[31]

But miners had to balance their schedules with other concerns—namely death and dismemberment. For years, coal mining was regarded as the most dangerous occupation in America. Risks ranged from cave-ins, gas explosions and poisoning, electrocution, and, especially, roof falls. Mine explosions—including dramatic ones at Switchback and Layland, West Virginia; Pocahontas, Virginia; and Briceville and Rockwood, Tennessee—claimed one hundred workers per year in the 1920s. Less infamous but more destructive were falling slate and coal, which killed 50,000 miners between 1906 and 1935. Then there were respiratory ailments, which the industry pooh-poohed for years. An incalculable number of miners fell because of chronic bronchitis, silicosis from breathing rock dust, and the now-infamous black lung, or pneumoconiosis. Workers' compensation, begun in most states during the 1910s, might pay as little as $4,000 for a death and $2,200 for permanent partial disability.[32]

Hazardous-duty pay? No way, although pay in the southern mines rose steadily from the 1910s through the late '20s, from about $1.50 for a ten-hour day to $4 for an eight-hour stint. During boom years, pay might go as high as $6 per day—and it fell during the Great Depression to under $3. Pay varied greatly from mine to mine: At some, miners were paid by the ton, elsewhere by the carload. Some were paid by the day, others by the shift.[33]

Was there something about coal mining that compelled abuse of the miners? Two thoughts come to mind: First, the work was disagreeable and brutal, combining dangers almost comparable to those of combat with inescapable grime and illness. And that might have been enough to compel workers to flee—if they had not somehow been held fast by their bosses. Second, the bituminous industry was very competitive, with many smaller mines just eking by even as the big operators raked in the profits. Such conditions naturally led to stinginess—which in turn likely prompted some coal operators not only to skimp on wages but also to squeeze money, in the form of rents and company-store earnings, from their workers. Then again, maybe there's just something about mining:

Both George Orwell in Britain and Emile Zola in France reported oppressive conditions in those countries' coal-mining areas.

A logical response was unionization, the very thing the coal operators most reviled. The dispersed nature of the mines—spreading across the Midwest, into western states such as southern Colorado and northern New Mexico, and southward through the Appalachians—and the isolation of the miners meant that many struggles were local, spontaneous, and short-lived.

Pennsylvania miners of the 1870s formed a union called the Miners' National Association; elsewhere in years to come, the Knights of Labor, the Industrial Workers of the World (IWW), and the Communist National Miners Union (NMU) were active. In some struggles, including at Coal Creek, Tennessee, the Knights and the UMWA participated, and many rank-and-filers belonged to both. But the most enduring of the unions—as a result of a history that combined sacrifice and craven compromise, political idealism, opportunism, and corruption—proved to be the UMWA.

The organization was formed in 1890 at Columbus, Ohio, when the Knights of Labor Assembly 135 and the Ohio-based National Progressive Miners' Union combined. At first, the organization consisted almost entirely of native-born or British immigrant pick miners. After a strike that idled 100,000 miners in 1897, the UMWA won its first contract in 1898, the so-called Central Competitive Field (CCF) Agreement, providing wage increases and union recognition in five midwestern states. Next, the organization ventured into the anthracite fields of Pennsylvania, where miners were more ethnically diverse and more organized into the company-town system, and where child labor was common: The 22,000 working in the mines there included 5,500 "breaker boys" who sorted coal from slate and stone as it rushed by on a conveyor belt. In 1902, 150,000 anthracite miners struck and ultimately won a 10 percent wage increase in a deal brokered with magnate J. P. Morgan by President Theodore Roosevelt. Success drew in even more members, and by 1908 UMWA membership stood at 263,000. By 1914, it counted 377,688 miner members in twenty states. That figure would double again by 1919.[34]

In the South, despite oppressive conditions, miners were indifferent, Caudill observed. They felt that as miners they were more prosperous than they'd ever been as farmers, the author believed. Things were going well for southern mine operators, as the anthracite strike and resulting coal shortage allowed them to penetrate new markets, including the upper Midwest and Great Lakes area. By 1910, the supremacy of anthracite in such places was at an end, and bituminous coal from Appalachia and from fields in Illinois and Indiana was on its way to becoming the predominant U.S. fuel.[35]

Violence often accompanied both UMWA advances and setbacks. And out of one famous, violent incident grew a different kind of challenge.

In Colorado, coal mines and company towns were scattered over 1,000 miles, but the operations of the corporate behemoth, CFI—owned by the Rockefellers after 1903—were concentrated in Huerfano and Las Animas counties in the south. The UMWA began an organizing drive there in 1913, reasoning that it had a network in place dating from a bitter 1903 strike, and that the state government led by Democratic Governor Elias Ammons was a likely ally. As in Appalachia, workers came from many nations: The first on the scene were Brits and Welsh, but soon came Irish, Greek, Italians, Mexicans, and Croats. But national divisions didn't appear insurmountable—miners of every ethnicity seemed to want a union.

Following a great parade of 3,000 marchers through the streets of the small city of Trinidad, all singing a union chorus set to the tune of the Civil War anthem "The Battle Cry of Freedom," delegates to a UMWA meeting heard from a variety of speakers, including spellbinder Mary "Mother" Jones. Then they came up with a series of strike demands, including union recognition, a 10 percent increase in all pay scales, an eight-hour working day, elected checkweighmen to double-check company tonnage figures that determined miners' pay, abolition of "the notorious and criminal guard system," and three demands that challenged company-town prerogatives: the rights to trade in any store they wished, to choose their own doctors, and to live wherever they pleased. The unionists set September 23 as their strike date. CFI, along with the other leading coal firms, Rocky Mountain Fuel and Victor American Fuel, immediately rejected the union demands, and as mine guards began evictions, thousands of miners began moving themselves into ten tent cities. The largest of these, Ludlow, was set up around a railroad depot eighteen miles north of Trinidad at the edge of CFI property, and consisted of four hundred tents housing 1,000 people, over a quarter of whom were children.

With John D. Rockefeller Jr. vowing to a CFI executive to "see the thing out, not yielding an inch," the company's in-house detective branch and the Baldwin-Felts firm began hiring dozens of thugs from as far away as Kansas City and Chicago.

Violence began almost immediately. Even before the strike vote, Baldwin-Felts agents murdered a union organizer on the streets of Trinidad, and soon there were union killings, too, including the shooting of a rifle-wielding deputy sheriff. October saw four battles between strikers and guards in which at least nine men were slain. Baldwin-Felts had constructed a sort of armored car with a mounted Gatling gun, and that same month it attacked the tent city at Forbes, killing two men and wounding a nine-year-old boy.

At the end of October, the governor sent in the Colorado National Guard, approximately 1,000 troops, with orders to disarm everybody—meaning chiefly the strikers, as company guards retained their arsenal—and to see to it that whoever wished to return to work was allowed to do so. The Ludlow encampment turned out in their Sunday best to greet the Guard, which they saw as neutral. In fact, the Guard's ranks were increasingly filled by former deputies, mine guards, and detectives—hardly the disinterested types the strikers hoped for. Troops were soon escorting strikebreakers into the mines.

In November, the governor attempted to broker a settlement, but talks collapsed over the issue of union recognition. Meanwhile, the National Guard began arresting strike leaders, and union efforts to turn away strikebreakers prompted federal indictments against the union for conspiracy to restrain trade. After a period of calm, the governor withdrew most of the National Guard troops in early April, leaving only two companies heavily salted with mine guards and CFI foremen.

On April 20, the final reckoning came to pass. At 9 a.m., with many in the camp still asleep following a Greek Orthodox Easter celebration, the Guard attacked Ludlow. Machine-gun fire ripped the tents. The assault went on all morning and into the afternoon, with strikers, who included veterans of European conflicts, returning fire. Then in the late afternoon, with many dead, the militiamen entered the tent colony. No one can say how the subsequent fire started, but two women and eleven children perished in the flames.

Ludlow was only the beginning of the violence, as leaders of the UMWA, the Colorado Federation of Labor, and the Western Federation of Miners (WFM) two days later called their members to arms. The resulting labor uprising produced further battles at several camps and widespread destruction of mine building and bridges. Unionists killed more than thirty strikebreakers, mine guards, and guardsmen.

In late April, Woodrow Wilson sent in federal troops. By July, with thousands of nonunion men entering the Colorado mines, CFI output had returned to 70 percent of pre-strike levels. Five months later, the UMWA recognized reality and formally ended the strike.[36]

It was another bitter defeat for the UMWA. National press coverage, however, helped create sympathy for coal miners and their union and left an evil stain on the Rockefeller reputation. "The charred bodies of two dozen women and children show that Rockefeller knows how to win," one Cleveland paper darkly intoned. Demonstrations led by the likes of author and political gadfly Upton Sinclair became a regular feature at Rockefeller's Manhattan headquarters and at the family compound, Kykuit. One beneficiary of the events: public relations pioneer Ivy Lee, who landed on the Rockefeller payroll, working to redeem the family reputation. Soon, John D. Rockefeller Sr. was out on the streets of New York in the guise of a kindly paterfamilias, handing out nickels to small children.

More significantly, John D. Rockefeller Jr. realized that he should perhaps moderate his antilabor attitude. As fortune would have it, he made the acquaintance of William Lyon Mackenzie King, a former Canadian deputy labor minister, who soon became the head of the Rockefeller Foundation's new industrial relations department. King was pro-union, but he also believed in labor-capital accommodation in the spirit of Christian brotherhood. By the end of 1914, he'd devised a complex plan for a company union at CFI, which Rockefeller laid out in October 1915 to a Pueblo, Colorado, meeting of company managers and workers. There would be an elected representative for every 150 employees, and every four months these reps would meet in a conference called by CFI.

"Joint committees" would discuss and make recommendations regarding safety, sanitation, health and housing, recreation, education, and "industrial cooperation and conciliation"—meaning wages and working conditions. Workers might lodge grievances via these representatives, with the possibility of appeal to a district joint committee or the company president. It had been only one year since the strike's brutal and demoralizing end, but a majority of CFI workers voted for the plan. Even Mother Jones seemed to endorse it.[37]

Rockefeller himself became a vocal advocate for progressive industrial relations, publicly excoriating U.S. Steel over its labor policies and instituting employee-representation plans at other Rockefeller companies, including Standard Oil of New Jersey and Standard Oil of Indiana. The Rockefeller Plan—or Colorado Industrial Plan, as it was also known—gained further traction as the federal government's War Labor Board adopted similar machinery in 1917. By 1919, 225 other companies employing 500,000 workers followed suit. By 1922, 725 such plans existed, and by 1928, they covered 1,547,766 employees. General Electric, Westinghouse, DuPont, International Harvester, General Motors, Procter & Gamble, the Pennsylvania Railroad, and Goodyear Tire were all influenced in one way or another. As late as 1937, twenty-seven Harlan County coal companies had created and promoted such company unions as part of a campaign against the UMWA.[38]

Such employee-representation plans, or company unions, represented a powerful alternative to labor organizations. Historian David Brody has argued that a broad program of welfare capitalism, including such representation plans, had won the support of most workers in the 1920s and may have become the prevailing model of U.S. industrial relations if not for the Great Depression and the New Deal.[39]

That doesn't mean that the UMWA disappeared in the interim. In fact, CFI followed the union's lead when it came to wage increases, mimicking each of the six wage hikes the union negotiated for the Central Competitive Field (CCF) between 1916 and 1920. Moreover, Colorado miners struck for representation and better conditions again and again following the Ludlow events—in 1919, 1921, and 1922. A 1924 study by the Russell Sage Foundation found the employee representatives at CFI to be "timid, untrained, and ill-prepared to argue the grievances of the miners." But unions can achieve little when employment falls dramatically, as it did in Colorado that decade, as oil and natural gas supplanted coal as fuels of choice in the western states.

Nationally, the events in Colorado provided union members the sense of being part of a historic struggle in which they had a duty not to allow martyrs to have died in vain. The years of World War I saw the UMWA in an agreement with the federal government that provided for pay increases, but these failed to keep up with inflation, paving the way for a decisive confrontation in 1919. That year, more than 400,000 miners walked out and stayed out despite federal injunctions demanding that they yield. In the end, the federal Fuel Administration brokered an agreement with CCF operators that granted the miners a 14 percent wage increase, and later, a bituminous coal commission granted even higher pay hikes.

By the end of 1920, though, economic hard times had clearly arrived, and few coal miners were employed full time during the following year. The union reached an organizational zenith with 500,000 members, but that fact disguised a chronic weakness, due in part to the ever greater introduction of labor-saving machinery such as the hand-loader. What's more, high wartime demand led to an expansion of bituminous mining that meant a glut of coal on the postwar market. CCF operators asked for givebacks and pay cuts even as the union demanded a thirty-hour week with the same pay. A UMWA plan called for "democratic management" of a nationalized coal industry, wages fixed by national collective bargaining, and labor representation in government backed by a labor party. Instead, 1922 saw a CCF lockout that lasted for five months, benefited the nonunion coal companies, and pushed unionized mines further toward mechanization. Hundreds of companies declared bankruptcy, and 200,000 miners abandoned coal mining for other work. By 1928, union membership was one-fifth its 1922 level.[40]

Things only got worse from there. The early '30s were a period of privation, impotent unions, and broken strikes marked by sectarian division. Falling prices for coal led to lower wages, short time, and unemployment.

A social worker in the Illinois coal country in 1931 found hundreds of children who hadn't had a balanced meal in two years, while a miner's lunch might consist of a sandwich of stale bread and lard. Incidences of disease, especially tuberculosis, rose. Meanwhile, the company towns fell into decay and decrepitude. Even though the vast majority of Appalachian men seemed to want a union, the UMWA existed only in scattered pockets.

Harlan County, Kentucky, was one of these. A 10 percent wage cut in 1931 prompted 11,000 miners to join up with the UMWA, vowing to "strike while we starve." A gun battle broke out near the town of Evarts between strikers and machine-gun-toting deputies: Three deputies and one miner died. The governor sent in the National Guard, arrested union leaders, and escorted in strikebreakers, many of them black. When the UMWA bailed out, the Communist-led NMU entered the fray and drew visits to the area from such intellectuals as Theodore Dreiser, John Dos Passos, and Edmund Wilson. But that union did no better against coal-operator force and surveillance. Meetings were broken up, gunplay was frequent, and a number of people were charged with "criminal syndicalism," the broad, antilabor legislation that was used to crush the IWW.

In West Virginia, the independent West Virginia Mine Workers Union (WVMWU) signed up as many as 23,000 miners by the end of 1931. Perhaps 60 percent of that state's miners had been UMWA members by 1919, but in the years following the 1921 Blair Mountain battle, that union had disintegrated. In mid-summer, 8,000 West Virginia miners followed the WVMWU out on strike. Brutal evictions followed, and a shortage of food doomed the strikers, whose effort collapsed after one month.[41]

Demands for wage cuts in Indiana and Ohio also led to violent confrontations and union defeats. Pennsylvania saw rioting and armed clashes in which three miners died, fifty-five were hospitalized, and more than 2,000 were gassed or injured. The NMU, behind most of the activity, could claim few accomplishments.[42]

Things turned around quickly after the June 1933 enactment of the National Industrial Recovery Act. The act created the National Recovery Administration, which called for industry-specific codes of fair representation to be hammered out between labor and trade groups. Section 7(a) of the act said that all codes must provide that employees had a right to organize and bargain collectively via representatives of their own choosing. Moreover, the act stipulated that no employee or job applicant could be required as a condition of employment to join a company union. Many employers, particularly in the steel industry, reacted as though the law had endorsed company unions—so long as employees weren't "made" to join them—and the Bureau of Labor Statistics observed a great expansion in the number of company unions. But coal miners expressed an immediate and overwhelming preference for representation by the UMWA. On the day after the act's passage, 80 percent of Ohio miners had joined up. By mid-June, the formerly union-free Logan County, West Virginia, was completely organized. During the same period, eastern Kentucky's coalfields were likewise unanimous for the UMWA, and by the end of the month, there were 128,000 new members in Pennsylvania's bituminous area.

Union organizers expressed astonishment at how the miners were "flocking into the union by the thousands." UMWA official John Brophy concluded that the miners had "moved into the union en masse . . . they organized themselves for all practical purposes."

Events continued to develop with eye-popping dispatch. The CCF system had collapsed in the 1920s, leading to wide disparities in wage rates: Pay varied from $1.50 per day in parts of the South to $5 per day in Illinois. By the end of September 1933, a new bituminous agreement, along with a new bargaining structure, was in place. With the considerable arm-twisting of the federal government, the union and bituminous operators from Pennsylvania, Ohio, West Virginia, Virginia, eastern Kentucky, and Tennessee agreed to wage rates of from $3.40 a day in the South to as high as $5.63 in the Northwest. The pact stipulated an eight-hour day, forty-hour week, a grievance procedure, automatic withholding of union dues from workers' pay, and rank-and-file election of checkweighmen. No boy younger than seventeen would be allowed to work in a mine, and it was forbidden to pay wages in scrip, to require workers to live in company housing, or to mandate that workers make purchases at the company store.

The agreement did not require miners to join the union, but they had pretty well seen to that matter on their own. As icing on the cake for the UMWA, in one of the first labor board elections conducted under the act, workers at Colorado Fuel and Iron dumped their company union, the Industrial Representation Plan that dated from right after the Ludlow events, and chose the UMWA by a vote of 877 to 273. The company had made wage cuts of 15 percent in 1932 despite the protests of representation-plan officers, undercutting any notion that these reps had bargaining clout. Shortly after the 1933 election, CFI abandoned its plan and negotiated the first UMWA contract.[43]

By 1935, collective bargaining had become a way of life in the coalfields—with the exception of Harlan County, which remained an antiunion redoubt. The county was dominated by corporate giants including International Harvester, U.S. Steel, Peabody Coal, and Ford Motor Co., which liked Harlan's low-sulfur coal for producing auto-body sheet metal. Harlan was cursed with higher freight rates than its northern rivals, and that alone was enough to drive the operators to wage war on unionism. Equally significant, Kentucky was the sole remaining state to allow deputization of private mine guards: Both West Virginia and Pennsylvania had outlawed the practice by 1933. In effect, Harlan operators had a private army backed by local government to enforce their dictates. These deputies, many of whom were mine supervisors, and sheriffs were virulently antiunion in their attitudes. But for some, there were extra incentives to keep things as they were: Sheriff Theodore Roosevelt Middleton acquired five coal mines of his own during his 1934–1937 term; he was also joint owner of the company store at Varda, where annual profits were 170 percent. Deputies in Harlan County and elsewhere were paid on a "fee system"—$2 for an arrest, 25 cents for summoning a witness, and so forth—giving them an incentive to crack down on "lawbreakers." The result was what a 1935 Kentucky state investigatory commission termed a "virtual reign of terror" directed at union organizers in Harlan, singling out Middleton for specific mention.

By the spring of 1935, bombings of union members' houses, shootings of organizers, and a generally unrestrained campaign of violence led miners to conclude that it wasn't safe to attempt organization in Harlan. Operators flagrantly violated Section 7(a) of the National Industrial Recovery Act, and the passage of the National Labor Relations Act in that year changed nothing. Foreshadowing the civil rights years, it took the U.S. Department of Justice to bring the mining companies around: In 1937, it prosecuted sixty-nine coal operators for engaging in a conspiracy to violate federal labor law. Kentucky state police were sent to Harlan expressly to protect union organizers. In 1938, Kentucky abolished the private-deputy system, and 65 percent of the formerly terrorized Harlan miners quickly signed up with the UMWA. At long last, the union won contracts covering 6,000 miners at U.S. Coal and Coke and six other firms. Other Harlan operators tried one final ploy—company unions. The phenomenon that had reached its peak elsewhere in the United States during the 1920s resurfaced at twenty-seven Harlan companies in 1937. In fact, in labor board elections held that year, seven such company unions won recognition as certified bargaining agents over the UMWA.[44]

The years to come would see further union advances in wages and working conditions—along with more strike activity, including controversial clashes during World War II despite labor's no-strike pledge. But the coal company towns were passing from the national stage.

Several changes doomed the fortress/prison-style company town. New Deal labor legislation backed by the possibility of federal prosecution of flagrant scofflaws made widespread union organization possible. Key, too, was the end of the use of private deputies, upon whose depredations the operators had depended. Finally, the declining national demand for coal meant the number of employed coal miners fell from 15,864 in 1941 to 2,242 by 1961. Harlan County saw a mass exodus of onetime miners to Midwestern industrial cities. There would be further violent strikes in the 1960s and even in the 1980s.[45] But the coal company town would play an ever-declining role in the drama.

Still, something like the coal company town lives on in the copper-mining territory of the American Southwest.

Perhaps the preeminent company in the region was for years Phelps Dodge Corp., now part of Freeport-McMoRan, the top U.S. copper producer in 2009. Originally a New York mercantile house created in the 1830s by two stern Calvinist families, Phelps Dodge long was guided by the Golden Rule, in the words of company biographer Robert Glass Cleland. Phelps Dodge developed what it saw as model communities in Bisbee, Morenci, Ajo, and Douglas, Arizona, and it offered workers company-welfare provisions such as hospital care, pensions, and voluntary insurance plans. But neither early company president James Douglas nor his son Walter, who succeeded him in the post, looked at all kindly upon union organization. In 1917, when the WFM and the IWW began a recruiting drive in the Arizona mines, Walter Douglas ordered a roundup of 1,200 union members by local vigilantes and the Bisbee sheriff. The detainees were then loaded into railroad cattle cars, trucked off to the middle of the New Mexico desert, and abandoned.

The events hardly seemed appropriate in a country that had only recently entered World War I with the announced intention of making the world safe for democracy. President Woodrow Wilson ordered an investigation, conducted by a commission headed by no less than Felix Frankfurter, a future justice of the U.S. Supreme Court. But after hearing hundreds of hours of testimony about the events—and taking note of the U.S. military's de facto custodianship of the stranded and suffering workers—the commission issued only a tepid report that recommended arbitration of disputes. Phelps Dodge executives were later indicted on federal criminal charges, but a trial court dismissed the charges.

With the war's end, an oversupply of already mined copper led to a slump in demand, idled operations, and industry consolidation. As sales revived in the 1920s, Phelps Dodge absorbed the holdings of rival Arizona Co., claiming absolute control over the Morenci area. It built an elaborate company store—in time, the multi-location Phelps Dodge Mercantile Co. would generate income in its own right—the lavish Hotel Morenci, and the whites-only Morenci Club featuring a bowling alley, library, and gymnasium. Although sales slumped again in the 1930s, the company anticipated prosperous years to come by building new housing and schools and a $100,000 hospital.

Production revived with World War II. Open-pit work—involving the extraction of ore from a giant, tiered hole in the ground—had replaced underground mining in the 1930s. Basically, though, operations were the same: Thousands of pounds of rock were blasted loose and carted away, then crushed until fine, mixed with chemicals, and baked at

2,000 degrees to separate slag from copper. Mines and smelters in Morenci and Ajo ran full bore to meet wartime production demands, with a federal subsidy of $26 million to develop a new open-pit mine in Morenci. Uncle Sam's watchful eye also allowed a union-representation vote in 1942, won by the Mine, Mill and Smelter Workers, which, however, did not win its first contract with Phelps Dodge until 1946. (Skilled-crafts unions already represented a small number of employees.) The successful negotiations made the local union president, charismatic David Velasquez, something of a legend among his fellow miners, and he would hold office for the next fourteen years.

The company built hundreds of new housing units—with whites segregated from Mexicans by neighborhood—a swimming pool, a playground, a fifty-two-bed hospital, and a baseball diamond. It also constructed a new crushing plant, smelter, and power plant. By the war's end, the company had spent $42 million on Morenci, which was becoming one of the most prominent company towns in the West. When some corporations were dumping their company towns—mining rival Kennecott, for instance, would sell its eight Arizona towns during the 1950s—Phelps Dodge seemed ever more committed to its wholly owned communities. In unincorporated Morenci, the company operated everything from the utilities to the bakery, and the mine superintendent hired teachers and other municipal workers and functioned as the town's mayor.[46]

As the second-largest U.S. copper producer, Phelps Dodge at midcentury appeared to have moved beyond the rowdy ways of its youth, including its penchant for confrontations with labor. Its operations were as far-flung as Peru and the Philippines. Ajo, Arizona, would be perhaps the most carefully planned of its U.S. sites, with an Anglo sector that contained such public facilities as a company store and movie house and separate neighborhoods for Mexicans and American Indians. But strikes continued to be a regular feature of company life: In 1967, an industrywide walkout shut down production. Every three years thereafter, hard bargaining that often included a brief strike ended in a union contract. In these, there were no violent confrontations and no management attempts to evict or replace strikers. Phelps Dodge commonly shut down operations, using walkouts as occasions for retooling. Even more noteworthy, strikers continued to receive credit at the company store, where a purchase-rebate system provided a form of profit-sharing to many. (Phelps Dodge Mercantile also managed the company's scrip system, known as "merchandise coupons.")[47]

In the 1980s, copper prices again fell, and Phelps Dodge laid off 100,000 salaried employees and furloughed its entire mining, smelting, and refining workforce. After five months, half of these employees were back at work, but management's impulse to return to the days of labor confrontation and union-free operations was strong. In 1982, CEO George Munroe—a soft-spoken product of Dartmouth College, the Boston Celtics, and white-shoe law firm Debevoise & Plimpton—toured Ajo, Douglas, Bisbee, and Morenci, where he held a series of meetings with miners reminiscent of John D. Rockefeller Jr.'s 1914 visit to Colorado. But Munroe's message was not exactly conciliatory: After describing the low wages of South American copper miners, he called for "a substantial and immediate decrease" in U.S. miners' remuneration.

The following year, 1983, other copper companies, including Kennecott and Magma, settled with unions on hard-times terms that stipulated no wage increases outside of cost-of-living agreements. Phelps Dodge, though, refused to go along with even this, calling for cuts in pay and concessions in benefits. When its thirteen unions—led by the Steelworkers, which had subsumed the Mine, Mill and Smelter Workers union—went on strike in June, the company continued operations in Morenci. At first, it depended only on supervisory personnel, but in August it urged strikers to cross their own picket lines and began hiring permanent replacements for all who stayed out.

A near riot resulted. In a frightening confrontation, 2,000 demonstrators took on state troopers near the plant gate and threatened to overturn a bus of strikebreakers. Arizona Governor Bruce Babbitt got the company to agree to a brief moratorium on hiring replacement workers, but with federal mediation making no progress, in mid-August Phelps Dodge again began hiring—this time, aided by the arrival of the Arizona National Guard and hundreds more state troopers. Ten strikers were arrested and charged with felony rioting. Gradually, more and more replacements crossed the line, and the smelter resumed something like regular operations. Within months, the company announced that it was curtailing hiring, having recruited an entirely new and nonunion workforce.

The Arizona events would provide the template for successful union-breaking tactics that would be replicated at numerous U.S. companies. "Greyhound followed us and used our techniques," reflected Richard T. Moolick, company president and architect of the antiunion campaign at Phelps Dodge. A former geologist and product of the Southwest, the abrasive Moolick evinced none of the Ivy League and Wall Street graces that had eased Munroe's way into the corporate suite. "Suddenly people realized, hell, you can beat a union," Moolick went on. "We demonstrated that nobody was invincible." Other imitative corporations came to include Continental Airlines, the *Chicago Tribune*, Hormel, International Paper, Eastern Airlines, and Caterpillar.[48]

In 1985, with replacements constituting the entire workforce, Phelps Dodge workers voted to decertify their unions. The company had long since reclaimed its worker housing, evicting strikers during Thanksgiving week of 1983 and cutting off their medical benefits. Phelps Dodge's Arizona operations were now completely union-free.[49]

Momentarily, copper appeared to be a terminally sick industry, with slumping prices along with less expensive and government-subsidized operations abroad putting a squeeze on U.S. companies. In 1985, the *Wall Street Journal* predicted that the U.S. industry would "be transformed permanently from a major world supplier to a marginal producer." Nevertheless, Phelps Dodge, which had ended smelting in favor of lower-cost chemical-extraction and electrolysis processes, announced a return to profitability one year after its strike. And contrary to the doomsayers' forecasts, by 1990 prices had risen and the company's net income reached $455 million, on sales of $2.6 billion.

Prices would fall drastically again in the late 1990s, nearly double by 2004 thanks to demand from China's electronics and construction industries, then fall again in 2007, perhaps guaranteeing the takeover of Phelps Dodge by the smaller Freeport-McMoRan. That deal delivered the town of Morenci and other Arizona properties into the hands of new managers. The new company's 2008 annual report announced a 50 percent cut in production in Morenci, and in January 2009, some 1,550 workers—half of the town's labor force—were laid off.[50]

What lies ahead for the town of Morenci, with its 1,132 company-owned houses, twenty-room Morenci Motel, and Merc general store? More of the same, as demand for copper waxes and wanes? Although it's overlooked by many observers of the U.S. economy, Morenci offers solid testimony to the enduring presence of the dystopian company town in America.

Meanwhile, less than three hundred miles from the Appalachian coal region, a separate company-town tradition emerged in the late 1800s and lasted into the late twentieth century: the textile towns of the Piedmont region, which runs from North Carolina down through Georgia. Some textile towns would outlast many coal towns and perhaps make an equally lasting mark on American culture. They were not as totalitarian as the coal towns—but neither might they be held up as the quintessence of the democratic American way.

CHAPTER 4

A Southern Principality

We govern like the Czar of Russia.

—A Carolina textile mill manager in the 1920s[1]

He was just folks: a small, "round, ruddy-faced man with an arthritic limp who wandered the cavernous textile mill in a work shirt, back-slapping and jawing with workers," in the words of one southern journalist. In formal portraits, he was a stolid and bespectacled figure in an off-the-rack business suit—seemingly a Rotarian bore you would never want to be seated next to at a dinner party. But he could be ferocious: In the 1930s, he stormed into Washington and, before a congressional committee, railed bitterly against New Deal "unjust economics dreamed up by a bunch of jackasses."

He was not a man of culture or even much learning, having dropped out of Davidson College at age nineteen to take a job as an executive in his father's mill. Although his white-columned home in Concord, North Carolina, was spacious, it would be the envy of none of today's hedge-fund billionaires. Clearly this was a man for whom the textile industry and work were everything.

Such was his power in the near-feudal fiefdom of Kannapolis, North Carolina, that the *Wall Street Journal* once likened him to Monaco's Prince Rainier. When the workers at Cannon Mills dared to go on strike, he got the governor to call in state troops to break the walkout and starved them into submission. "There was never a hint at compromise," in the words of one historian.[2]

But Mr. Charlie, aka Charles Albert Cannon, president of Cannon Mills Co. and the force behind the town in its glory years, was a benefactor in his way: Kannapolis was no backwater burg for cotton-mill rats. Along with its 1,600 tidy clapboard millworker houses and seven textile mills, the town was home to the company-funded Cabarrus Memorial Hospital, the Cannon Memorial YMCA, and the *Daily Independent*, owned by the Cannon family. With a population of 36,000 in the 1970s, Kannapolis was the largest unincorporated town in the state.

All normal government functions—including utilities, police and firefighting, street maintenance, and trash collection—were within the purview of Cannon Mills. In this, it resembled the Appalachian coal towns that were, after all, only a few hundred miles away as the crow flies. Kannapolis, though, lacked the prison-camp attributes of the coal towns and more resembled the benevolent despotism of a Lowell or Pullman, albeit less luxuriously. Not exactly a utopia, Kannapolis was a tad like Scotia insofar as isolation made it a universe unto itself. Moreover, some profitable companies have made a practice of sharing their bounty with the hired help—but that wasn't Cannon's way, or for that matter the custom in the scores of southern mill villages across the Piedmont region. Not that Cannon Mills was short of bounty that it might have shared: Charles Cannon built the company into THE LARGEST MANUFACTURER OF TOWELS IN THE WORLD, as a massive illuminated sign atop the company's Mill No. 1 declared.

The mantle of company leadership descended on Charles in 1921, upon the death of his father and Cannon's founder, James William Cannon.

James Cannon started building his manufacturing empire in the late 1880s. A decade earlier, the blond, brown-eyed former errand boy for a Charlotte grocery store had, along with his brother David and two others, founded a general merchandise store in Concord, a town twenty miles northeast of Charlotte that had been home to cotton mills since the 1830s. This was a simple country store, and they were simple, rural people: James and his wife, Mary Ella, the daughter of a miller, rode around Concord in a small mule-drawn wagon, their bare feet hanging from the buckboard. Nevertheless, like many merchants, James soon branched out into buying cotton, and by 1888 he had a 4,000-spindle mill employing eight hundred hands. By 1892, Cannon was operating a second mill, at Cabarrus, and further plants followed in China Grove, Albermarle, Salisbury, and Mt. Pleasant. David became the president of the company, and James, who bought the cotton and raised the capital, served as treasurer.

At first, Cannon produced only yarn, but the company soon began to sell its own much-sought-after cloth—Cannon cloth—used to make clothes.

In 1906, James, who had become president of the company, approached textile engineer Robert Dalton of the leading engineering firm of Stuart W. Cramer Co. "Meet me at Glass," he told Dalton, referring to a whistle stop on the Southern Railway near Concord. Cannon had purchased six hundred acres of land there, and he had plans to build a new kind of textile mill—a terry-cloth towel factory, the first in the South. Cannon had made flat-weave towels in Concord, but the new plant would help popularize the absorbent fabric: Up to that time the rich had used linen towels, and poor folks resorted to flour sacks.

Dalton drew up blueprints for the buildings and figured out what machinery would be needed. He helped Cannon arrive at $75,000 as the necessary capitalization. Cannon amassed the sum from his own savings and by turning to investors in Boston and Philadelphia. And he began constructing what would soon be named Kannapolis, home to a modern, electricity-driven cotton mill and a growing collection of millworker houses, which surrounded the mill in a circle. A five-room schoolhouse and a two-story, white-columned YMCA were completed in 1908.

Unlike, say, George Pullman or Milton Hershey, Cannon seemed to have few grandiose plans for Kannapolis. The construction of Piedmont mill villages dated back to the antebellum years, and he was likely just following established custom. In most such places, there would be a few houses, a little school, a small church, the mill, and the residence of the owner-manager. Kannapolis would end up being so much more than that. But in the main, James Cannon was responding to what was a sheer necessity. In the words of one local newspaperman: "Mr. Cannon had to build houses, because the people coming in from farms to work in the mills had to have a place to live. They were broke. They didn't even dream about building houses."[3]

During World War I, more than 86,000 North Carolinians fought in Europe, in such affrays as the Second Battle of the Marne, St. Mihiel, and in the Meuse-Argonne, and more than 2,000 died of wounds or disease. The war meant windfall profits and expansion for Cannon, as the government took all the towels the company could produce. One specialty product was the Patriot Cannon towel, emblazoned with the words TO HELL WITH THE KAISER.

James died of a stroke in 1921 after a two-week illness. At the time, he was the master of twelve mills that turned out 300,000 towels each day. The company employed more than 15,000 workers and enjoyed an estimated $40 million in annual sales.[4]

Quickly a quarrel broke out among family survivors. David, who had no children, had died some years earlier. But James's sons disagreed over the disposition of the estate, with Joseph threatening to sue Charles, the youngest of six boys. In the end, Charles and daughter Adelaide's husband, David Blair, were named trustees of the estate. Joseph was forced out of the textile company's management. And in accordance with James's wishes, Charles took his place at the helm of the company, where he remained for the next fifty years.

Charles showed little interest in diversification: Cannon Mills focused on what it knew best, soon producing half of all the towels purchased in the United States, along with sheets and women's hosiery.

When Charles took over the Cannon empire, the Kannapolis mills and worker houses were pretty rudimentary. Each house "sat on brick pillars, and the wind blew under it and through the knotholes in the floor," as one resident recalled. There could be as many as ten people, including boarders, living in each four-room house. Until the 1930s, everyone shared outdoor privies.

The company commissary was a "jot-'em-down store," selling groceries, shoes and clothing, coal, and furniture, all on credit to the cotton millworkers. (No one store dominated, though; there were many neighborhood shops in town.) Cannon Mills paid the workers in cash, with a 75-cent deduction for rent every two weeks. In the 1920s, typical earnings for an adult might be $18 for 110 hours of work—ten hours a day through the week and five hours on Saturday. It was not uncommon in such mills for a quarter of the workers to be under the age of sixteen— and children's wages were, of course, much less.[5]

Over the next several decades, the company built more worker housing, schools, and office buildings. In 1919, it completed two large dorms for single women—Mary Ella Hall, named after James's wife, and Cabarrus Hall—housing hundreds of residents. Denominations erected a half-dozen churches on land Cannon donated.

Main Street and the downtown area featured a number of substantial, two-story brick buildings, home to the A&P, Woolworth's, a hardware store, and more. But the closest hospital was in Concord until 1937, when Cabarrus Memorial Hospital opened in Kannapolis. Charles Cannon served the institution as board president for more than thirty years. Nor was the leisure of the workers neglected, between the YMCA and a local, semi-pro baseball team, the Towlers, which played in the Carolina Textile League. Cannon even built a large lake in a park right across from the main plant.[6] But for all that, Cannon could not stop the clock—nor could he gain social peace just by wishing for it.

In the post–Civil War years, the South was a study in contradictions. Well into the second half of the nineteenth century, visitors to the region commented on the poverty and idleness of the natives, along with the decay and lack of vitality in what had once been thriving cities. At the same time, the area was seen as a land of opportunity, notably in a body of "get-rich-quick" literature. Both land and natural resources were abundant there, according to eastern newspaper reports, and everything was available on the cheap. Books bearing such titles as *How to Get Rich in the South* echoed the sentiments of prominent New York attorney and future U.S. Senator Chauncey M. Depew, whose 1890s address to fellow Yale alumni was titled "Go South, Young Man."

Across much of the Piedmont, the local merchant became the pivotal economic figure. Plantation agriculture supported by black slavery was gone, but given that land ownership remained concentrated, new institutions emerged: tenant farming and sharecropping. A new merchant class—backed by the crop-lien system, under which much of a farmer's crop was pledged to whoever put up seed money—became the supplier for this smaller-scale agriculture. As merchants got more and more involved with buying and selling cotton, trading centers grew up around their stores. Before long, many merchants, such as James Cannon, became cotton-mill entrepreneurs.

Soon they found themselves part of a much-hyped crusade. Starting in the 1880s, newspapermen and development-minded townspeople initiated a passionate campaign urging the construction of a southern textile industry on the scale of that in New England. The enthusiasts promised that the textile industry would reinvigorate the region and its institutions, raise up a new rank of leaders, and offer economic betterment to the millhands. With a fervor rivaling that of the region's evangelical preachers, the agitators thundered: "Bring the mills to the cotton," in the words of the *Charleston News & Courier*. "Where the cotton is produced here and manufactured elsewhere, South Carolina is in the position of furnishing the elements which make other communities rich," reasoned another writer. Towns competed against one another to win development, some offering free land equipped with water power to whoever would build.

This propaganda and organizational effort culminated in the 1881 International Cotton Exposition in Atlanta, where apostles of the new industrial order gathered and drew attention from northern investors. The principal exhibition building there resembled a cotton mill, chockablock with textile machinery, including two Corliss steam engines, knitting and lace-making machines, wool combers, pickers, carding engines, and more. Before long, lawyers and bankers, merchants and teachers were abandoning their former professions to become cotton-mill executives.[7]

There was rapid expansion of a number of southern industries, from mining and lumber to railroads and tobacco, encouraged by an inflow of northern and British capital. But it would be the textile mill that became the leading symbol of the New South, and with good reason: Between 1860 and 1880, North Carolina doubled the value of textile-mill output, while that figure tripled in Georgia and quadrupled in South Carolina. The number of mills rose from 161 in 1880 to 239 in 1890 and to 400 in 1900. Meanwhile, in the old textile-producing region of New England, production was decreasing. Southern mills featured competitive new technology and a burgeoning number of workers, up from just fewer than 17,000 in 1880 to nearly 100,000 in 1900.[8] And the scale of southern enterprises quickly rose: In 1880, the typical South Carolina mill had fewer than 6,000 spindles; by 1910, this figure would be more than 25,000. Whereas the South was first primarily home to small factories that produced for a local market, it was soon characterized by integrated cloth mills competing in international markets.[9]

Yet the textile industry was much like other enterprises that thrived in the region: It was marked by low-skill, low-wage work and products of little added value. To attract the mills, southern promoters followed a formula that still operates today, promising low taxes, cheap power, municipal subsidies, and hostility toward organized labor. Most important, the mills were ensured a steady supply of would-be wage laborers thanks to the hardships of rural living. Increasingly, when rough weather or even minor economic difficulties hit tenant farmers, who already subsisted on meager plots of land, ruin followed. The first migrant millworkers were farm widows. Next came whole families, migrating to one of the roughly one hundred mill villages that stretched across backcountry North and South Carolina and part of northern Georgia.

This "cracker proletariat" was looked down on by many people from the professional and business classes. Common terms of approbation included "factory rats" and "lintheads" or "cotton-tails," easily identified by the cotton dust on their worn clothes and the fluff in their hair. Particularly by the early twentieth century, middle-class people began to express concern over the "cotton mill problem" and the lawless, "shiftless" social types who migrated to labor there.[10]

The heyday of southern mill villages was between 1880 and the 1930s. At the turn of the twentieth century, 92 percent of southern textile workers lived in such hamlets, from Roanoke Rapids, North Carolina, to Honea Path, South Carolina, and Columbus, Georgia.[11]

⟶

At the simplest level, such a village consisted of the mill and a few rows of worker housing—some two-story, four-bedroom clapboard houses set on brick piers, others one-and-a-half-story structures comprising two rooms and a hallway downstairs, a kitchen in back, and a sleeping loft. (For all, the privies were out back.) Far from innovative, these were typical country town dwellings.[12] In addition, there would be a company store for provisions, a church, and maybe a schoolhouse. For journalist W. J. Cash, the son of a textile-mill superintendent and the author of the influential *The Mind of the South*, the model was clear: "a plantation, essentially indistinguishable in organization from the familiar plantation of the cotton fields. . . . Many of the new towns were not regularly organized municipal corporations at all, but merely the fiefs of the mills."[13]

Given that wages were often startlingly low (perhaps only 60 percent of those paid in New England), what would keep anyone in such places? A chief draw, especially for widows and those who'd been unable to make ends meet on the farm, was the cheap rent the textile companies charged, traditionally 25 cents weekly per room.[14] Into the twentieth century, some mill villages were little more than country crossroads. Low wages were less burdensome given that many workers kept chickens and other livestock and maintained vegetable gardens adjoining their small houses and supplemented their diets with hunting and fishing.[15]

But bear in mind that these formerly rural folks had not internalized industrial discipline—the necessity of reporting to work on time every day for long shifts (six twelve-hour days in the late nineteenth century, later adjusted to five ten-hour days plus five hours on Saturday), or the idea of committing oneself to years of work for a single enterprise. Instead, some who came saw themselves working in a factory—or, as they called it, doing "public work"—only until they could amass sufficient means to return to the farm. Like coal miners, many were afflicted with what mill owners would come to call "the wandering habit": a tendency to pick up at a moment's notice and move away to . . . whatever.

Compare such attitudes with the high-flown expectations of cotton-mill enthusiasts and entrepreneurs. Such townsfolk proclaimed themselves to be public philanthropists, saviors of a near-destroyed southern civilization, benefactors of the white race and, specifically, of the formerly rural white poor. Blacks had worked in textile mills since antebellum times, but increasingly, and almost absolutely by the turn of the twentieth century, textile labor was for whites only, excepting the most menial tasks. As one mill manager testified before Congress in 1902, the mills had passed on using cheaper black labor, as "mill life is the only avenue open today to our poor whites." Whites resisted racial mixing and, moreover, it would be wrong, said the mill manager, to have blacks working alongside white women and children, who made up more than half of the millworkers.[16]

Given such assertions of paternalism, it's no wonder that measures were taken to ensure that the new industrial working class would behave itself. As in Appalachian coal-mining towns, textile companies provided preachers and teachers to offer frequent reminders of the workers' duty. Some mill owners themselves, or their hired police, would monitor workers' private hours. And if the carrot of wages and cheap rent didn't hold the workers, there was the stick of indebtedness to the company store. Paydays might be spread out, but stomachs needed to be filled regularly. Company-store bills, along with rent, could be deducted from workers' earnings—and before long, many were in arrears, guaranteeing that they couldn't walk away from their jobs.[17]

Under James, the Cannon company had made strides toward modernity. Like the early New England mills, most outfits in the South had begun by using water power from nearby streams and rivers to run their machinery. Cannon first employed coal-fired steam turbines to power its equipment in Kannapolis, but it soon converted to electricity from hydroelectric provider the Southern Power Co. And in 1916, it broke with the established practice of maintaining an independent, commission-based sales force and developed its own New York City–based sales organization.[18]

Not long after Charles Cannon assumed the helm, he began making the company into a modern corporation. By 1928, he'd consolidated its nine separate units, with plants in seven different towns, into Cannon Mills Co., headquartered in Kannapolis, and the corporation was listed on the New York Stock Exchange. (The family also managed six independent mills that were outside of the corporation.)

Cannon Mills began building a unique brand that came to stand for quality, utilizing as the Cannon trademark an antique artillery field piece. This, executives felt, was a fitting symbol of an enterprise that had emerged successfully "from the shambles of the Reconstruction Era." And in an important innovation, in the mid-1920s, it began spending millions of dollars on national advertising, particularly in women's magazines and the *Saturday Evening Post*. Cannon products demonstrated unusual flair, courting consumers with fancy packaging and stylish designs. Towels came in flower patterns and polka dots, and in colors to complement bathroom decor.[19]

The town of Kannapolis also continued to develop. Even though children and adolescents still worked in the mill, the town built new educational facilities, notably the eight-room Old North School, completed in 1917, and J. W. Cannon High School, in 1924. But the academic year was only six months long in 1925, extended to eight months in 1927.[20] Legal restrictions on child labor and state laws for compulsory school attendance—pressed by middle-class progressives who worried about the detrimental impact of the millworker population on society—came into force by the early 1930s. By 1931 all southern states had outlawed factory labor for those under age fourteen and restricted those under sixteen to working no more than an eight-hour day.[21] But such restrictions were largely unnecessary, given that the Depression had largely eliminated underage workers from the ranks and reduced the hours of all workers.

Given the labor-saving nature of machinery in southern mills, much of the work was rudimentary. Workers were little more than unskilled or semiskilled machine tenders. Whether they labored on a picker, a card machine, a slubber, or a stripper, a spinning frame or a loom, plenty of jobs were interchangeable. Spinning, spooling, and duffing were tasks that could be learned in only days. More demanding jobs included weaving, winding, and beaming, and it could take weeks for one to become proficient at these. Becoming a loom fixer, on the other hand, required a lengthy period of apprenticeship.

But even if the jobs weren't demanding intellectually, the work was often punishing. Lint filled the air, covered everything, and got into workers' lungs—ultimately causing a medical condition known as byssinosis, or brown lung. Still today, after decades of improvement, the noise in a textile plant is deafening. Before air conditioning, mills in the subtropical South were stifling in the summer and warm even in winter months.[22]

Life was not always peaceful in Kannapolis: In 1921, there was a bitter strike at Cannon Mills involving 9,000 workers. That decade featured a series of geographically dispersed job actions, prompted by uncertain times, textile overcapacity, and wage cuts. The events culminated in a 1934 general strike of hundreds of thousands of workers across the southern textile region. That major uprising threatened Kannapolis, although in the end Cannon experienced little disruption.

Before the 1920s, the most common form of protest among southern textile workers was simply quitting a job. World War I saw an expansion of the South's textile industry. With European manufacturing disrupted and global and domestic markets for textile products strong, jobs were easy to come by and family and social networks kept workers informed of likely openings across the region.

But with the coming of peace, there clearly was too much textile capacity. As companies began cutting the wage and bonus rates established during wartime, friction rose. The United Textile Workers (UTW), an American Federation of Labor craft union with its roots in New England, expanded across the South. Then beginning at Charlotte's Highland Park Mills in 1919, a series of walkouts intended to secure the pay levels won during the war. Lockouts were common that year, including at Cannon facilities in Concord and Kannapolis, where workers made no demands of management but seemed to support the union. In more than one community, workers formed armed patrols and threatened gunplay. North Carolina's governor, Thomas W. Bickett, stepped in. After defending workers' right to organize, he denounced the potential turn to violence, for which he seemed to place the most blame on the "unwise, unjust" owners. Surrendering to this suasion, Highland Park's president agreed to a settlement that included a fifty-five-hour week at wages calculated on the former sixty-hour rate and said there would be no discrimination against union members. Within weeks, Cannon agreed to the changes as well. Across North Carolina, the UTW enlisted 40,000 new members.

Then, after the textile depression of 1920 hit, companies cut wages once again. In June 1921, the UTW struck three companies—the Chadwick-Hoskins and Highland Park mills at Charlotte and Cannon's plants at

Concord and Kannapolis. Union leaders worried that victory was unlikely in the midst of an industrywide downturn. But they gave in to the
rank-and-file militancy, taking on "some of the strongest mills in the
country" because that was where union organization seemed most solid.

Charles Cannon refused to rescind the wage cuts or deal with the
union at all. Instead, he joined with the mayor of Concord to call upon
the state's new and more conservative governor, Cameron Morrison, to
send in the National Guard "to preserve law and order."

For strikers, hunger soon became a real issue. Union commissaries
supplied only a few staples, and as the summer gardening season neared
its end, even union stalwarts grew concerned. As the mills reopened in
mid-August under the armed protection of the militia, Cannon workers
began crossing picket lines and returning to work. Observed journalist
Gerald Johnson of the *Charlotte Labor Herald*: "The overwhelming nature of the mill owners' victory can hardly be overstated."[23]

All the same, the fat years were at an end for management and labor
alike. Overcapacity would continue to plague the industry for decades
to come. In New England a long period of downsizing continued, as 40
percent of that region's textile mills would close during the next decade.
The South was afflicted with an oversupply of willing employees: Ever
more people abandoned the rural life even as manufacturers installed
labor-saving equipment and applied scientific management to squeeze
workers ever harder.

This "stretch-out," which had workers tending acres of machines at a
backbreaking pace, in time sparked a new round of labor troubles. In
March 1929, another strike wave began in the small Blue Ridge Mountains town of Elizabethton, Tennessee, and soon thousands of workers
from thirteen different mills walked out. In April, workers at the Loray
Mill in Gastonia, North Carolina—called "the South's City of Spindles"—
joined in, demanding a $20-per-week minimum wage, equal pay for
women and children, an end to the stretch-out, and recognition of their
union, the Communist-led National Textile Workers Union.

The city of Gastonia outlawed picketing, the state sent in the National Guard, and Loray began evicting families from company-owned
housing. Through the summer and into the fall, there was a spasm of violence that saw the murder of the town's police chief, a terror campaign

aimed at unionists and union property, and finally the murder of a key union activist.

The rebellion continued despite the collapse of the Gastonia uprising in September. UTW-led strikes took place in Marion—where six more unionists were shot and killed—in 1930 and 1932, in Danville and High Point. Everywhere unions were met with force and crushed, although there were some gains such as shortened workweeks at Gastonia and Marion.[24]

Then in 1934, the UTW declared a general strike of all textile workers. The New Deal's National Industrial Recovery Act had encouraged unionization, at least rhetorically. The voluntary National Recovery Administration (NRA) textile industry code of fair competition, facilitated by that law, said all companies should provide minimum wages of $12 per week ($13 in the North), limit the workweek to forty hours, and discontinue the use of child labor. But nothing in these restrictions prevented a further stretch-out, which required workers to perform as much work in eight hours as they had before in twelve. Many companies experienced impressive profits despite the Depression. "The Blue Eagle has learned to cover a multitude of sins since he alighted in the Piedmont area," one Cannon worker wrote to NRA head General Hugh Johnson, referring to the agency's avian symbol. In the end, it was all too much, and UTW delegates to a national convention voted for the massive walkout to begin on September 1.

Across the country, perhaps as many as 325,000 textile workers struck. It became the largest labor conflict in U.S. history to date. Flying squadrons of cars and trucks crossed the countryside, going from one isolated mill town to another, forcing a great many plants to shut down. But the strike was hardly totally effective. In Gastonia, throngs of angry millworkers paraded through the streets, some threatening to confiscate the property of the respectable citizenry. In Durham, energetic strikers were highly effective in shutting down operations—but in Burlington the strike failed to take hold. In Concord, pickets closed four plants—but in Kannapolis, Cannon Mills continued to run uninterrupted, despite the appearance of three hundred pickets on September 10.

All in all, the action closed around two hundred North Carolina mills, while more than three hundred remained open. In response, the state governments of the Carolinas called out 14,000 National Guardsmen, and Georgia declared martial law. In Kannapolis, a contingent of the National Guard was billeted at Mary Ella Hall, the women's boardinghouse.[25]

Violent incidents multiplied. In early September, a striker and a deputy were killed during a gun battle in Trion, Georgia. In Lowell, Massachusetts, 2,500 workers rioted. At Honea Path, South Carolina, strikebreakers and deputies killed seven pickets and wounded many more. In Saylesbury, Rhode Island, a three-day pitched battle occurred between pickets who were attempting to shut down a plant and authorities armed with shotguns and machine guns. At Woonsocket, Rhode Island, police and National Guardsmen fought with a crowd of 8,000 workers before the city declared martial law.[26]

The violence prompted a federal board of inquiry to urge the UTW to end the strike—and the union complied. The government appointed committees to investigate the stretch-out complaints, and the Federal Trade Commission studied whether the industry could afford higher wages. President Franklin Roosevelt implored the companies to rehire strikers without discrimination, but in the end few companies complied. Despite the clear defeat, UTW officials asserted that it had been an "amazing victory." The end result was to leave a generation of millworkers embittered and disillusioned with unionism. In the words of one Kannapolis local union member: "Our local is gone and it don't seem there is any use to try now as they have lost faith in the union. . . . It looks like Cannon Mills are running the whole thing. We want to know if they run the whole country."[27] In the late '30s, the Congress of Industrial Organizations (CIO) set up a Textile Workers Organizing Committee, envisioning rapid unionization of the hundreds of thousands of workers in the field. But it had little success in the South, where workers were suspicious and fearful.[28]

⌒

The 1930s also witnessed another sweeping change in southern textiles: the beginning of the end of mill villages.

Disparagement of such villages dated from at least the turn of the twentieth century, when critics began faulting their rigid caste-bound social structure and frowned upon the companies' restrictions on occupants' personal lives and occupations. The National Industrial Recovery Act's textile code echoed the criticism with suggestions that perhaps the southern mills should get rid of their villages.[29] Moreover, the automobile meant that workers no longer had to live within walking distance of the factory. As the powerful Burlington Co. began buying up bankrupt mills, it declared that it didn't want the accompanying villages—and the old owners began selling the worker houses to their inhabitants. By 1939, a dozen companies had sold at least thirty villages, and by the 1940s, some sixty villages in Virginia, the Carolinas, and Georgia containing 7,000 homes had been similarly disposed of. After a pause during World War II, the trend resumed in the late 1940s.[30]

One holdout, of course, was Cannon. Instead of disposing of the company's property in the town of Kannapolis, Charles Cannon—inspired by a trip to Colonial Williamsburg in Virginia—decided to develop the place even more, upgrading the town's business district. Over a period of many years, every building in downtown Kannapolis was refashioned in the Georgian style.

The town also featured sixteen churches, including two for the town's five hundred black residents, although there was no Catholic church. Liquor wasn't available in any restaurant or other establishment. Overall, the result wasn't to everyone's liking: In 1933 a reporter from *Fortune* magazine found the town of 15,000 inhabitants to be "a medieval city" standing "aloof and self-contained in the midst of an empty country, suspicious of all strangers, loyal to its feudal lords."[31]

During the next thirty-odd years, not much changed in either the town or the textile-production process. Just after World War II, one hundred prefabricated houses were added to the stock of around 2,000 company-owned houses in a section that became known as G.I. Town. Aside from church, the townsfolk's primary recreation centered around the large, company-subsidized YMCA, located adjacent to the company headquarters: Its 12,000 members paid annual dues of $2, or $1 for youths.

In 1962, the company celebrated its seventy-fifth anniversary, saying that its annual sales had reached $231 million. Two years later, in the first significant alteration in production for years, it announced plans for a new highly automated facility, which would become known as plant

16. Recognized as the largest textile mill built since World War II, it added 550 workers to the more than 25,000 employed by Cannon in Kannapolis.

Notably, the southern civil rights movement had little impact on Kannapolis. The Y's membership remained all-white until 1966. With only 15 percent of the citizenry being African American (and only fifty Cannon houses occupied by blacks), the town had no NAACP chapter. The Ku Klux Klan, on the other hand, was well-established and provided the lead contingent in the town's 1968 Christmas parade.

The following year, the U.S. Justice Department sued Cannon to force integration of company housing. But the legal papers included no formal complaints by Cannon workers. A front-page *Wall Street Journal* article that profiled Charles Cannon, his company, and the town asserted that Cannon "has the support of most residents in town who enjoy living under his paternalistic eye." The article even quoted a retired black janitor who'd worked in the plant, noting: "There's not a thing I could say against Mr. Cannon. It's a fact he has a one-man town, but he's a good man."[32]

Charles was now chairman, having retired as president in 1962. His wife died in 1965, and he lived alone with a police dog as his only companion.

In 1971, Cannon Mills signed a consent decree, ending the federal lawsuit. The agreement admitted no wrongdoing and simply said that the company would from that time not discriminate in employment matters or in housing.

A few weeks later, Charles suffered a stroke while sitting at his desk beneath a large portrait of his father and surrounded by small replicas of artillery field pieces. He refused a stretcher or an ambulance, but allowed the company president, Don Holt, to help him to his car and on to the hospital, where he died after a few hours. He was seventy-eight.[33]

At the time, Cannon Mills was the largest employer in North Carolina, with 24,000 workers. Kannapolis remained unincorporated—its citizens disenfranchised when it came to local issues—an alien presence in the modern world. If incorporated, the town would become North Carolina's tenth-largest city.

For those fearful of change, the signs were increasingly ominous. Symbolically, the Crescent Ltd., the last privately operated, overnight luxury train in the United States, discontinued its stop in Kannapolis right after Charles's death. Out near I-85, shopping centers first began appearing in the 1960s, posing a clear danger to all small-town enterprises.[34]

Signs abroad were equally menacing, as all U.S. textile production was endangered. Since the industry requires little skilled labor, textiles are one of the first products to which developing nations turn. And just as the South had used cheap labor to steal jobs away from New England, so were such places as Asia and Latin America now taking textile work away from the South.

Cannon and other manufacturers stayed one step ahead of organized labor for decades. Beginning in the 1950s, the Textile Workers Union of America made efforts to organize—and Cannon generally turned these efforts away, frequently doling out small wage increases to keep its workers relatively content.[35] When the union finally forced an election in 1974, workers in fifteen Cannon plants voted against it, 8,473 to 6,801, with many abstentions.[36]

But within thirty years, there would be no company left to fight over.

The company's once-high-quality products had lost their luster by the 1980s, becoming the stuff of bargain stores. The town itself was looking increasingly threadbare. It was at that moment, in 1982, that corporate raider David Murdock launched an offer of $413 million for all 9.38 million shares in the company. Charles's son William agreed, and Cannon, along with its 660 acres of surrounding property, became a privately held outfit. Murdock said he intended to upgrade the company's facilities across the South and redevelop the community. He built a spacious guest lodge in Kannapolis to house business guests, along with a new YMCA. And he began selling the worker housing to its occupants, for an average of $20,000 per house. Kannapolis's citizens voted to incorporate the town in 1984, and within a few months, they elected its first city council.

Three years later, in 1985, Murdock abruptly sold Cannon to Fieldcrest Mills for only $250 million. A dozen years later, Fieldcrest Cannon, as it had become known, was itself sold for $700 million to Dallas-based Pillowtex Corp., which in turn filed for Chapter 11 bankruptcy protection within three years. Pillowtex announced its complete bankruptcy in July 2003. Suddenly 4,340 Kannapolis residents—all that remained of textile employees in the town—found themselves unemployed.[37]

The former Cannon headquarters was demolished in 2005, and the site was taken over by the North Carolina Research Campus, the brainchild of Murdock, who remains active in the town. A variety of universities say they will have facilities at the complex, including the University of North Carolina, Duke, and Rowan Cabarrus Community College.[38] If all of this happens, Kannapolis could become a center of research in areas from nutrition to agriculture and medicine. It would be quite a transition.

Meanwhile, over the very same span of years that saw Kannapolis's rise, industrial America's preeminent enterprise fathered a very different company town, halfway across the continent on the shores of Lake Michigan. That startling, near-instant metropolis would be the crowning achievement of America's company-town builders.

CHAPTER 5

The Magic City

Made-to-order cities are the spectacular civic by-product of the new industrialism. Accustomed though Americans of this day are to rapid accomplishment, not one who visits the suddenly created city of Gary fails to experience a new thrill of amazement.

—GRAHAM ROMEYN TAYLOR,
Satellite Cities (1915)

In 1904, Elbert H. Gary determined that U.S. Steel, of which he was chairman, was in need of vast new expansion. The huge trust had been created only three years before, when banker J. P. Morgan, Carnegie Steel executive Charles M. Schwab, and others had pulled together "the combination of combinations," embracing such large outfits as Federal Steel and Carnegie Steel, and representing 65 percent of the American steel industry. And already, demand for steel had outpaced U.S. Steel's resources, benefiting its competitors. "Judge" Gary, as he was always called thanks to his two terms as a county jurist, delegated the corporate expansion to Eugene Buffington, president of the subsidiary Illinois Steel. And like George Pullman a decade earlier, Buffington and his colleagues decided to build on the edge of Chicago's spreading metropolitan region.

The corporation considered locations in Waukegan and South Chicago, but the final decision favored 9,000 acres on the Lake Michigan shore across the state line in Indiana. The barren site offered plenty of elbow room at a good price, along with water, railroad access, and proximity to the Chicago labor pool. The corporation went on to build the largest steel mill in the nation there for a new unit called Indiana Steel, along with facilities for corporate holdings American Bridge, American Sheet and Tin Plate, American Car and Foundry, American Locomotive Works, American Sheet and Wire, National Tube, and Universal Portland Cement.

And it built a new city to support the works. Gary, Indiana, as the judge allowed the community to be named, would come to be the largest company town ever constructed in the United States. Gary's warp-speed incarnation led its promoters to dub it "the Magic City"—a moniker that others, including the mixed-industry town of Middlesborough, Tennessee, had tried to claim but that seemed to fit Gary best of all.

Like most steel men, U.S. Steel's executives were not eager to become involved with housing for employees. "We are manufacturers, not real estate dealers," the head of a large Pittsburgh steel outfit haughtily announced in 1908. "The most successful places in the United States are those farthest removed from suspicion of domination or control by an employer," averred Buffington. At first, company executives thought they could simply lay out the grid, supply a sewer system and gas lines, and let the community itself take care of the actual residential construction. Before long, though, the corporation was driven to build many residences, since undeveloped lots weren't selling particularly well and home-building hadn't taken off. In the end, U.S. Steel built "half a city," in the words of writer and social reformer Graham Romeyn Taylor. This inclination to abstain from residential building meant Gary was dissimilar from many company towns that had come before, including Lowell, Pullman, Hershey, and even southern textile towns or the towns of the coal belt.

In his article for *The Survey*, a journal published by the Charity Organization Society of the City of New York, a social-welfare group, Graham Taylor wasn't altogether flattering toward Gary. But neither could he help but be impressed: With a population nearing 50,000 only nine years after the first brick was laid, Gary was "probably the greatest single calculated achievement of America's master industry," in Taylor's opinion.[1]

Judge Gary's personal history reads like a pop-psychology case study. His childhood took place in an atmosphere of repression marked by occasional bursts of self-expression. Raised on an Illinois farm by a strict Methodist family, he spent much time in Bible study and was told that no unnecessary work should be done on Sunday. His father was a spare-the-rod authoritarian who beat young Elbert with a belt—once for allowing a family cow to stray into a neighbor's pasture and eat his corn, another time for using forbidden curse words. Work, study, obedience, and punishment were the cornerstones of his youth, reported biographer Ida Tarbell. But Elbert would stand up for his rights if need be: "I never allowed a teacher to punish me if I didn't think I deserved it," he told Tarbell as he related a tale of false accusation. On that occasion, he seized a brandished ruler from the teacher and broke it before she could land a blow.

He enjoyed being clean, his mother said, and wearing his Sunday-best clothes. (Photos taken of him later in life invariably show a dandyish, balding gentleman with a trim moustache and stiff white collar, not dissimilar in looks from Parker Brothers' Monopoly game tycoon.) But Elbert knew when it was time to remove such garments and put on his informal duds. That meant his dress things lasted much longer than those of his brother. In all matters, Gary seemed to learn that getting the proper balance was key: Acknowledge authority and traditional values, but assert yourself when you believe you should. Even a bit of personal display, within limits, can earn the approval of others.

Gary was fourteen when the Civil War broke out, and he soon left the Wesleyan Methodist college where he was studying and enlisted. But he was shortly mustered out to be with his family, as his brother had returned wounded from the fighting. By 1865 Gary had begun to study law, and within three years he'd become a clerk in the Illinois Superior Court and gotten married. He developed a reputation for rectitude: Gary did not drink, smoke, or allow racy stories to be told in his presence. Before long, the young man had become mayor of his small village of Wheaton, where he joined the successful effort to make it a Prohibition town, free of alcoholic beverages. In 1882, he ran for a county judgeship and won, serving two four-year terms.

By 1892, he had been a lawyer for twenty years and was president of the Chicago Bar Association. He was approached by John W. "Bet-a-Million" Gates, a renowned steel man and gambler, to help combine five companies into Consolidated Steel and Wire Corp. Gary joined the company's board and later assisted in another consolidation, that of American Steel and Wire Corp. At every turn, he was earning a wider reputation for his skill as a patient and trustworthy bargainer who knew how to get what he wanted. In 1894, when Gates became president of Illinois Steel, he made Gary general counsel of that enterprise. Four years later, financier J. P. Morgan appointed a surprised Gary—a man who knew a lot about mergers but almost nothing about making steel—president of the new combination of Federal Steel.

The next combination would be U.S. Steel, of which Gary became chairman of the executive committee and Charles Schwab, the flamboyant former president of Carnegie Steel, became president. But the two struggled. Initially, the idea was that the executive committee would make all the fundamental decisions and the president would be in charge of day-to-day administration. But Schwab was not one to be led by others. After all, he had been one of the prime movers behind the creation of U.S. Steel—putting the bug in Morgan's ear at a testimonial dinner, working out details during a midnight meeting in Morgan's study, getting a price for Carnegie Steel from Andrew Carnegie during a round of golf, and drawing up a list of other properties that would make the giant trust into a "rounded proposition." However, it was becoming ever clearer that Gary rather than Schwab was the one to whom Morgan turned—that whatever Gary desired would receive the financier's support.

Gary favored stability and a low corporate profile, while Schwab was never reserved about his inclination to battle workers and unions. More problematic was Schwab's penchant for high living. He began building a giant New York City chateau for himself, modeled on the fanciful Loire palace Chenonceau. He gambled and celebrated the high life in Monte Carlo, drawing tabloid headlines—and withering criticism from his old colleague Andrew Carnegie. In the end, the patron's decimating fire resulted in Schwab's nervous breakdown. He took a leave from work and in 1903 resigned from the corporation. Gary shortly was named to a new position, chairman of the board, where he would set company policy for the next twenty-five years.

It was Judge Gary's code of ethics that drew the most comment from colleagues and onlookers, in many ways reflecting the point of view of enlightened financial men rather than that of the steelmakers. The judge first broke with tradition by having the corporation issue quarterly financial reports—and distributing them to the public and to board members simultaneously. Such a practice restricted the ability of board members to profit personally from early access to information, and led to grumbling from the likes of board member Henry Clay Frick. But this was only the first of Gary's innovations. He also insisted that stockholders be allowed to speak at stockholder meetings, and that the opinion of the general public be considered when making policy. He even advocated applying "Sunday school principles" to business affairs—partly as the right thing to do, but also because it would enhance public relations. Appearances, after all, counted for a lot, especially in an age that distrusted all trusts.

At the same time, for years he resisted the biblical injunction—and calls from the public and his own board members—to give workers a day of rest on Sunday. He did not want to make such a change "simply because a public sentiment compelled them to do so," he pompously announced at one point. In 1912, responding to criticism from attorney Louis Brandeis, he said the company had largely eliminated twelve-hour shifts, but the statement was untrue. At least 50 percent of U.S. Steel workers still endured such lengthy workdays, according to a 1911 stockholders report, and the twelve-hour day continued into the 1920s. Not every Sunday school principle, it seemed, made sense in the real world.[2]

The shadow of three earlier industrial communities lay over Gary, Indiana. First was Pullman, the company town repeatedly cited by the judge and others as a negative example. "Time and again the paternalistic mistakes of Pullman were given as justification for a 'do-as-little-as-you-have-to' policy in shaping town conditions," Taylor reported. Meanwhile, Judge Gary was a vociferous advocate of various corporate-welfare policies—

including expenditures on visiting nurses, libraries, and playgrounds—
that might be regarded as paternalistic. Moreover, the corporation trained
a watchful eye on steel towns including Gary: In 1907, when one entrepreneur proposed to open a movie house in a company-owned building,
Buffington and Gary originally said no, then agreed only after it was suggested that the theater could double as a venue for church services. An
executive was assigned to review all films, with the power to veto any he
considered unsuitable. In short, to U.S. Steel executives, the dreaded term
"paternalism" only applied to a policy of residential development. Instead
of assuming from the first the task of planning and organizing the community of Gary, the corporation would be drawn into town-making
grudgingly and haphazardly.[3]

The second community experience that shaped Gary was that of
Homestead, Pennsylvania, America's quintessential steel town. Located in
the Monongahela River valley fourteen miles south of Pittsburgh, Homestead began as a small village in the 1870s, housing a glassmaking works
and 1,000 inhabitants by the end of that decade. In 1881, a group of Pittsburgh iron and steel men established one of the country's most up-to-date
steelmaking facilities there, the Homestead Works. Shortly thereafter, a
plague of labor problems prompted the owners to sell out to Andrew
Carnegie, who transformed the works into an awesome production facility.

Carnegie, too, eschewed landlord duties, leaving further development
of the town to private developers and speculators. Soon, rows of cheap
frame housing spread across the hills above Carnegie's works. Carnegie's
most significant contribution in this regard came in the nearby area of
Munhall, where he offered homes for sale to his workers with low-interest
mortgages. Other aspects of town planning went begging: The largest
green space in Homestead would be the lawn of the superintendent's
mansion. In 1910, a study of the area backed by the Russell Sage Foundation and known as the Pittsburgh Survey decried Homestead's open
sewers and chaotic organization.[4] Braddock, across the Monongahela
River from Homestead, experienced a similarly congested sprawl. In the
words of novelist Tom Bell, whose *Out of This Furnace* (1941) looked at
three generations of immigrant life in Braddock, the housing thrown up
by speculators there was "characteristic of the steel towns, long, ugly rows
like cell blocks, two rooms high and two deep, without water, gas or con-

veniences of any kind, nothing but the walls and the roofs. . . . They were filled as soon as they were finished and made no apparent impression on the housing shortage or the rent level."[5]

In 1906, Homestead was perhaps best known for its pivotal steel-worker strike in 1892. Henry Clay Frick, master of the Carnegie mill, had determined that year to destroy the established union, the Amalgamated Association of Iron and Steel Workers, which he saw as standing in the way of plant modernization. Although the company had negotiated an agreement with the union following a strike in 1889, this go-round management demanded cuts in skilled workers' pay and the elimination of numerous jobs. Frick made his late-June offer in the form of an ultimatum: Take it or we'll run the plant nonunion. Then he fortified the works, erecting an eleven-foot-high wooden fence topped with barbed wire, backed by towers with searchlights. On July 6, he attempted to reopen operations: Three hundred armed Pinkerton guards boarded two barges and attempted to slip up to the plant via the Monongahela River under the cover of darkness. Meanwhile, the strikers had also organized themselves along military lines, going so far as to acquire artillery and to patrol all river and land entrances to the town. The barge was greeted by a barrage of rifle and cannon fire from the riverbank. Before the Pinkertons surrendered, nine strikers and seven detectives had been killed during a twelve-hour battle.

The state militia entered the fray, management imported strikebreakers, and by the end of the year the Homestead mill was operating without a union, just as Frick had wanted. Within another year, thirty more of the area's sixty-odd iron and still mills had likewise broken their unions.[6] But U.S. Steel was not eager to repeat the Monongahela Valley experience in the town of Gary if it could help it.

The planning of Gary, such as it was, reflected this sentiment. The various Gary plants stretched all along the lakefront, allowing town residents virtually no access to the water. In the event of trouble, supplies, guards, and willing workers could be brought directly into the plants by boat. On the other side of the factories was the Grand Calumet River, which separated all the plants but one from the residential areas of town. In effect, the river might act as a defensive moat should events like those in Homestead be repeated in Gary.

Finally, a third community provided inspiration for Gary—this time in a more positive fashion. Lying thirty-odd miles northeast of Homestead, the Kiskiminetas Valley town of Vandergrift, Pennsylvania, was built from scratch in the 1890s by the Apollo Iron and Steel Co., which in time, like so many other independent companies, became part of U.S. Steel.

Apollo Iron and Steel's first home was in Apollo, Pennsylvania, one mile from where Vandergrift would be built. Keeping up with technological developments and growing demand, the iron mill at Apollo was transformed into a steel mill in the 1880s. But residences, mostly owned by the workers, got crammed into the existing town boundaries, encroaching ever closer upon the mill, and the company had difficulty getting room to expand the works. Thus in 1892, Apollo's chief executive, George Gibson McMurtry, began contemplating expansion elsewhere, and for that purpose purchased 640 acres of land upriver in Westmoreland County.

The major depression of 1893 led steel prices to collapse. Apollo announced a wage cut, which precipitated a strike at that mill by the Amalgamated, which of course had only recently experienced the bloody defeat at Homestead. After two months, Apollo reopened after announcing that it would employ only those who renounced the union. It hired skilled workers from other, nonunion mills and promoted laborers to fill the ranks of the semiskilled. There was no violent explosion at Apollo—the Amalgamated's spirit, it seemed, was for the moment broken.

McMurtry was not present for these events. Instead, he was in Europe visiting celebrated model industrial towns, including the Krupp estates near Essen, Germany, various English factory villages, and the foundries at Le Creusot, France. His trip was not unlike the grand tours taken by Francis Cabot Lowell and Milton Hershey. McMurtry saw landscaped European towns in which companies provided schools, housing, and social programs.

Two years after returning to the United States, McMurtry hired the celebrated landscape architecture firm of Olmsted, Olmsted and Eliot to design a model industrial town for him. The legendary Frederick Law Olmsted Sr. had made his reputation with the rolling landscapes and rustic motifs of New York's Central Park and pastoral middle-class suburbs.

Olmsted's successors, partner Charles Eliot and stepson John Charles Olmsted, envisioned for McMurtry a town of curvilinear boulevards dominated by a large village green.

McMurtry had stipulated that the new town would have a modern sanitary infrastructure, including water mains, sewers, and gas lines, all of which he believed would mean a stronger, healthier workforce. Like Apollo, and for that matter like Homestead and Braddock, the company would not build housing for workers, instead leaving this to private interests. Lest this have the same undesirable result as in the other towns, the Olmsted consultants recommended a series of restrictive covenants that would define the use of town space and ensure that only desirable structures were built. They would, for example, bar tenements and stipulate the size of yards, and all houses would require approval by a board of architects.

Immediately, McMurtry began tinkering with the designers' grand vision. More and more space would be needed for the mill itself, he determined, much of which came at the expense of the greensward. As for the restrictive covenants, he approved only one: barring the sale of liquor. The town, he decreed, would be named Vandergrift in honor of Apollo's largest investor, Jacob Jay Vandergrift Sr.

It wasn't long before the architects washed their hands of the project. But Apollo's board at least was pleased with the outcome. The board set up a separate company to handle real estate, the Vandergrift Land and Improvement Co., and within six months of its announcement of lots for sale in the budding town, two-thirds of residential properties had been sold. This meant Apollo had practically recouped all of its $200,000 initial investment.

The land company carefully evaluated all prospective property buyers, with an eye primarily to weeding out any union men, and it advanced money to help those it favored build homes. Supervisors and skilled operatives made up the ranks of the first buyers. The land company built a good number of houses to be rentals. Even so, the size of lots and their $750 price tag meant that only elite workers could afford to live in Vandergrift's main residential area. The town soon offered a second subdivision, dubbed Vandergrift Heights, and in time that $150-per-lot area filled up with housing built for lower paid operatives. In a third area,

Morning Sun, immigrant laborers settled, and that region grew into a facsimile of the "Hunkytowns" common among the steel communities of Pennsylvania.[7] In a *Harper's Weekly* article saluting Vandergrift, Eugene Buffington described how the foreigners had "segregated themselves . . . on the outskirts of the borough," requiring Vandergrift officials to keep an eye on their sanitary habits and enforce "regulations for cleanliness and health."[8]

Vandergrift borough was incorporated in 1897, and citizens elected a town council to set a tax levy and to hire a constable and policeman. On more substantive matters, the council, which consisted of skilled workers from the mill, regularly deferred to the company. McMurtry agreed to provide a firehouse and a cemetery, and to donate land for the seven churches that were established by 1903.

Vandergrift was far from exhibiting the tidy, model looks of Pullman, Hershey, or early Lowell. Those who bought lots in Vandergrift immediately began subdividing them and constructing rental housing, while Vandergrift Heights was notable for its rutted, unpaved streets, cowsheds, and privies. But homeownership in the area seemed to have the effect the steel managers desired: A 1901 strike called by the Amalgamated drew little support in Vandergrift, where a union observer found the employees to be "bound up by their property interests." The strike's failure there offered McMurtry a "crowning vindication," raved trade journal *Iron Age*: "With such a splendid proof of the value of an industrial town laid out on modern lines, and of a management fostering close relations with the men based on absolutely fair dealing, it is to be hoped that in the future Vandergrift will have the distinction of being only the oldest of a series of similar communities."

As further evidence of the community's harmonious labor relations, in 1902 Vandergrift citizens held a ceremony in which they presented McMurtry with a silver punch bowl. Engraved thereupon were the words A TRUE FRIEND OF THE WORKING MAN.[9]

An instinctive American "self-helpfulness" prompted Vandergrift workers to build their own houses, Buffington said. Surely that impulse, the town's homeowner spirit, and its company loyalty could be duplicated at Gary, the corporation figured.

Accordingly, it established the independent Gary Land Co., resembling the Vandergrift Land and Improvement Co., under executive Horace S. Norton. Following a $7.2 million anonymous land purchase of nearly twenty square miles, including eight miles of Lake Michigan shore frontage, the Gary Land Co. filled in seven hundred feet of the lake, dredged a twenty-five-foot ship canal a mile inland, and relocated a straightened and narrowed Grand Calumet River a half mile southward. Indiana Steel, with its eight blast furnaces, fifty-six open hearths, coke ovens, and the largest rail mill in the world, was the first plant to be constructed and became the nucleus of the industrial complex. It would be flanked by American Sheet and Tin Plate's factory and that of National Tube, with the Universal Portland Cement factory located farther to the west along the shore. Located slightly inland were the American Bridge and American Locomotive plants. The Elgin, Joliet & Eastern Railway—which circled Chicago's outer rim and connected the Gary Works with Illinois Steel finishing plants in south Chicago—located its terminal yards at the southwest corner of the industrial area.[10]

As for the town, the Land Co. hired no city planners, merely turning over the layout to engineer A. P. Melton. There would be no curvilinear boulevards or pastoral inspiration in Gary. Instead, Melton plotted the town as an unvarying grid centered on an axis of Broadway—the thoroughfare that ran straight south from the front entrance of the Indiana Steel plant—and the east–west commercial street called Fifth Avenue. The avenues south of Fifth would simply be numbered; the streets running parallel to Broadway would get the names of U.S. presidents and states. The Land Co. built a sewer system sufficient for a city of 200,000 and later would donate land for schools, churches, a library, a hospital, and municipal buildings.

By June 1906, hundreds of men were at work building the new town. Adjacent to each company's property, Melton plotted subdivisions for its workers' homes. The first subdivision, intended for Indiana Steel, consisted of eight hundred acres immediately to the south of the mill site, plotted into 4,000 lots. Streets were graded and paved, concrete sidewalks built, sewers dug, and electric and gas lines installed. Lot-sale agreements stipulated simply that building plans had to be approved by an agent of the Land Co., that houses had to be completed within twelve to eighteen months, and that, with very few exceptions, no liquor could be sold. (Five sites obtained exemptions from this prohibition, Buffington explained, as a safety valve necessary to a large town, since the foreign element "would otherwise be enticed to groggeries of the lowest type.") But unlike in Vandergrift, this near-laissez-faire approach was not greeted with an explosion of home-building. Instead, within three years only 250 private homes had been constructed.

Consequently, the Gary Land Co. soon found itself in the home-construction business, erecting around eight hundred homes that rented for anywhere from $42 to $14 per month. Many of these were houses of five to ten rooms, and, as in Vandergrift proper, the rents made them affordable only to executives and the most skilled workers. Beginning in 1909, the company built three hundred apartment houses for workers at American Bridge and more than one hundred single homes for American Sheet and Tin Plate employees.

It was a departure when the company constructed fifty uniform, wood-frame, four-room houses in a corner of the first subdivision. With rents a bit lower—$12 to $13 per month—less-skilled, lower-paid workers could afford to live there. But fifty units hardly put a dent in the need for inexpensive housing, and in any case, Land Co. executives decided they did not approve of the results and in 1911 tore down the already-disheveled structures. The majority of Gary's 16,000 low-paid immigrant workers had to fend for themselves. Many commuted from Pullman, a twelve-mile round trip.

Finally, private enterprise stepped in—exhibiting its least attractive attributes. The South Side area beyond U.S. Steel's property but still within Gary's incorporated limits beckoned to real estate promoters, including the president of the town board, a pol by the name of Tom Knotts, whose older brother Armanis had organized the original, anonymous land purchase for U.S. Steel. Tom Knotts—who once likened his real estate success to "picking leaves from trees"—ensured that land lying to the south would soar in value by seeing to it that the town's streetcar franchise went to an ally. The Gary and Interurban Railway Co. went on

Kirk Boott, the great
potentate of the early days
of Lowell, Massachusetts.

Lowell's
Boott Mills
in the
late 1800s.

The Illinois National
Guard assembling before
the Arcade Building in
Pullman during the great
railroad strike of 1894.

George M. Pullman, head of the Pullman Palace Car company, felt his model town would have an "ennobling and refining" effect on his workers.

Chocolate magnate Milton M. Hershey in 1927 with one of the orphan boys from the Hershey Industrial School.

Hershey workers in 1937 producing one of the company's signature products, Hershey's Kisses.

Corning Inc.'s current headquarters in the town of Corning, New York, incorporates a decades-old tower that's emblazoned with the image of Little Joe the lightbulb glassblower.

Founded in 1912, Jenkins, Kentucky, was one of the dozens of coal-mining towns that sprang up across Appalachia.

At the coal face, a miner prepares a fuse and charge of explosive powder to dislodge a layer of coal.

Into the twentieth century, companies employed Pinkerton guards to help break strikes, as they are doing here during an 1880s coal strike in Ohio's Hocking Valley.

In the early 1900s, laborers at Cannon's Cabarrus Cotton Mill in Concord included child workers as young as eight years of age.

Charles Cannon, president of Cannon Mills, ruled the town of Kannapolis, North Carolina, from the early 1920s until his death in 1971.

A sign on Kannapolis's south main street and another atop Cannon Mills' works proclaimed the company as the world's largest maker of towels.

The use of labor-saving machinery across the South's textile belt doomed rival producers in New England and meant much of the work was simple enough to be performed by children. This photo was taken in 1908.

As head of U.S. Steel, Elbert H. Gary presided over a vast expansion of the company's productive facilities and construction of the Indiana town that bore his name.

The intersection of Broadway and Fifth Avenue, here under construction in 1907, would become the central axis around which company engineers plotted Gary, Indiana.

Frank Phillips, a former barber and bond trader, built Phillips Petroleum into a vertically integrated, $130 million company by 1925.

Bartlesville, Oklahoma, was the site of several major oil strikes in the early 1900s, but the town also became a major administrative center for Phillips and other oil companies.

Henry J. Kaiser was a pioneer of welfare capitalism, offering twenty-four-hour childcare, workplace-safety programs, and comprehensive medical care to his World War II shipyard workers.

A woman welder at the Kaiser shipyard in Richmond, California, in 1943.

The "liberty ship" SS *George Washington Carver* just prior to its launch in 1943.

The so-called "hillbilly girls" who worked at Oak Ridge's Y-12 facility during World War II had no idea that they were producing U-235 for use in an atomic bomb.

Like other company towns discussed, Oak Ridge is today a tourist destination complete with souvenir postcards.

to build a Broadway-centered, north–south line, not the Fifth Avenue–oriented, east–west line the Land Co. preferred. Then, Knotts and others built hundreds of South Side boardinghouses and cheap frame houses for the immigrant workers. The results were slums, given that there were no restrictions on lot sizes and no codes requiring running water, toilets, or sewers. Typical were the one hundred–foot-by-eighteen-foot shacks split up into two-room units, each of which rented for $6 to $9 per month. And unlike Vandergrift and the subdivisions of the Gary Land Co., the South Side had no limitations on drinking establishments. By 1908, there were eighty-seven saloons on Broadway alone. An infamous area known as "the Patch" emerged just south of the Wabash Railroad tracks, which defined one edge of the Land Co.'s holdings. By 1911, Gary featured one saloon for every eighty-eight citizens; in Chicago working-class wards, the ratio was 1 to 231.[11]

Political struggle between local politicians and corporate interests continued for several years. The 1909 mayoral election pitted Knotts against the Land Co.'s candidate, Republican John A. Brennan. The town's only newspaper, the *Gary Daily Tribune*, supported Brennan, but Knotts created another paper to support his candidacy, the *Evening Post*. Affairs quickly turned messy: The county's Republican sheriff arrested Knotts on a charge that he had defamed Brennan. There were near riots as Republicans brought in dozens of immigrants to cast votes for the GOP. Knotts won by seventy-one votes, but his triumph was short-lived. The Republican-controlled Lake County government harassed Knotts continuously, filing fourteen charges against him, ranging from embezzlement to perjury and election fraud. No trial ever took place, but the charges damaged his reputation. Then in 1913, he was opposed by Citizens Party candidate Roswell O. Johnson, whose backers included independents, Bull Moose progressives, unhappy Democrats—and U.S. Steel. Spies observed Democratic rallies, and company foremen punished workers who attended them while ushering right-voting employees to the polls. Immigrants, who played little political role elsewhere, were eligible to vote in Indiana shortly after they declared an intention to become U.S. citizens—and ethnic bosses or foremen herded them to the polls. Johnson won by 1,516 votes. Republicans would dominate city politics from that time into the 1930s.[12]

By 1909, Gary had 12,000 inhabitants, residences valued at $2 million total, fifteen miles of paved streets, two banks, six hotels, three daily newspapers, two schools, ten church denominations, and many stores and shops. It had only two parks, neither with any playground or recreational facilities and one of which was dominated by a large water tower. Thousands of men were already at work making steel.

To attract workers, the corporation had advertised Gary's progress in newspapers across the United States and Europe, and real estate interests circulated promotional pamphlets. ("Come to Gary," urged one Land Co. newspaper advertisement: "Become a factor in the building of this model city. Own your own home in Gary.") The foreign publicity was particularly effective, pulling large numbers from twenty-two countries including especially Ireland, Croatia, and Serbia: Before Gary was three years old, 50 percent of its population was foreign-born. U.S.-born professionals including teachers, lawyers, newspapermen, architects, and would-be merchants came, too, in search of adventure and a new start. By 1914, Gary's citizenry had more than quadrupled to 50,000. For all of its shortcomings, the town's schools were up to the standards of most progressive cities, according to Graham Taylor. What's more, the city featured such impressive institutions as a $65,000 Carnegie-donated library and an elaborate YMCA constructed with a $250,000 personal gift from Judge Gary.[13]

The city of Gary was only four years old when U.S. Steel began building another city, this one in the South. Fairfield, Alabama, a suburb of Birmingham, would be a manufacturing hub for the Tennessee Coal, Iron and Railroad Co., American Steel and Wire, and other corporation subsidiaries. Once again, U.S. Steel shied away from residential construction and ownership, this time not even generating a separate land company to manage development. Instead, in Fairfield the company turned over these tasks to a private real estate firm that founded the Corey Land Co., named after the town's first appellation. Here, though, as in Vandergrift but not in Gary, Corey Land hired an expert landscape architect to develop an overall plan.

It was another Bostonian, George H. Miller, who developed four main residential zones for Fairfield. Dwellings ranged from double three-room bungalows to two-story homes with baths and electricity. These were a far cry from the simple wood-frame dwellings in Kannapolis and even farther from the coal-town shacks. There was no grid in Fairfield—instead, streets adhered to the meandering local topography.

Yet there was one respect in which Fairfield adhered to southern custom: the town was closed to African Americans. Those who purchased lots encountered restrictions that specified that the "lot shall be used by white persons only." That didn't mean that the industrial firms in Fairfield employed only whites—as ever, the sweatiest, most punishing labor was reserved for blacks. Soon a cluster of Negro shanties emerged just over the Fairfield city line.[14]

A score of such medium-size steel towns were scattered across the industrial heartland. Where U.S. Steel had Gary, Fairfield, and more, Bethlehem Steel had works at Steelton, Pennsylvania; Lackawanna, New York; and Sparrows Point, Maryland. Jones & Laughlin made steel at Aliquippa, Pennsylvania (which was run through the 1920s much like a coal company town by plant superintendent Tom Girdler); Inland Steel, at Indiana Harbor, Indiana; Colorado Fuel and Iron, at Pueblo, Colorado; and Weirton Steel, at Weirton, West Virginia (another virtual dictatorship, presided over by private company police). Such one-industry communities were home to 60 percent of U.S. steelworkers.[15]

Sparrows Point provides a noteworthy contrast to Gary. The town and mill, located on a peninsula at the confluence of the Chesapeake Bay and Baltimore Harbor, were projects of the Pennsylvania Steel Co., a subsidiary of the Pennsylvania Railroad. While Midwestern plants depended upon iron ore from the Mesabi Range and the western United States, Pennsylvania Steel got ore from Cuba, and later from South America. Company executives figured that meant an Atlantic shore location made more economic sense. Development moved quickly: In the 1880s, company point man Frederick Wood traveled to Cuba to contract for the ore, scouted out potential sites for the U.S. works, and recommended the Maryland location. The company quickly and quietly acquired the land for $57,900. Before a stone was laid, Luther Bent, president of the steel company, came to an agreement with Maryland's Democratic machine politicians that Pennsylvania Steel would have absolute political control over Sparrows Point—everything from hiring teachers to controlling the police. In 1891, Bent signed papers incorporating the Maryland Steel Co. of Baltimore County. He named Wood as president of the new enterprise and his brother Rufus as general agent in charge of town affairs.

Interestingly enough, the Woods were born in Lowell, Massachusetts, sons of a Boott Mills weaving-room foreman, and they brought a Boott-like sense of social hierarchy with them to Maryland. After laying out and constructing Sparrows Point on a grid of rectangular blocks, with streets named simply for letters of the alphabet, the company allocated houses according to one's place in the corporate pyramid. Avenues A through D, closest to the water, were for executives; Avenues E through F were for foremen and skilled workers; and remaining lettered streets were for workers of lesser rank. Homes became smaller and neighborhoods denser as the alphabet progressed.

The company owned all buildings directly and rented them out to employees, meaning that, of course, tenants had to leave if they lost or gave up their jobs. The houses were substantial and inexpensive, renting for between $5.50 and $12 a month. Once again, of course, the company's primary housing concern was for managers and skilled workers: On the far north side of the peninsula was a group of shanties for unmarried immigrants and single black men—six-room affairs housing up to four men per room, with no running water, and privies out back.

There were two schoolhouses in town, one for whites and another for blacks. Seven churches were present on land rented from the company for $1 per year, and no alcohol was allowed in the town.

Although many of the residences in Sparrows Point were above average for a company town, there were similarities to coal-mining communities. Rents, for example, were deducted from pay. There were no independent stores in Sparrows Point, only a company store where credit was extended in the form of scrip. Company executives got stock in the store and bonuses based on its earnings, which ran between 10 percent and 12 percent a year.

And in what was standard practice in steel facilities, the plant ran long hours: The day shift was eleven hours, followed by a thirteen- or fourteen-hour night shift and a twenty-four-hour swing shift on Sunday. (Every two weeks, the shifts reversed so that those working days went onto nights and vice versa; on the day of the shift turn, half of the workers had to pull a twenty-four-hour stint.) There were no vacations, and two unpaid holidays per year. The Sparrows Point facility was a self-declared open shop—no union allowed.

By 1910, 4,000 men were employed there, 75 percent in the works and the rest in the shipyard. It had already become the largest employer in Maryland. But following a drop in global sales of rails, and drastic cuts in the workforce, the company sold out to Bethlehem Steel in 1916. Bethlehem president Charles M. Schwab, who'd come to that company only a year after resigning from U.S. Steel, saw Britain, France, and Russia as profitable wartime clients and courted them even when the United States was supposed to be a neutral power. Munitions and armor-plate sales abroad allowed Schwab to transform Sparrows Point into a much larger works, employing 12,500 men at its peak.

Wartime production demands, it turned out, weren't altogether to the liking of steel executives. President Woodrow Wilson's National War Labor Board sought a détente with organized labor and began proceedings against Bethlehem Steel, forbidding it from blocking union activities and requiring the organization of shop committees. In response, the company began an employee-representation plan much like the one at Colorado Fuel and Iron. Employees elected representatives who met annually with top management; elected plant committees met six times a year to discuss such issues as transportation, the company bonus system, safety, housing, and grievances. Management, however, could simply terminate any grievance.

Altogether, the Sparrows Point formula seemed to work even without offering home ownership, which seemed to be a key to worker contentment in Vandergrift. When pent-up wartime demands and grinding, dangerous work shifts combined to explode in the form of a national 1919 steel strike, only five hundred Sparrows Point men walked out.[16]

During the 1910s, the steel industry seemed to arrive at a formula for avoiding industrial strife. The corporations were not above coal-industry-like repression, albeit of a less violent nature: Many workers were required to sign "yellow-dog" contracts vowing not to join unions, and suspected violators were discharged and blacklisted. Companies maintained elaborate and efficient departments for spying on employees. But equally important, the steel towns themselves, along with other corporate welfare measures, seemed to reconcile workers to lives of nearly ceaseless, low-paid toil.

Steelworkers likely viewed home ownership or even low rents, as in Sparrows Point or the Carnegie-built dwellings at Munhall, as a pay subsidy. Moreover, the central place of the factories in the towns, and of the guiding and beneficent hand of the plant managers, probably shaped residents' sensibilities. Company largesse was evident: Over a twelve-year period ending in 1924, U.S. Steel spent more than $22 million on playgrounds, schools, gardens, clubs, and a visiting-nurse program. Town sanitation facilities were another big expense. U.S. Steel funded Boy Scout troops and sports teams, and Bethlehem Steel, a ninety-piece, touring military band. Such efforts built a sense of pride and company loyalty among workers and a positive attitude toward these corporations among the public at large.[17]

There were other corporate welfare measures, too. In 1903, U.S. Steel began a stock-purchase plan that allowed model employees to buy shares on installment at below-market prices, and more than 26,000 employees immediately took part. Republic Steel, Cambria, and Youngstown Sheet and Tube copied the program. By 1921, Bethlehem Steel workers owned company stock worth $40 million. Under Schwab, that company particularly favored paying monthly bonuses tied to productivity increases— "a cash premium on personal efficacy and endeavor," in his words. These bonuses went to managers and skilled workers only, however. As in most regards, the semiskilled and particularly the unskilled, who got a flat 37 cents per hour at Bethlehem, were neglected.[18]

Skilled workers were also made aware that there were clear avenues for promotion and that they were ever being prepared to ascend the job ladder. The unskilled received little in the way of pay or perks, as most seemed content with what they got. Before World War I, the immigrant ranks included a great many unmarried men who believed they were in the United States only temporarily, just long enough to gather sufficient funds to buy property back in their home countries. They expected to endure a period of harsh sacrifice, doing unpleasant and even dangerous work, and their greatest complaint came when they felt there was not sufficient work to go around.

Perhaps the biggest problem for the steel companies before World War I came from the period's influential social critics and reformers. The 1909 Pittsburgh Survey, and a series of articles for *American Magazine* summarizing the survey findings, exposed the industry's relentlessly long work hours, speed-up, low pay, and repressive attitude that "stifles initiative and destroys healthy citizenship." The U.S. Senate's labor committee denounced U.S. Steel's "brutal system of industrial slavery," while the *New York World* ran a series of articles on steel-town conditions, which the newspaper called "a crime against humanity."

Judge Gary, for one, was contrite—at least a little bit. He responded by enhancing the corporation's social welfare programs. The company initiated a new "boost for safety" program in the mills, adopting a variety of effective safety devices and practices along with a generous compensation plan for the injured. But despite the fact that much of the criticism was focused on the steel industry's long workdays, U.S. Steel clung to the two-shift, seven-day system.

At one of the regular, lavish dinners that industry executives held for the purpose of praising themselves (and fixing prices), Gary announced: "The man who has the intelligence and the success and the capital to employ labor has placed upon himself voluntarily a responsibility with reference to his men. We have the advantage of them in education, in experience, in wealth, in many ways, and we must make it absolutely certain under all circumstances that we treat them right." Such a responsibility, it almost goes without saying, did not extend to permitting unionism. There, too, a matter of principle was at stake, the steel companies argued before a congressional investigation of the steel industry: No man's right to work should be abridged by a requirement that he join any organization.[19]

During the run-up to the war, maintaining wages rather than cutting them had become a consensus policy within the industry, even during financial downswings. The question of unionism seemed largely moot: Outside of U.S. Steel, all steel mills were nonunion after 1908, and Gary's corporation adopted a policy of starving the union out, regularly idling mills where the union had any membership. The war, however, changed all that. In Gary, 11,896 men were employed in steelmaking by 1917. Although wages increased by 21 percent by 1916, growing demand for steel first from Europe and then from the U.S. government led profits to double, then to triple. A persistent scarcity of labor and of living space—Gary experienced a shortfall of 4,000 housing units, according to its *Daily Tribune*—led to worker restiveness and even a revival of the Amalgamated Association. By war's end, that organization had a membership of 15,000, up from 6,500 in 1914.[20]

Organized labor seemed to have an ally in the Wilson administration. Its National War Labor Board—which primarily sought labor peace to guarantee industrial productivity—asserted that workers had a right to organize in unions without interference. It ordered Bethlehem Steel to stop blocking the union and to organize shop committees. As a halfway measure and in what they hoped the government would regard as a show of good faith, the companies threw ever more energy into organizing employee-representation plans, notably at Midvale, Bethlehem, Youngstown Sheet and Tube, Inland Steel, and more. U.S. Steel held back from employee-representation plans, saying that its wage policies and welfare spending, which had tripled during the war, should be sufficient to satisfy employees. Meanwhile, companies stepped up their patriotic-propaganda efforts: Illinois Steel asked its workers to sign a "pledge of patriotism" vowing to oppose disruptive actions; flag days and patriotic signs were common; in Gary, there were dramatic patriotic parades through the streets, one featuring 25,000 marchers and delegations from Greek, Romanian, Hungarian, Serb, Croat, and Russian societies.[21]

By 1919, with the war over, the workers were ready to reap the reward for their patriotic efforts. The American Federation of Labor's National Committee for Organizing Iron and Steel Workers demanded improved wages, an eight-hour day and a six-day week, abolition of the twenty-four-hour shift, and collective bargaining. It set a strike date of September 22.

Reporting on how steelmakers were gearing up for the strike in the Pittsburgh area, the *New York World* wrote: "It is as though preparations were made for actual war." The sheriff of Allegheny County mobilized 5,000 deputies on the eve of the strike, and 3,000 more were sworn in at McKeesport, Pennsylvania. Publicly, steel company executives said they expected few workers to back the walkout. However, by the union's count, 365,000 men, or perhaps half of U.S. steelworkers and many more than the companies expected, responded, shutting down about half of the industry.

Across the land, police broke up workers' meetings and beat and jailed strikers, and the steelmakers brought in strikebreakers, including some 30,000 southern blacks, to run the mills.

In Gary, patriotism—that last refuge of a scoundrel—showed its usefulness again. With 85 percent of the city's 18,000 steelworkers honoring the strike, there was calm at first, then clashes with black strikebreakers on October 4, prompting intervention by 1,500 federal troops under General Leonard Wood. The military declared martial law, prohibited all outdoor meetings, and began arresting pickets and strike leaders, putting the miscreants to work sweeping the city's streets. Wood—who incidentally as a U.S. presidential candidate enjoyed the backing of Judge Gary as well as Morgan partner and U.S. Steel board member George W. Perkins—ardently fell to his work, repeatedly identifying the union with radicalism. "Gary is a hotbed of anarchy," he announced. The strike, he found, had been instigated by a "dangerous and extremely active group of IWW and the Red anarchist element." Wood was joined in his scare campaign by the Loyal American League, a business-backed group that worked to sway native-born workers away from the "Hunky" strike, and the *Tribune*, which ran banner headlines declaring RED PLOT UNCOVERED and REDS' BOMBS MADE HERE. By November, most Gary strikers had returned to work.

The strike served as a catalyst for a national "red scare," with the U.S. Justice Department under Attorney General A. Mitchell Palmer raiding political meetings and arresting nearly 10,000 alleged radicals across the country. The government deported dozens of recent immigrants. Meanwhile, the steel strike lagged under the combined corporate-government attack, and the union called off the walkout in January.[22]

With that conflagration over, both the company and the city of Gary looked ahead to the 1920s, which they saw as fat times. In reality, the two were headed in different directions: The city, already a flawed effort, would by the end of the decade enter a period of decline; the steel industry would revive after the Great Depression and emerge in a period of unmatched productivity and prosperity.

As the original city infrastructure no longer sufficed, Gary authorities called for a raft of new building, including new streets and sanitation facilities and a new civic center. The city went so far as to contract for a professional city plan that would allow improved transportation, street layouts, and zoning—but the move came to a halt when U.S. Steel, the railroads, and real estate interests showed a distinct lack of interest. Even so, a building boom brought new skyscrapers, office buildings, hotels, and apartment buildings. The large Gary State Bank Building was erected at the corner of Broadway and Fifth Avenue; not far away were the twin Gary City Hall and County buildings.

In addition to being the home of the Gary Works, the city was becoming a commercial center for the region. By the end of the 1920s, there were 1,300 retail stores employing 4,000 workers. The presence of 1,800 hotel rooms facilitated convention business, and thirteen movie houses provided distraction from the world of toil.[23]

For steelworkers, the long workday gradually shortened despite the company's best efforts to fight off change. The U.S. Labor Department reported in 1920 that the twelve-hour shift was still as prevalent as it had been in 1910, while 25 percent of blast-furnace, Bessemer, and open-hearth workers were enduring seven-day weeks. Christian reformers at the Interchurch World Movement issued a voluminous report criticizing the long hours. U.S. Steel responded by circulating a pamphlet written by Reverend E. Victor Bigelow of Andover, Massachusetts, calling demands to shorten the workday "the hobo doctrine . . . [that] glorifies leisure and denounces toil." In 1921, U.S. Steel stockholder Charles M. Cabot of Boston financed an engineering report that considered the impact of switching to a three-shift system of eight-hour days. It found that although the change would raise costs, it would also result in a better finished product. U.S. President Warren G. Harding endorsed the Cabot report and called steel men to the White House to discuss the matter. But once again

Judge Gary and U.S. Steel were unmoved: The corporation issued its own study showing that 60,000 more workers would be needed to make the change, and besides, workers didn't really want shorter days if that meant lower wages. U.S. Steel's seeming callousness and disrespect for a presidential request roused a further storm of public protest—and adoption by 1923 of a three-shift day across the steel industry.[24]

Gary's foreign-born workers still smarted from the harsh verbal attacks they'd received during the 1919 strike. Even those who had fought for the Allies or marched in the World War I–era patriotic parades had been branded as radicals and Bolsheviks. By 1920, immigrants represented 60 percent of the city's population of 55,000, with the largest groups being Polish, Slovaks, Serbs, Croatians, Italians, Greeks, Russians, and Hungarians. Some returned to Europe and warned their compatriots against coming to America. Then in 1924 Congress passed a law restricting further European immigration. The company turned to African-American émigrés from the Deep South—more than 2,000 were employed in Gary by 1920, and by 1930 they represented 18 percent of the population, the largest percentage of any northern industrial city. The Gary Works recruited workers from Mexico as well: Mexicans held 19 percent of semi-skilled jobs by 1928. Throughout the 1920s, steel production increased in Gary, where there were more than 24,000 industrial workers by 1930.

Meanwhile, the old problems continued: In 1922, the Indiana state housing department called conditions in the city's South Side among the worst in the state, citing overcrowding in the area's shacks and unsanitary conditions. The following year, a U.S. Labor Department report also decried South Side conditions. Gary began condemning some of the worst slums, but end-of-the-decade prosperity meant a further rise in population and even worse congestion. African Americans settled in what became known as the Central District—the old Patch and a new area created by draining the Little Calumet River. Segregated, slum housing predominated. Mexicans settled nearby in some of the worst housing in town; most of these newcomers were young, unmarried men employed as laborers at the steelworks.[25]

The corporation, which had built 1,250 housing units and advanced $4 million in building loans to employees before World War I, withdrew from construction altogether. In the 1920s, private interests built 14,000 new residential units.

Parts of Gary were becoming increasingly dangerous. In 1925, the city experienced thirty-two murders, a rate that encouraged comparisons to Al Capone's Chicago. Businesses complained that it was impossible to get theft insurance for properties along Broadway south of the Wabash tracks.

The company's executives seemed to take as a given the town's uneven development—pockets of prosperity surrounded by larger pockets of poverty. Through the end of the 1920s, the corporation wielded considerable power in the city. Its power base was a gentlemen's organization known as the Commercial Club, and among the many company officials holding posts in the city government was mill assistant superintendent Ralph Rowley, who between 1910 and 1935 served continuously on the city council, was council president, and controlled the city budget after 1913. Land Co. chief Horace Norton, who was also head of the town's chamber of commerce, was a top leader of the city's Republican Party, which remained dominant even though its policies hardly favored the Catholics, immigrants, and blacks who constituted half of the population. In 1925, the victorious mayoral candidate Floyd Williams was backed by both the corporation and another increasingly powerful force, the Ku Klux Klan.

Judge Gary also took a keen interest in city affairs and during his occasional visits had many words of advice for Gary's political and economic leaders. He would tour the city with his wife and bask in the way his name was featured in many institutions' titles, including the imposing new Gary National Bank Building. In 1927, though, Gary died, a victim of the heart troubles that had plagued him for some years.[26]

In 1932, Myron Taylor, a tall, stern-faced, and equally formal gentleman of patrician ancestry, took over as chairman and CEO of U.S. Steel after serving for several years as part of a ruling triumvirate that included J. P. Morgan and financier George F. Baker. Although Gary and Taylor were both lawyers, their business careers differed greatly, mirroring the changing times. Judge Gary had risen as a skilled merger-and-acquisitions man, but Taylor's specialty was in helping streamline and rationalize operations at long-established companies, including textile firms in Lowell and Newburyport, Massachusetts. With the onset of the Great Depression, Taylor brought in younger managers who encouraged innovation in finance, production, and employee relations.

In 1934, U.S. Steel's Chicago-area plants, including the Gary Works, turned out as much steel as was generated in all of Germany, the world's number-two steelmaking country. But behind that startling statistic lay an unhappy reality: Many U.S. Steel plants were obsolete and expensive to run. The company's managerial approach was antique, as centralized as the Vatican, and practically oblivious to such essential matters as cost accounting and technical innovation. Taylor responded by closing some obsolete facilities and forcing a merger of the corporation's two big subsidiaries, Carnegie Steel and Illinois Steel (which included the Gary Works), forming Carnegie-Illinois, but he also pioneered a change in employee relations. At first this involved developing a company union, an organization Judge Gary had shown no interest in. But following the 1933 National Industrial Recovery Act with its pro-labor Section 7(a), Taylor brought in a leading exponent of employee-representation plans, Arthur H. Young of the Rockefeller-subsidized Industrial Relations Counselors Inc., to produce such a plan for U.S. Steel. "Word has been passed around that company unions will suffice in meeting the requirements of 7a," reported industry trade journal *Steel*. Questioned by a U.S. Senate committee, Young strongly advocated for the U.S. Steel program: "The works council plan is a supplement to the Golden Rule as given to us by the Carpenter of Nazareth," he declared.

The company-union approach backfired. Under John L. Lewis, the new industrial-union umbrella organization, the Congress of Industrial Organizations, placed a priority on steelworker unionization, turning the task over to its Steel Worker Organizing Committee (SWOC). And SWOC adopted the crafty approach of encouraging militants to take over employee-representation plans. Many aggressive union leaders emerged within the supposedly tame groups, including at the Gary Works. By the end of 1936, it was evident that the company unions were either dysfunctional or surprisingly confrontational.

Moreover, the Depression and Franklin Roosevelt's New Deal had prompted a new union mobilization nationally—most notably in auto production, which witnessed sensational sit-down strikes in Flint, Michigan. Taylor saw that the unionization of steel was probably inevitable, and after a series of private meetings with Lewis came to terms. By March 1937, Carnegie-Illinois had signed a tentative pact with SWOC that recognized the union as the bargaining agent for the company's workers and granted a $5 hourly wage along with the eight-hour day and forty-hour week. Within two months, the union had 110 contracts covering some 300,000 workers at U.S. Steel and other companies. Unionization was hardly complete—major holdouts included Bethlehem and the other "Little Steel" companies—but a corner had been turned at the Gary Works and other U.S. Steel plants. Perhaps not entirely coincidentally, that corporation's share of the nation's steel output rose from 35.4 percent in 1936 to 36.6 percent in 1937.[27]

The World War II years continued the expansion at the Gary Works. The federal government poured money into the steel industry, especially into new facilities near Pittsburgh, but Gary benefited as well with a $12 million expansion. By 1945, the Gary Works, with a raw steel capacity of 5.72 million net tons, was the most productive of U.S. Steel's facilities and the largest steel plant on Earth. By the late 1950s, production at Gary would approach 8 million net tons. Other companies grew as well, including Bethlehem's Sparrows Point works, which would pass the Gary Works to become the largest steel mill in the world in the 1950s.[28]

But steel towns were another matter. Bethlehem regarded the town of Sparrows Point as expendable, and in time most of it would be demolished to make room for factory expansion. In Homestead, the company tore down perhaps a third of the town during World War II to construct five new complexes. In Gary, the problem was instead a matter of neglect: In the 1930s, the U.S. Census Bureau had classified as substandard 20 percent of the city's white-owned housing and 50 percent of its black-owned housing. U.S. Steel encouraged the building of federal housing during the decade, on the grounds that it could house steelworkers making less than $1,000 per year, of whom there were many, according to company spokesman Norton. The federal government financed hundreds more units built during the 1940s and early '50s, but many sections of town continued to be slums.

In fewer than fifty years, Gary had gone from being a sandy wasteland to a booming industrial area to, finally, an older city in decline. Overall, it had never been an especially good place to live, with its spotty residential properties, limited cultural resources, and wanting educational institutions. Even as the number of African Americans in the city grew from 18 percent in 1940 to 39 percent in 1960, many Gary institutions resembled those of the Deep South. Public schools—which had been involved in an impressive educational experiment in the 1910s—were segregated because of neighborhood composition. Into the 1930s, major hospitals and numerous restaurants, theaters, and churches were for whites only.[29]

In 1967, the city's African-American majority elected its first black mayor, Richard G. Hatcher. White flight, already under way, accelerated. Within a dozen years, the town became truly depressed and crime-ridden. Although the Gary Works had 30,000 employees as late as 1970, steel employment began falling. In the mid-1980s, U.S. Steel closed its rail plant in Gary along with 150 other facilities around the country, including most of those in the Pittsburgh area. And there was little in Gary to replace U.S. Steel as an employer.

In 1996, Gary won the distinction of being the most dangerous city in America, with one murder for every 1,000 inhabitants. Gary neighborhoods, marked by gang violence, drugs, and prostitution, seemed the epitome of urban decay. Formerly bustling Broadway had become a strip of boarded-up stores and dilapidated buildings. The Palace Theater, once the fanciest movie house in the Midwest, was an abandoned wreck, and a former Sears store was now a welfare office. The most visible enterprises in the business district included a Goodwill Industries shop and several bail bondsmen's offices. To distance itself from the blight, the *Gary Post-Tribune* dropped the word "Gary" from its title.

Today, the Gary Works and U.S. Steel still sound impressive on paper: The Gary Works is U.S. Steel's largest American facility, with an annual capacity of 7.5 million tons, and the corporation remains the fifth-largest steelmaker in the world. In 2007 the company completed a major renovation of Gary's largest blast furnace, but the Works now employs fewer than 7,000 people. Gary's other primary employers: the school system, the Methodist Hospital, and two Majestic Star Casinos.[30]

The promise of 1901 was fulfilled for neither U.S. Steel as a business nor Gary as a community. At the time of the great trust's creation, technological innovation no longer provided steelmakers with a competitive edge—and so they tried combination in hopes of gaining winning economies of scale. But this strategy worked only for a while: By 1920, the company was producing about half of the nation's steel, down from the 66 percent it had made in the trust's first year. And by the late 1990s, U.S. Steel was responsible for only one-eighth of the steel produced in America.[31]

Had the trust fared better—demonstrating a greater agility and a willingness to adopt new technology—would things have turned out better for Gary, Indiana? Perhaps not, for the combination of combinations was never much interested in developing a corporate utopia. Like an adolescent who never grows into maturity, it sought to receive the credit for the Magic City while accepting little in the way of responsibility.

CHAPTER 6

On the Road to the Consumer Economy

The rise of large-scale advertising, popular magazines, movies, radio, and other channels of increased cultural diffusion from without are rapidly changing habits of thought as to what things are essential to living and multiplying optimal occasions for spending money.

—ROBERT S. LYND AND HELEN MERRELL LYND,
Middletown (1929)

Near the end of the nineteenth century, consumerism took a dramatic upward leap in American life—and propelled a fundamental shift in the U.S. economy. The number of mass-produced goods had been on the rise since the early 1800s, but for the middle class, the post–Civil War years brought new retail outlets, intermittent prosperity, labor-saving technology, and shorter hours of work, all conspiring to recommend the replacement of homemade goods with store-bought things. In the cities, such emporia as Boston's Jordan Marsh & Co., Philadelphia's John Wanamaker, and Chicago's Marshall Field & Co. brought a cornucopia of stuff into the public eye. Mail-order houses such as Sears, Roebuck and Montgomery Ward began doing big business selling national brands to rural customers. By the mid-1890s, F. W. Woolworth had established twenty-eight stores in various eastern cities, and such food chains as the Great Atlantic and Pacific Tea Co. grew in importance from about 1910. Advertising was mushrooming, too: The first prominent advertising agency, N. W. Ayer & Sons, opened its doors in 1877, and by 1900 corporations were spending $95 million a year on ads. Even the utopian Edward Bellamy in his *Looking Backward* celebrated the efficiency of modern retailing while proposing a streamlined version that overcame the unpleasantness of overproduction.

By the late 1920s, when Robert and Helen Lynd published their study of life and changing behavior in the emblematic, midcontinent Middletown—actually, a disguised Muncie, Indiana—the consumer paradise seemed at hand. The Lynds cited an extensive list of phenomena that were new must-haves for the community's middle-class consumers: hot and cold running water, appliances ranging from toasters to washing machines, telephones, refrigerators, green vegetables and fruit available year-round, a great variety of clothing, cosmetics, commercial hair dressing, movies, automobiles, phonographs, radios, and cigarettes. Households had even given up making their own bread, relying instead on bakeries. The greater availability of canned goods and refrigeration were leading to a decline in homemakers' cooking skills, they found. Around 1915 the automobile industry introduced installment selling, which the Lynds said "turns wishes into horses overnight"; it exploded during the '20s, encompassing 15 percent of all sales by 1926.[1]

Economist and Wharton School professor Simon N. Patten was an early celebrant of this era of abundance, particularly the "rapid distribution of food." In his 1907 work, *The New Basis of Civilization*, he wrote that "each gain upon nature adds to the quantity of goods to be consumed by society, and lessens the labor necessary to produce them."[2]

Of course, the culmination of consumerism would take place after World War II. Spending on the war had helped pull the country out of the Depression, and U.S. political leaders at first worried that without that level of arms spending, hard times could return, much as they had after the first war. But there was no need to worry. The private expenditure on mass-built, single-family homes in dispersed and zoned suburbs, modern appliances including washers, refrigerators, and televisions, and, of course, automobiles provided a more than adequate replacement.[3]

Company towns played their part in this transformation of American life. Cloth from New England and southern textile mills was an early factory-made consumer product. Pullman's luxurious railroad cars facilitated a growing public interest in tourism and travel. As Milton Hershey realized in the early 1900s, food too could be the stuff of mass consumption, while the lightbulbs Corning manufactured allowed more hours in which to work, to shop, and to enjoy leisure.

One catalyst was essential to the consumer economy: The discovery of vast pools of oil in the American Southwest. Dozens of new towns and cities emerged, dedicated to pursuing and refining petroleum. Without oil, one can hardly imagine that the array of other consumer-goods industries, from autos and appliances to meat, could have been nearly as vast.

Black gold. Texas tea: Oil has been the most mythologized, fantasy-conjuring substance in American life, the stuff dreams are made on. Its pursuit and use dominated twentieth-century civilization, prompting and facilitating wars, uneven global development, and postindustrial consumerism. But like the Golden Fleece of ancient lore, America's oil was bait for a race of wanderers rather than for city-builders, at least in the industry's early days. Boomtown—a word once associated with the California gold rush—for a time was applied almost exclusively to the haunts of the moving crowd that sought oil riches.

Consider the ups and downs of Beaumont, Texas. In January 1901, it was a southeast Texas ranching and lumber town of 9,000 people about ninety miles east of Houston and thirty miles north of the Gulf of Mexico. The state's legendary oil reserves greeted the new century with Texas's first and most celebrated gusher, Spindletop, located on a sulfurous hillside four miles outside of town. For almost ten years, a one-armed mechanic and lumber merchant named Patillo Higgins had argued that oil could be found there. The obsession made Higgins and his partner, an Austrian engineer named Anthony Lucas, a joke among geologists. Finally, Lucas got Pittsburgh wildcatters James Guffey and John Galey to take a flyer on Higgins's intuition. After months of drilling through hundreds of feet of sand, an ear-splitting eruption of mud and rocks preceded a gusher of gas and then heavy, green oil. Before long the flow from Spindletop reached 75,000 barrels a day.

Spindletop's petroleum was up for grabs. Land prices near Beaumont soared from $10 per acre to $900,000 per acre. Both land-buyers and the landless descended upon the area, which soon became a warren of tents and shacks, lean-tos, whorehouses, and gin mills. Beaumont's population tripled in a year, and within two years stood at 50,000. Within months, 214 oil wells owned by one hundred or more companies jammed the hill. Among the outfits that lasted were Gulf Oil, operated by the Mellon banking family out of Pittsburgh; Sun Oil, whose pioneering figure was J. Edgar Pew, also out of Pennsylvania; and Texaco, whose chief executive was Joseph Cullinan, who became for a time the foremost oilman in Beaumont. London-based Shell Oil, already a power in the Russian oil fields at Baku, contracted to take half of the Guffey-Galey-Lucas production.

Spindletop itself was depleted within four years. "The law of capture," which dictated that the oil belonged to whoever could grab it, encouraged drillers to suck the stuff out as quickly as possible. With the oil all but gone, people scattered, many moving on to the next strike—or rumored strike. Beaumont remained an important refining center, but its population plunged by 20 percent, to 40,000.

Similar events occurred over and over in the Southwest. In 1903, oil was discovered at Sour Lake, Texas, twenty miles northwest of Beaumont. Within a few months, 10,000 people settled there. At Ranger, about eighty-five miles southwest of Fort Worth, population increased from around 600 to 30,000 within a year of a 1917 strike. In August 1921, a discovery at Mexia in central Texas prompted a tenfold increase in population—from 4,000 to 40,000—within a few days. Other spectacular oil finds came in the Panhandle region and in East Texas.

Who were these thousands of on-the-move people? In the first strikes, skilled workers, including drillers and rig builders, came from such states as Pennsylvania, which already hosted oil production. After former Texas plowboys picked up the necessary expertise, they, too, became drillers and rig builders, earning as much as $5 a day for a seven-day week. Depending on the size of the strike, there could be lots of skilled workers: At Buckburnett, the purported site of the 1940 Clark Gable–Spencer Tracy movie *Boom Town* and the location of repeated strikes after 1912, eighty derricks were under construction at one point, each occupying a fifteen-to twenty-man crew. Hordes of unskilled laborers also descended on new fields, finding employment as roustabouts, doing whatever heavy labor was needed, and as teamsters, delivering necessary supplies to the work area. Other arrivals included speculators and would-be wildcatters, sure that they could strike pay dirt on their own, plus managers from established oil companies and keepers of stores, boardinghouses, and hotels. Other avocations: prostitution, gambling, and various sorts of thievery.

Once production was under way, swarms of pipeline workers—who worked in crews of up to 150 men—and tank builders would come. Of course, both exploration and production might be going on simultaneously, but after a time, a smaller number of workers would be needed to operate and service wells, pipelines, and tanks. Some exploration workers might stay on if the production jobs seemed enticing enough, but others, including the great multitude, would leave. The lure of the next big thing was an ongoing attraction for young and rootless workers and drifters, as well as for much of the disreputable demimonde. Model T Fords, loaded down with possessions and stuffed with family members, crisscrossed Texas, stirring up virtual dust storms as they followed the drilling rigs to successive boomtowns.

Since a boom began abruptly and could be short-lived, no one cared to invest in building housing for such people, so they were left with tents or shacks. Many swarmed into flophouses that rented cots at 50 cents for an eight-hour shift. Some resorted to sleeping under sheets of galvanized iron that were propped up a few inches above bare ground. In Ranger, an enterprising landlord set up a large circus tent filled with row upon row of cots (the solution was much copied thereafter), and one farmer there rented out his hog shed.

There were hotels—often barracks-like flophouses. Those lucky enough to land a bed there would share a room with another person and, after eight hours, would have to make way for a second shift of sleepers. It was not unknown for hotel proprietors to move their buildings from boomtown to boomtown.[4]

By the 1920s all the major oil companies had erected more permanent "company camps," with substantial housing renting for as little as $3 per month, aiming to retain a skilled workforce. The area around Midland alone contained thirty-eight camps. Humble Pipe Line's Kemper Station

Camp consisted of orderly rows of houses painted in uniform colors. That company's camp near the town of Wink housed four hundred refinery workers and featured a community center, baseball field, playground, and swimming pool. Around the town of McCamey, seven companies had camps. Some houses there were even relatively luxurious, with two bedrooms, a kitchen, a dining room, and a single bath. And Big Lake Oil's Texon camp in the remote Permian Basin offered such amenities as a hospital, nondenominational church, clubhouse, swimming pool, theater, and golf course. Its pleasant two- or three-room bungalows featured running water and electricity, hardwood floors, and front lawns.

Some camps evolved into more substantial settlements: Oklahoma-based Phillips Petroleum built a large camp at Pantex in the Texas Panhandle, which eventually became the town of Phillips. The Amarillo-area camps of Skelly and Roxana came together to form a town of several hundred, Skellytown, with two refineries and a carbon black plant.

Many were unsavory places. At Mexia, bootlegging became so flagrant in 1922 that the Fifty-Sixth Cavalry of the National Guard was dispatched to support federal agents. One of the most notorious towns was Borger, near Amarillo. Founded in 1926 by Oklahoma town-site promoter A. P. "Ace" Borger, the rough-and-ready village featured numerous hotels, cafés, a plethora of decrepit wooden buildings, gambling halls, brothels, and speakeasies within weeks of an oil strike. Borger's citizenry showed little interest in observing the law, and the moonshine and narcotics trade flourished. In 1929, an area district attorney was murdered prompting Texas Governor Dan Moody again to send in the National Guard and to place Borger under martial law.

Wink was equally rowdy, dominated in its boom years by an allied group of bootleggers, gamblers, and corrupt politicians. At first the settlement had no law officers, and the closest sheriff was an hour away. With lawbreaking rampant, the Texas Rangers raided the town on several occasions in the late 1920s, to little lasting effect; in 1929, four people were killed in a murder spree. Such goings-on contrasted strongly with life in the nearby Humble Oil camp, which was reserved for supervisory workers such as "gang pushers." Strict camp rules required house inspections by the company and prohibited the keeping of dogs or livestock.

But most company camps proved temporary affairs. By the late 1950s, the companies had come to see them as expensive and outdated. Improvements in the Texas roads meant that workers could live in established towns and commute to the oil fields by automobile. Humble sold off its houses to workers and even subsidized their removal to other locations.[5]

Some towns retained a sizable population by becoming specialists in refining or administration. Beaumont and Port Arthur had the advantage of being near the Gulf Coast and so remained refining centers even as oil production shifted from that region to as far away as the rich Glenn Pool in Oklahoma. Port Arthur, which had a negligible population in 1890, was home to 22,000 residents by the 1920s, when both Gulf Oil and the Texas Co. had built large refineries there. By 1909, it already had become the fastest growing port in the United States and increasingly participated in global markets, with shipments to England and the Netherlands.

Texas is such a large state and the oil fields covered such a wide area that several regional oil centers emerged. Among these were Wichita Falls, which became home to the headquarters of several independent oil companies and refineries; Amarillo, a former cattle town that housed regional offices for Phillips and Shamrock Oil and Gas; and Fort Worth, a onetime railroad hub where Gulf, Marland, the Texas Co., Skelly, and Phillips all opened offices.[6]

In Oklahoma, the town of Bartlesville, forty-five miles north of Tulsa, became an administrative center for Phillips Petroleum and Cities Service Co. after booming in the early 1900s. Frank Phillips, an ambitious onetime barber and bond trader, came to the area in 1903 and found a frontier town already jammed with oil derricks and crowded with roughnecks and speculators. Oil had first been discovered on Cherokee land near Bartlesville in 1897. Phillips, a bespectacled sharpie who had once invented a baldness "cure" based on rainwater, was casting about for a new opportunity and had been tipped off to the area's potential by an acquaintance who had become a Methodist missionary to the area's Indians. After one glimpse of Bartlesville's frantic oil activity, Phillips rushed back to his home in Creston, Iowa, recruited his brother L. E. to the cause, and enlisted financial backing from his banker father-in-law. By February 1905, Phillips—who of course knew nothing of the oil trade—had begun drilling on leases acquired over several trips to Bartlesville.

He quickly struck oil, but his first well produced very little. Then within six months, he hit a gusher on land leased from a Delaware Indian girl, Anna Anderson. Eighty-one producing wells followed. But rather than place all of their bets on petroleum, the Phillips brothers also opened the Citizens Bank to cater to area oilmen. The Phillipses didn't believe in doing anything by halves, and soon they had built a two-story bank building with three vaults and impressive marble counters. Within three years, they had absorbed the Bartlesville National Bank and, by 1920, the much larger First National Bank of Bartlesville.[7]

For a time, Oklahoma was producing more oil than Texas. Tulsa-area oil strikes in 1901 were followed by the discovery in 1905 of the richest oil allotment ever, the so-called Glenn Pool on the Ida Glenn farm outside of Tulsa. The central Oklahoma Cushing field, discovered in 1915, was shortly responsible for 20 percent of the oil produced in the United States. Then in 1917, Phillips drillers hit a huge gusher in the Osage Hills.

The Osage strike, along with the impending world war, prompted Frank Phillips to transform his partnership into a public company, Phillips Petroleum Co. With its twenty-seven employees and stash of oil leases, Phillips Petroleum issued 15,000 shares of preferred stock, mostly to insiders.

As in Texas, Oklahoma's oil workers lived close to the derricks. The area known as the Burbank Field near Ponca City was producing 32 million barrels of oil in its peak year of 1923. The field, which included such settlements as Webb City, Carter Nine, Shidler, Lyman, and Whizbang, became home to 45,000 people.

Meanwhile, Bartlesville continued to develop as an oil-company administrative center, with Cities Service Co., the Indian Territory Illuminating Oil Co., and 157 other oil companies headquartered there. Phillips Petroleum, the largest such outfit, erected a new seven-story headquarters in 1925, complete with mahogany-paneled offices for its executives. The company's assets, $3 million in 1917, had soared to $130 million. It owned 1,759 producing oil and gas wells and supported a total payroll of $5.36 million. Such were its ambitions that it opened a research wing and, in the late 1920s, an "aviation department," intended largely to publicize the company's products via skywriting and such stunts as an air race from Oakland, California, to Honolulu. Among the company's products were an airplane fuel, dubbed Nu-Aviation, and automobile gasoline, to which it assigned the moniker Phillips 66, after the federal highway that spanned much of the continent. And in a further exercise of daring, Phillips Petroleum entered the arena of gasoline retailing: By 1930, it had opened 7,000 English-cottage-style gas stations in twelve states. With a refinery in Borger, a pipeline that stretched from there to East St. Louis, Illinois, a bevy of filling stations, and numerous administrative departments, Phillips entered the 1930s as a vertically integrated company.

In the late 1930s, with Frank Phillips entering his last decade, he created the Frank Phillips Foundation with a $66,000 higher-education fund devoted to scholarships for employees' children. He also donated $50,000 toward completing a new senior high/junior college for the area. Phillips didn't seem to care much what other people thought of him: He was fond of dressing up, sometimes in Indian war bonnets, or in Hollywood-cowboy gear complete with tooled-leather chaps and a holstered six-gun. Combined with his owlish accountant's face and physique, the costumes made him look like the silliest tenderfoot at the dude ranch. No matter—let them laugh. In his own mind, Phillips was a tough guy and also a philanthropist who willed his 3,600-acre ranch and wildlife preserve, Woolaroc (woods-lakes-rocks), and his private museum of western artifacts, to the foundation, intending that they serve educational purposes. Phillips died in 1950, a year after retiring from the company.

Phillips Petroleum emerged from the 1940s as the largest marketer of liquefied petroleum gases, an innovator in chemicals, and the producer of 93,000 barrels of crude oil in 1945. It sponsored foreign oil field exploration in Venezuela, Colombia, Mexico, and elsewhere—in 1969, Phillips pioneered discovery in the North Sea.[8]

Bartlesville, where half of all local economic activity was tied to the company in one way or another, was proud to be thought of as the home of Phillips. In 1978, a locally produced coffee-table book described the town's colorful history and devoted several chapters to "the company that stayed home." (Cities Service, by contrast, had moved its headquarters to Tulsa in 1968.) The town's identification with and dependence upon Phillips was made very clear in the 1980s, when two corporate raiders—T. Boone Pickens in 1984 and Carl Icahn in 1985—made independent runs at the company. To fend off the raiders, Phillips bought back half of its stock, taking on $8.6 billion in debt. Many in the town of 35,000, where 8,000 were on the company payroll, freaked out. Some attempted to amass nest eggs—and the number of bad checks soared by 41 percent. Episodes of domestic violence rose as well, according to the local women's crisis center. The First Baptist Church sponsored a round-the-clock prayer vigil, calling upon the Almighty to aid Phillips management in its defense. And one Bartlesville citizen mailed a shocking package to Pickens: a five-foot-long coffin-shaped box . . . containing not a bomb but a letter detailing the sender's anxieties over the possible takeover.

The combination of company debt, Phillips's cessation of oil exploration, and the 1986 fall of oil prices, from $27 a barrel to $10, seemed to portend that the company might disappear in the way of Bartlesville's other historic oil concerns. But by 1996, Philips had paid off much of its debt, resumed its profitable North Sea activities, and begun employing sophisticated technology in pursuit of new discoveries in Mexico, China, Algeria, and Indonesia. The following year, Phillips doubled in size by buying Atlantic Richfield's Alaska production facilities, and then it became the second-largest U.S. refiner with a purchase of the independent Tosco Corp.

Bartlesville is less of a company town today. In 1999, Phillips merged with Houston-based Conoco—really a takeover of Conoco in which Phillips shareholders emerged with more than half of the new entity's stock and the Phillips CEO, James Mulva, became head of the new entity, but ConocoPhillips moved its headquarters to Houston. Nevertheless, ConocoPhillips continues to have operations in Bartlesville, including a global data center and a company-history museum, employing around 3,000 people. Like much of U.S. capitalism, the company is at the time of this writing taking some lumps due to the U.S. recession—in 2008, it posted a net loss of $17 billion.[9]

Oil at first drew its chief economic value from its use in making kerosene, a fuel for lamps. But around the turn of the twentieth century, the automobile began to catch on, and 8,000 were registered to individual owners in 1900. Within a decade, gasoline sales surpassed those of kerosene. By 1920, there were 9.2 million autos on America's roads.[10]

U.S. automobile production was of course long centered in Detroit, an economically diverse metropolis that hardly merits consideration in this account. But the Ford Motor Co. built its largest plant in one area—the town of Dearborn—that qualifies as a company town situated within metropolitan Detroit.

Henry Ford was born on a farm near what would become Dearborn, ten miles west of downtown Detroit. As a youth, Ford worked as a machinist in Detroit, and in time he became a master mechanic at Detroit's Edison Illuminating Co. He tinkered by night in his shed, attempting to build an early automobile. His first two attempts at founding auto companies failed before he began Ford Motor Co. in 1903, operating out of rented shops in Detroit, and then at the giant Highland Park complex north of the city. By 1917, ten years after the opening of Highland Park, Ford had sold 1.5 million Model Ts and become a billionaire. Finally, in the 1920s he established the huge complex that would become synonymous with his company: the two-thousand-acre River Rouge plant in Dearborn, a few miles from his family's farm. By 1929, the average hourly workforce there was more than 98,000. The once bucolic area was transformed into an industrial wilderness. Ford and his son Edsel owned the whole company personally—no partners, no stockholders, and no back-talkers.[11]

The nature of Dearborn was made perfectly clear during the Great Depression, on March 7, 1932. Detroit-area Communists organized the Ford Hunger March with the intent of trooping from downtown Detroit to the Rouge plant, where a petition demanding jobs for the jobless, free medical care at the Ford Hospital, and much more would be presented to Ford management. A crowd of 3,000, composed largely of the unemployed, formed, and police escorted them to the Dearborn town line. There a contingent of thirty to forty Dearborn police awaited and warned the marchers to disperse. These police took their instruction from Chief Carl Brooks, formerly a member of Ford Motor's private police squad—the euphemistically titled Ford Service Department—and Clyde M. Ford, who was Dearborn's mayor, a cousin of Henry Ford's, and the owner of a Ford dealership. When the marchers attempted to advance, they were tear-gassed, hosed with icy water, and finally fired upon. Four marchers and a teenage newsboy were shot dead and fifty were wounded.[12]

Like employers in many company towns, Ford was very much interested in his employees' private lives. In fact, his Sociological Department was the very prototype of the corporate social welfare agency–cum–management espionage apparatus, alternately helping workers with housing and loans and having them discharged for such infractions as smoking or owning a General Motors car.

But the Ford fiefdom of Dearborn was quickly integrated into the Detroit metropolitan sprawl. Ford steadfastly refused to be involved in building worker housing, and consequently, as in Gary, Rouge plant employees commuted from across the city. And of course, there were other employers of equal prominence in the metropolis, notably General Motors, which maintained its own company town at Flint, seventy miles north of the center of Detroit. There lay giant Chevrolet, Fisher Body, and Buick plants, along with the AC Spark Plug Division, employing 40,000 people even in hard times and supplying 80 percent of Flint's jobs. GM held sway over the local media, including the town's one newspaper, and over the years many of Flint's officials including the mayor and chief of police were tied to the company.[13]

Automobile production soon spread across the continent. By the late 1930s, for example, Ford had assembly operations in California, New Jersey, Chicago, Louisville, and Kansas City, not to mention plants in Canada, Mexico, and six other countries. In the 1940s, General Motors had 102 plants across the United States and a headquarters building in New York City.

In addition, Ford created nineteen "village industries" in small towns across Michigan, all within sixty miles of Ford headquarters. Many of these "little industries out in the country," in the words of company organ *Ford News*, were situated in rehabilitated gristmills and staffed by part-time farmers. They, along with workers who transferred from the Rouge plant and elsewhere, made such small parts as gauges, horns, valves, ignition locks, and starter switches. It was a typically eccentric and ill-explained exercise, but Henry Ford seemed to see these operations as a way of employing rural people and as an experiment toward a decentralized industrial future. In any case, Ford insisted that they were not company towns, as the company did not own the areas around the small plants and there was no effort to build housing, establish company stores, or exert political sway over the villages. When journalist Drew Pearson asked Ford if he intended to create any model towns near the outfits, the Flivver man responded: "No, I am against such things. If people want to get things done they can do them themselves." After Henry Ford's death in 1947, Ford Motor gradually sold off all the village-based operations.[14]

Many glory years followed for the U.S. auto industry, but a period of very slow decline began with the oil shocks of the 1970s. Today, despite all of the industry's travails, including a takeover of Chrysler by Fiat and the near-bankruptcy of General Motors, nearly half of all cars and trucks sold in the United States are produced by U.S.-owned companies.[15]

What's more, 38 percent of all cars and trucks made in the United States are produced in Michigan and Ohio. But in the 1980s, a new group of auto-production facilities began appearing, many in southern states that discouraged unionization. These were run by Japanese and European automakers. Honda opened its facility in 1982 in Marysville, Ohio, forty miles northwest of Columbus. The following year, Nissan opened a facility in Smyrna, Tennessee, near Nashville, and five years later, Toyota followed with a plant in Georgetown, Kentucky, not far from the Bluegrass center, Lexington. In 1989, Subaru-Isuzu opened a car-manufacturing plant in Lafayette, Indiana, a small city sixty miles northwest of Indianapolis. And in the 1990s, German maker Daimler opened a facility in Vance, Alabama, and BMW in Greer, South Carolina. As of 2008, there were fifteen foreign-car assembly plants in eight states. Toyota alone was responsible for more than a quarter of all U.S.-made cars.

The move of Japanese carmakers onto U.S. soil came after the companies had significantly penetrated the American market, doubling sales during the 1970s, to 24 percent of all cars sold. The migration was at least in part a response to U.S. critics who charged the foreigners with dumping exports. Once the Japanese arrived, they brought along corporate practices that emphasized quality and a sense of common purpose. Managers carefully selected American production workers for youth, education, and an ability to fit in; not a few traveled to Japan for training. The cautious approach paid off, as unions have regularly been defeated in representation elections—losing by 2 to 1 at Nissan in 1989.

The Japanese also brought along many executives—who avoided any conspicuous presence in the small, center-of-the-continent towns. The companies are very concerned not to come across as an alien presence: "We constantly need to think about the potential backlash against us," Toyota CEO Katsuaki Watanabe told *Business Week* in 2007. So they worked at demonstrating their good citizenship. Nissan made record contributions to the United Way, and Toyota donated $1 million for a community center in Georgetown, where its workforce totaled 7,000. Toyota has gone on to fund literacy programs and university research institutes. It has also ramped up its spending on corporate lobbying, to $5 million a year.[16]

Controversy has still dogged the interlopers, including charges that they have engaged in racial discrimination and placed inflated demands on communities. Nevertheless, in 2010 the foreign companies have a foothold in the United States—apparently permanent and maybe growing. Volkswagen for one plans to open a $1 billion, 2,000-worker plant near Chattanooga, Tennessee, in 2011.

At the same time, all automakers have a tougher road ahead, as U.S. consumers have at least momentarily stopped buying and millions have lost their credit standing. Toyota in particular has an unpredictable future, given its 2010 recall of 6 million vehicles in the United States as a result of problems with accelerator pedals and braking systems. Globally, some thirty significant carmakers are fighting over a market that has shrunk by 30 percent in the past couple of years. With a capacity of 90 million cars, the companies are selling only about 55 million.[17] Earlier, many U.S. industrial communities ripened into full-fledged company towns over a period of several years. It remains to be seen whether the likes of Georgetown, Kentucky, or Vance, Alabama, will ever attain that status.

The United States today is a country filled with gadget freaks, people addicted to everything from personal digital assistants to digital radio. But what made Americans that way? Labor-saving appliances, from telephones to phonographs and toasters, taught generations of citizens to be wowed and eager for the next cool thing. Washing machines and other devices freed people from exhausting, time-killing tasks and helped build interest in mechanical gizmos among women.

Maytag Co. was a pathbreaker in the field of washers. It evolved from small-town beginnings in Newton, Iowa, to become a major international corporation by the mid-twentieth century. Never straying from its small-town domicile, Maytag prospered as a result of a commitment to quality rather than flash, successful innovation pioneered by an inveterate tinkerer, and the growth of the vast consumer market. The founding Maytag family was, like so many others in this book, quirky, possessive, sometimes exploitative of its town and workforce, and anti-union but not suicidally so. Finally, like too many other U.S. manufacturing concerns, Maytag no longer exists, having been absorbed after a period of crisis by a larger competitor, Whirlpool Corp.

Frederick L. Maytag, a farm boy born near Elgin, Illinois, moved with his parents in the late 1800s to Newton, a village of 2,500 souls thirty-five miles east of Des Moines. In time, he found employment as a lumberman. In 1892, Maytag joined with inventor and entrepreneur George Parsons to market a "band cutter and self-feeder"—a threshing-machine accessory. Peddling their device directly to farmers, they had modest success, and in 1896, to help them make refinements they hired a talented mechanic out of Austin, Minnesota, Howard Snyder. Snyder would prove his worth many times over, rising to be head of the company's "experimental department," then plant superintendent, and finally a company vice president.

After the turn of the century, Newton had become home to several makers of hand-operated washing machines, including the One Minute Washer and the Automatic Electric Washer. In 1907, Parsons and Maytag began producing a washer, too—the Pastime—basically a wooden tub with a crank mechanism that dragged clothes against a corrugated surface. Although they viewed the product as a sideline, it had several advantages. Unlike farm equipment, the Pastime could be sold in all seasons. And its manufacture would draw upon skills and materials similar to those the outfit already employed. Mechanic Snyder turned his hand to the machine and never stopped making improvements.

Within a few years, the company—now known as Maytag Co. after F. L. Maytag bought out Parsons—was producing a model that ran on a gasoline engine and another that was electric-powered. A prime venue for exhibiting and market-testing the machines: state fairs across the Midwest.

By 1915, Maytag's washing machines were outselling its farm implements, a field it would soon abandon. The Maytag Multi-Motor, which
ran on gasoline, became a hot seller, and the company's production more
than doubled. In part, the machine's popularity was due to the fact that,
while in operation, its engine could also serve as a power source for other
appliances, such as butter churns and ice cream freezers. Ads in the *Saturday Evening Post* showed a housewife blithely reading a book while the
Multi-Motor labored away, its flywheel propelling three household appliances simultaneously.

Although some 120 manufacturers were making washing machines
at this time, four companies in Newton, Iowa, made more than one-third
of them. Maytag produced several pioneering models that utilized metal
cabinets, electric motors, and the "millrace washing principle," which
tumbled clothes and forced hot water through them. By 1920, the company had the largest factory in Iowa, a network of thousands of dealers,
and a backlog of orders. Early in that decade it introduced a model employing an innovation that would become standard in modern machines:
a bottom-of-the-tank agitator that used water alone, rather than any sort
of corrugation, to do the cleaning. Maytag's employment in Newton rose
above 2,000, and it erected a new 600,000-square-foot factory.

Maytag became a public corporation listed on the New York Stock Exchange in the 1920s, establishing a separate Maytag Acceptance Corp. to
help facilitate installment-plan purchases. But, for better or worse, the company continued as a family-run operation, with F. L.'s sons taking turns as
chief executive and the founder keeping an active hand in the game. Corporate welfare measures included a piecework-pay plan that allowed factory
employees to set their own pace of work. Then there were other acts of
questionable benevolence: CEO Elmer Maytag joined with a Newton contractor to buy vacant lots around town and build hundreds of homes that
they sold to employees. Mortgages, paid via payroll deduction, were offered by a savings bank where Elmer was an officer. A company gasoline
station accepted scrip-like coupons that were also charged against workers'
pay. The Maytags funded a local YMCA—workers were required to join
and pay dues. They gave away free tickets to various concerts and public
performances and sponsored a yearly family picnic that included a parade
to the fairgrounds site and speech-making. For employees, attendance at

the picnic was also mandatory. In 1935, city fathers dedicated F. L. Maytag Park as a memorial to the aging founder, and the dedication was delivered by a local radio personality, Ronald "Dutch" Reagan.

In the late 1930s, union activism swept the Midwest, and it would have been surprising if Maytag had not been affected. But the enthusiasm for a union was startling to family members, who imagined that workers appreciated the family's beneficence: Within nine days in 1937, the United Electrical Workers signed up 1,400 Maytag employees. Among the issues motivating organization, there was one oddball matter: A sure-fire way of getting a job at the company, it seemed, was to purchase a Pontiac, on credit, at a local dealership owned by one of F. L. Maytag's cronies. Maytag himself may have been part owner of the dealership, many figured, and that encouraged workers to feel that just maybe they weren't all one big happy family. Although the company quickly recognized the United Electrical as its workers' representative, two years later during a confrontation the union demanded a 25 percent pay raise and the company instituted a 10 percent pay cut. A three-month strike that brought the National Guard to Newton resulted in few changes.

During World War II, Maytag shifted all production away from washers, instead making parts for aircraft and armored vehicles. It returned to washer making after the conflict, where it faced a raft of new competitors including General Electric, Westinghouse, Ford's Philco, GM's Frigidaire, Amana, and—soon to emerge as Maytag's primary competitor—Whirlpool. In a marketplace once dominated by small appliance stores, the likes of Sears, Roebuck and Montgomery Ward took over. Opening a new plant in 1949, Maytag held its own and in 1967 began a series of popular television ads featuring the lonely Maytag repairman—underemployed as a result of the company's next-to-unbreakable products.

With management no longer in the hands of family members, Maytag began acquiring other companies. In 1982, it would purchase stove maker Jenn Air and in 1989, vacuum-cleaner maker Hoover.[18] (It would sell Hoover to an Italian company in 1995 and end its European operations.) In 2001, it purchased another small-town-Iowa appliance maker, Amana, which had twice changed ownership since its 1934 creation by members of the German pacifist religious sect at the Amana colonies, an hour's drive east of Newton. That acquisition made Maytag number three among appliance makers, behind only Whirlpool and GE. And a mid-1990s innovation, the pricey, energy- and water-saving Neptune washer, seemed to portend a brilliant future. The *Wall Street Journal* said Maytag was "faster-growing and more profitable than its main rivals" and called profits produced by the ecologically friendly machine "extraordinary." "We can't make them fast enough," a Maytag executive bragged of the machines.

Then came a nasty surprise. Uncharacteristically for a "dependable" Maytag machine, the Neptune developed a seemingly endless number of defects, from faulty seals and latches to failing circuit boards. A class action featuring more than 120,000 claims forced the company to pay out millions in claims and attorney fees.

Perhaps more significant, competition from makers that employed foreign labor prompted Maytag to outsource production abroad, skimp on materials, trim new-product investment, and introduce a low-cost line of products that tended to degrade the brand. Layoffs, strikes, and post-9/11 hard times all made an impact. By 2005, Maytag's share price and market share had tumbled, and customer surveys put Maytag in the appliance-field cellar. After a takeover battle involving several other parties, Whirlpool acquired Maytag in 2006. The new owner quickly announced that it would be closing Maytag's headquarters and two large factories in Newton, along with plants in Arkansas and Illinois.[19]

The purchase left 2,800 workers jobless, nearly a fifth of Newton's 16,000 residents. Whistling in the dark, the town's mayor, Charles Allen, wrote that the community was far from dead, having received commitments of $100 million in private investment, with $70 million going toward a new motorsports complex. He gamely predicted that Newton was "on the cusp of a paradigm change like no other the state of Iowa has seen."[20] Others pin hopes for economic revival on the likes of a new 150-employee wind-turbine plant that was promoted during a recent Earth Day visit by President Barack Obama.

But Maytag's specter continues to haunt Newton. Its presence lingers at such local landmarks as Maytag Park, the Maytag Bowl bandshell, Maytag Pool, and Hotel Maytag.

In my hometown of Memphis during my youth, I regularly passed a Purina plant that roasted and processed animal feed; the aroma, as writer Willie Morris has recalled, was comfortingly reminiscent of "ham in the oven." But the actual smell of the bacon cure at a meatpacking plant is far from lip-smacking. Rather, it is a stomach-turning stench, a daily rot that one hopes to avoid, an "odor that hovered in the air on the Northside and hit the rest of us with the wind," recalled memoirist Cheri Register of her hometown of Albert Lea, Minnesota. Nor is the actual labor involved in meatpacking something to savor. Remembering a school field trip to Albert Lea's Wilson plant, Register wrote of the "large, high-windowed rooms, some filled with steam from vats of hot water, others damp and cold as the inside of a refrigerator, where men hacked at red flesh, ground blades against bone, stripped blue veins still leaking blood, and scraped pale yellow globs of fat from foul-smelling hides." On the killing floor, newly dispatched hogs hung from hooks, the blood draining to vats below, before they were plunged into de-hairing tanks. Over the decades, this work became more mechanized—today instead of knives, much of the cutting is done with such power tools as the Whizzard, an electric knife with a spinning round blade—but fundamentally, the tasks have remained the same.[21]

From the Civil War through the 1950s, companies situated in such rail-terminal cities as Chicago, Milwaukee, Kansas City, and St. Louis dominated the U.S. meatpacking industry. But much as Milton Hershey decided to locate his chocolate-making close to key suppliers—in his case, dairy farms—smaller meatpackers began as early as the 1870s but especially after 1920 to locate in smaller towns near the farms that raised the animals. This was especially the case for pork packing in Iowa. That state experienced a pig-population boom in the twentieth century, producing 22 percent of the total U.S. hog supply by 1940. Ottumwa, where Liverpool, England-based John Morrell chose to locate in 1877, was a leading packing town from the 1870s on.

Chicago and other major cities were home to the so-called Big Five—Swift, Armour, Cudahy, Morris, and Schwarzchild and Sulzberg, which changed its name to Wilson in 1916. (This became the Big Four when Armour bought Morris in 1923.) These companies ran huge factories of death and dismemberment: Armour employed 6,000 to 8,000 workers by 1900, and Swift, between 4,000 and 6,000. Concentrated as they were, the Big Five enjoyed huge economies of scale, proximity to vast terminal-market stockyards, and good rail connections to eastern cities. They were also tech innovators: Swift famously developed the first successful fleet of refrigerated railcars, and Armour employed cold storage at its branch distribution points.

But the small-town packers had their own advantages. Their buyers developed close relationships with the farmer-suppliers, who learned that animals lost less weight and thus commanded higher prices if they could be delivered via short truck runs rather than lengthy trips aboard trains. Farmers who dealt with the independent packers also avoided other costs, including stockyard commission fees charged in cities such as Chicago. As for the costs of slaughtering and disassembling the animals, pork packing demanded fewer laborers and less sophisticated assembly-line activity than beef packing and so was more amenable to smaller-scale production.

Dubuque Packing began operations in the Iowa city of that name in 1891, and by the 1940s was one of the largest such operations in the country. It was outdone only by Rath Packing Co. of Waterloo, which had the largest plant in the state by 1920. Other nearby states were home to independent packers, too, including Sioux Falls, South Dakota's Morrell plant, and Madison, Wisconsin's Oscar Meyer facility. Another sizable operation was that of Geo. A. Hormel & Co. in Austin, Minnesota, which by 1933 was handling a million hogs and 186,000 cattle. Even some of the large companies joined the movement to smaller towns, including Wilson in Albert Lea, Minnesota.

Both Ottumwa and Austin were railroad centers before they became home to meatpackers. Waterloo—which along with Rath was home to a John Deere farm-equipment plant—and Dubuque were both considerable manufacturing centers. But the packing plants employed large numbers of workers relative to these towns' overall size: By 1935, Hormel employed 2,500 of Austin's 12,000 citizens, while Morrell provided work for the same number in Ottumwa, a city of 25,000.[22]

Austin, a town ten miles north of the Iowa border, fits the company-town model well. Although other businesses have existed there, Hormel has long been the only truly important enterprise. For years, the company has exerted strong influence over the local media, including the

Austin Daily Herald, and over what was taught in local schools. For a time, Austin teetered precariously between utopia and exploitationville, with Hormel a part of an industry not famed for its progressive employee and community relations. In the 1930s, plant foremen were dictatorial, asserting authority over everything from workers' family problems to their choices in the voting booth. But by the 1940s, Austin had in effect become a model town, with row after row of worker-owned single-family homes and a generous and philanthropic employer, namely Hormel. It was "as good a company as there is anywhere to work for," a worker told a 1953 industrial-relations researcher, who found that the overwhelming majority of workers had positive feelings about the enterprise.[23]

Founded in the 1890s by George A. Hormel, a traveling hide-buyer out of Toledo who started by taking over an Austin retail butcher shop, the company experienced slow expansion in the 1900s, erecting a refrigerated plant for slaughtering and packing pork and beef with a workforce of two hundred. Before long, Hormel developed distribution centers throughout the Midwest and the South and began running advertisements for its products in such national publications as the *Ladies' Home Journal*. In the 1920s, Hormel perfected a means of canning ham, which proved a popular item. Expansion and construction of a national market continued into the 1930s. In 1933, the company opened a new $1 million beef-slaughtering facility in Austin.[24]

Even after the development of ice houses and then refrigeration, meat-packing remained a seasonal occupation. Animals matured in the warm months, and slaughtering and other work was performed in the winter, largely by farm workers idled by weather. But Hormel's burgeoning facilities called for a year-round workforce. Shorter summer hours and consequent reduced pay led to friction and economic woes for the town as a whole. Recognizing these facts, beginning in 1931, the company initiated what it called a "straight time" pay plan, which paid employees a weekly flat rate rather than one adjusted to hours worked. You might spend more time on the job during winter and less during the summer, but your pay would not vary—and the company regarded workers as permanent, salaried employees entitled to a fifty-two-week notice prior to any layoffs. This approach seemed to offer greater job security and to benefit the company and workers alike.

Hormel extended its corporate welfarism with mandatory 20-cent weekly deductions for an annuity savings plan. An additional stab at do-goodism: enforced contributions to the local community chest. Neither of these two measures went over so well. The community chest "was for the poor people," one worker exclaimed. "Hell, *we were* the poor people." When gruff and tyrannical foremen attempted to browbeat employees into signing the necessary checkoff cards, they touched off a rebellion—which in turn led to a company-employee-community social contract that lasted for more than forty years.

The payroll deductions, arbitrary treatment by bosses, and low pay prompted a union drive led by a remarkable Trotskyist plant foreman, Frank Ellis. A former organizer and executive board member of the Industrial Workers of the World, Ellis had lived the life that killed IWW organizer Frank Little: He'd ridden the rails, been jailed from Texas to Minnesota, forced out of towns by gun thugs, and beaten by vigilantes. He'd become a Hormel foreman only because of meatpacking skills honed during stints in various midwestern packinghouses. Ellis and other radical employees—some of whom he'd hired—organized mass meetings and a series of in-plant sit-downs. In fall 1933, the workers shut down the plant altogether and escorted from the facility Jay C. Hormel, George's son who'd become company president. Hormel was surprised by the emergence of the union; he felt he had done a lot of good for employees. But the company quickly recognized the workers' union, the IWW-inspired Independent Union of All Workers (IUAW). "When the union was organized, I was fearful of its use," Jay Hormel told an audience some time later. "But I like the idea now."

All the same, friction continued between the union and Hormel management for several years. Anti-union vigilante groups emerged in Austin, sporting such dramatic names as the Secret 500 and the Citizens Alliance. Meanwhile, the union organized repeated sit-downs over plant grievances and began a regional organizing drive that recruited members from across southern Minnesota and northern Iowa. To counter the *Daily Herald*'s perceived antiunion barrage, the IUAW began its own weekly newspaper, *The Unionist*. In 1939, the IUAW affiliated with the CIO and became Local 9 of the United Packinghouse Workers of America.[25]

Small-town people are not known for ardent unionism, but such places as Austin, Albert Lea, Cedar Rapids, Ottumwa, and Waterloo proved fertile ground for militant labor activity. In Cedar Rapids, the independent Midwest Union of All Packing House Workers organized the Wilson plant, and Ottumwa's Morrell workers were among the first members of the CIO's United Packinghouse Workers in 1939. At profitable companies such as Hormel and Oscar Meyer—makers of such successful, value-added brands as Spam and Oscar Meyer wieners—union organization plus progressive company management resulted in high wages and a comfortable standard of living for small-town packers from the postwar years up to the mid-1980s. In fact, the average meatpacking wage in five midwestern states as of 1977 was nearly 30 percent higher than the average wages of all manufacturing workers.

Although workers enjoyed some of the highest remuneration in the industry, progressive developments at Hormel went beyond pay increases. In addition to the guaranteed annual wage, management agreed to institute an unusual group-incentive arrangement. The workload for each gang in the plant was prearranged. Once they'd finished the stipulated amount of labor, the gang could either opt to go home—the "sunshine bonus," they called it—or as a group they could decide to work more and receive a bonus for the extra production. With the speed of work self-determined, the once dictatorial foremen had less to do. "Formerly, you had to run your ass off to get them guys to work," one foreman said. "Now you just stand and watch." A worker added, "Some days, we do not see the foreman." The profitable company also instituted profit-sharing and, to reduce conflict further with the union, agreed that it would mimic whatever wage rates the Big Four packers agreed to. For more than forty years, there was no serious dispute between the employees and the company.

Hormel's success continued into the 1940s, as such products as Dinty Moore Beef Stew and Hormel Chili Con Carne sold well domestically and as the federal government shipped millions of tons of such products as Spam and other canned meats to allies abroad. In 1941, Jay and George Hormel created the Hormel Foundation partly to keep company stock in friendly hands—the foundation received a controlling number of shares—but also to support local charities and ensure "the welfare of the community in which [the company] was located." Prosperity continued after the war with company expansion into numerous other states, including California and Hawaii. In Austin, 75 percent of town residents owned their own homes, while it seemed that virtually all workers owned their own, relatively new cars.[26]

But by the 1980s, this state of affairs had come to an end: By one historian's calculation, meatpackers' pay, weighted for inflation, proceeded in that decade to fall by almost half. Recession, plant closings, union defeats, and Reagan-era pay concessions conspired to bring the average hourly wage for packinghouse workers down to 20 percent below the national average for manufacturing workers. Another key factor: the entry of aggressive new companies into the field. A new Big Three—Iowa Beef Processors or IBP (today part of Tyson Inc.), ConAgra, and Cargill's Excel—brought startlingly new technical innovations and marketing strategies, along with fiercely antiunion practices and very low wages. One key and highly disruptive innovation: the consolidation of slaughterhouse, meat-cutting, and packaging operations into single plants. Rather than shipping whole carcasses to retailers, popular cuts such as loins, ribs, or rumps could now be boxed up and shipped directly, allowing supermarkets and restaurants to do without their own skilled butchers.

Many older companies, including Wilson, Armour, and Rath, were driven from the business. The serene relations in Austin and elsewhere came to an end with a series of unsuccessful mid-1980s strikes prompted by once-enlightened companies' attempts to turn back the clock. Hormel's Austin plant is now run as a two-tier operation, with the least desirable work—the killing floor—subcontracted out to a low-wage employer.

Today, the prototypical meatpacking company town is a dystopia—a seeming throwback and at the same time very much representative of modern-day America. In Holcomb, Kansas, a town of 2,000 residents two hundred miles west of Wichita, IBP in 1980 built the world's largest beef-packing plant. The company entered pork processing two years later. These large-capacity operations ran very high-speed production lines: At a plant in Columbus Junction, Iowa, the company slaughtered 11,500 hogs a day. In Perry, Iowa, IBP took over an Oscar Meyer pork plant that had been handling 750 hogs per hour, and it upped production, slaughtering 900 hogs per hour. Where Oscar Meyer was union, IBP ran the Perry plant nonunion, and it cut wages from close to $10 per hour to $5.80.

When IBP opened its Holcomb plant, the fact that there was an insufficient local labor pool did not strike management as an obstacle: IBP proceeded to recruit workers from elsewhere—Mexicans from the Texas border, Laotians from California, and blacks from Chicago. Holcomb's population shot up by 6,000. Of course, there was insufficient housing for the newcomers, so many moved into crowded boardinghouses or trailer parks; IBP opened a trailer park specifically for its employees. Other plants depending largely on Hispanic migrants include ConAgra's Garden City, Kansas, and Marshalltown, Iowa, facilities and the IBP plant in Storm Lake, Iowa, which employs many Laotians as well. The changes represented a culturally destabilizing explosion of ethnic diversity in an area where, for generations, the population had consisted almost entirely of whites of Scandinavian and German extraction.

The unforgiving pace of work led to unprecedented worker turnover, with annual rates of as much as 96 percent at some plants. IBP regarded this level of turnover as a positive thing, one company executive testified before Congress, since it meant the company would neither have to pay for health insurance nor grant vacations to many workers since they never got past their probationary periods.

Then there was the horrific injury rate. At companies such as Hormel, it was bad enough: Workers equipped with knives and electric equipment gouged themselves and their fellows on a regular basis, and repetitive-motion injuries such as carpal tunnel syndrome were at epidemic levels. In 1986 Hormel predicted that some 36 percent of the Austin workers would be disabled due to injury in the coming year. But at IBP the injury rate was even worse: In 1988 the federal Occupational Safety and Health Administration (OSHA) fined the company more than $3.1 million for its neglect of workers at the company's Dakota City, Nebraska, plant. OSHA said IBP had made no attempt to solve its high injury rate due to repetitive job motions. In the intervening years, the injury rate has scarcely improved: The U.S. Bureau of Labor Statistics in 2005 reported an average of 12.6 injuries or illnesses per 100 full-time meatpacking workers, a number twice that of all manufacturing jobs.

With the coming of packing facilities, towns have experienced a spike in social problems, including every sort of crime, drug addiction, and poverty. "We get people who arrive with only the clothes on their back," one social worker in Columbus Junction, Iowa, told the *Wall Street Journal*. Crime in that town, where IBP moved in to take over a shuttered Rath plant in 1985, quadrupled, with as many as thirty big-city gangs appearing. Student turnover at the high school soared, to 25 percent. These ills are also spreading to towns where plants have been shuttered or where companies have cut pay and benefits, including Austin and Ottumwa.

There has also been a geographic shift in meat production away from the Midwest, to the Deep South. The largest pork-slaughtering plant—owned by Smithfield Foods, which has become the largest pork processor in the United States—is now in Tar Heel, North Carolina.[27] That state is experiencing the same problems that became commonplace across Iowa and the Midwest.

In the summer of 2008, a kosher meatpacking plant in Postville, Iowa, became the subject of frenzied news coverage. A raid by state labor investigators revealed that Agriprocessors, the largest U.S. kosher meatpacking plant, was employing more than three hundred illegal aliens from Guatemala. It was the largest immigration bust ever. But more important, the state found that fifty-seven of these workers were underage. There were "egregious violations of virtually every aspect of Iowa's child labor laws," in the words of the state's labor commissioner; a criminal indictment listed 9,000 such instances of lawbreaking. Workers told reporters that they were forced to work shifts of up to seventeen hours a day, received wages of between $6.25 and $7 per hour, and sometimes got no overtime pay. Two months later, federal authorities arrested the company's former chief executive, Sholom Rubashkin, and charged him with harboring illegal immigrants and abetting identity theft.[28]

The affair stirred local resentment and a wave of anti-Semitism against the Hasidim from New York and Israel who had established a colony in Postville and operated the plant. Rubashkin, who in June of 2010 was found not guilty of the child-labor law violations, made no comment at the time of his arrest. Perhaps he should have said: "Hey, what's the big deal? It's the American way." At least where meatpacking is concerned, he would have been correct.

CHAPTER 7

The Instant Cities of the Good War

A small band played "The Star Spangled Banner." A foreman made a speech. . . . At the minister's loud "God bless this ship," the young woman smashed the bottle with a will and, whistles blowing, the shining grey freighter began to slide. . . . Pushing out a white surging wave behind her dripping stern, she slid into the river.

In our group, eyes were damp. Throats were being cleared. . . . [Said one young man:] "Every day in some yard a ship is being launched. As many as I've seen go down, it always gives me a thrill."

—JOHN DOS PASSOS
describing a Portland, Oregon, shipyard
in *State of the Nation* (1944)

orld War II operated on the population like a milkshake machine, dislodging men and women from their places of residence and scattering them across the continent, to serve both the military and defense industries. Between 1940 and 1947, 25 million people, or about one-fifth of the citizenry, decamped for new situations. "Probably never before in the history of the United States has there been internal population movement of such magnitude," said a U.S. Census Bureau report.

By spring 1945, more than 12 million were in the armed forces, which shuttled them from base to maneuvers to base before sending many off to foreign shores. On the home front, unemployment, as high as 14 percent in 1940, vanished, as 15 million additional people entered the workforce, mostly in war-related industry. Under War Production Board orders that limited all nonessential production, factories switched from manufacturing automobiles to tanks, from toilets to submarine torpedo tubes. Companies enlarged existing plants and built gigantic new ones. Near Detroit, Ford Motor Co. built the sprawling, sixty-seven-acre Willow Run plant that employed 42,000 men and women making bomber planes, such as the B-24. Enormous Douglas Aircraft plants in Long Beach and El Segundo, California, employed 100,000 people working in three shifts around the clock. The most unlikely places abruptly became centers of industry: Sleepy Pascagoula, Mississippi, formerly home to 6,000 people, quadrupled in size as workers flooded in to man its shipyards.[1]

John Dos Passos, author of the celebrated *U.S.A.* trilogy of novels, went on the road during the 1940s to track the cultural upheaval. Among his stops: Detroit, Washington, Pittsburgh, San Francisco, Houston, Portland, and the Gulf Coast seaport of Mobile, Alabama. He found the last of these—home to an airfield, shipping operations, and shipbuilding facilities—to be a teeming boomtown, "trampled and battered like a city that's been taken by storm." On the edge of the town he discovered "acres and acres raw with new buildings," long lines of new houses, and "miles of dormitories, great squares of temporary structures" hammered together by mobs of tobacco-chewing construction workers. "To be doing something toward winning the war, to be making some money, to learn a trade, men and women have been pouring into the city for more than a year now," he reported. "For them, everything's new and wonderful."[2]

New towns emerged as part of this cataclysm—and two of these were extraordinary. The San Francisco Bay Area became a center of shipbuilding operations, and even more instantaneously than Gary, Indiana, a city mushroomed around new shipyards at Richmond. The most far-reaching war venture, of course, was the Manhattan Project: Of its several operations—which also included Los Alamos, New Mexico, and Hanford, Washington—Oak Ridge, Tennessee, was arguably the United States' most astounding and disruptive exercise of eminent domain. It, too, was an instant city, where 80,000 people migrated without any idea of exactly what work they would be doing.

⌐

In the early 1940s, Richmond, California, was a pretty quiet place. Just north of Oakland on the eastern shore of San Francisco Bay, the town was "a drab little industrial city," in the words of *Fortune* magazine, marshland backed by a few hills that were peppered with Standard Oil storage tanks. The fragrance from that company's refinery was an almost palpable presence. Along with the Standard facility, Richmond contained perhaps a dozen other industrial operations, including since the early 1930s a Ford Motor assembly plant.

Things were about to change—radically. Ford had been drawn to the area by its deepwater port, and local businessmen felt that other companies should be attracted as well. So in 1939, officials from the local chamber of commerce suggested to the U.S. Maritime Commission that the site was a natural for shipbuilding. War was already a reality in Europe, and where there is war, there is money to be made. Before long, the Maritime Commission and the Richmond officials were in contact with other parties, including a vigorous construction magnate named Henry J. Kaiser and his sometime colleague, W. A. Bechtel.

Kaiser and Bechtel had been the major figures behind such profoundly transformative projects of the 1930s as the Boulder and Bonneville dams. They didn't know much about shipbuilding—but such gaps in experience never stopped Kaiser. A baldheaded, 260-pound dynamo in a double-breasted suit, Kaiser would become nationally celebrated—and resented—as a can-do guy who seemed always to deliver on his ambitious, even outrageous, promises. And it didn't take Kaiser long to become very interested in Richmond.

In late 1940, a British commission arrived in New York looking to assign the building of sixty cargo ships. The Kaiser-Bechtel consortium, known as Six Companies, bid on the project and, against all odds, won it. Almost immediately, Kaiser dispatched a young executive from his company, Clay Bedford, who was working on a construction project in Texas, to Richmond to put together a shipyard. Solidifying the shoreline marshes with 300,000 cubic feet of rock, Bedford had a workable ship-yard in place within six months.[3]

That was only the beginning.

Pearl Harbor made Kaiser's shipyards into a major contractor for the U.S. government. The assignment: producing the freighters that would be known as Liberty Ships and Victory Ships. Kaiser and the War Man-power Commission proceeded to recruit workers from across the coun-try and abroad—targeting such surplus-labor pools as Minneapolis, Little Rock, Memphis, and St. Louis. They tapped idle mining and agricul-tural areas in California and called out to urban workers in Los Angeles. The result: Richmond's population jumped by 400 percent. By the end of 1943, the four Kaiser shipyards employed 100,000 workers.

Richmond became a boomtown, with experiences not unlike those of the Texas oil-gusher communities. The promise of high wages, aver-aging $1 per hour, drew workers, but expenses, especially rent, ate up much of that. And as in Texas, they were extremely fortunate if they could find any place to stay: Early arrivals in Richmond snatched up the available spare rooms. More than seventy trailer camps sprouted on the outskirts of town, and soon they were jammed, too. Families slept in cars, pitched tents along outlying creeks, and rented shelter in boats harbored near the shipyards. In one case, twenty-eight people cohabited in a converted storefront. Others found lodging in chicken shacks that a federal housing agent called "so horrible that the only possible solu-tion would be to remove their occupants immediately and burn the shacks." In another oft-described case, a single male worker volunteered for the graveyard shift at the Richmond yard, slept in the park by day, then shaved at a gas-station washroom and spent the evening in a bar before going off to work.

Schools operated in quadruple shifts, as juvenile delinquency soared. Other crimes, including prostitution, rose as well, and during one month police made 4,000 arrests. (The resulting fines ran to $34,000 and, no doubt, were welcomed by the fiscally strapped city government.) Al-though neither gambling houses nor brothels operated openly, plenty of both existed surreptitiously. Restaurants and movie houses ran full-out, round-the-clock. And as in Gary, a tough saloon district appeared, espe-cially along the main drag known as McDonald Avenue. "It takes a fairly hardy customer to walk into the Nutt Club, the Denver Club, or the Red Robin," reflected the *Fortune* writer.[4]

Kaiser's shipyard was like a city unto itself. Photos from the time show a vast industrial area dominated by towering cranes. In his collection of short stories, *Swing Shift*, Joseph Fabry describes a character's arrival at the facility after passing beneath a huge REMEMBER PEARL HARBOR sign. "The yard was arranged city-like," Fabry explains:

> F, G, H Streets running in one direction, 9th, 10th, 11th Streets in another. It was a city without houses, but the traffic was heavy. Cranes, trucks, trains nosed by. Finally, after a rather long walk, I came to the edge of the water. There were the ships—or rather, halves, thirds, quarters, and tenths of ships. There was a piece of a ship here and a piece of a ship there, and a hole in between. And then out of a clear sky a crane dropped the missing piece of a ship, big as a house, into that hole.

In *Swing Shift*, workers from a variety of backgrounds are thrown together, eagerly learn new skills, rapidly overcome initial stereotypes about gender and race, find romance, and finally triumph in the speed-record-breaking completion of a Liberty ship. A Viennese refugee from Nazism, Fabry saw American life and comradeship in a rosy hue. William Martin Camp's novel *Skip to My Lou* is much less Pollyannaish. Following a family of Arkansas migrants to Richmond, Camp offers images of brutish living conditions, furtive prostitution amid partially built ships, and racial friction that threatens to burst forth in street fighting. In one scene, the author describes the sweaty, miserable drudgery belowdecks:

> There they lay on their bellies and fitted the pipes and welded them, flanged, burned, bolted, riveted, working long, hot, hellish hours in those burning hulls where the slightest tap with a hammer on the steel hull reverberated and echoed and bounced back like the noise inside a big bass drum.[5]

Most employment in Richmond involved semi-skilled labor. In prewar shipbuilding, skilled trades dominated, represented by such AFL craft

unions as the Boilermakers. What Kaiser brought to the wartime enterprise was a promise of streamlined production, made possible by using
prefabrication, an approach his company had helped to pioneer during its
dam-building years.

Managers broke down skills into manageable parts or, where possible, eliminated skilled work to accommodate new employees. Large parts
of a vessel including boilers, forepeaks, and deckhouses were put together
in the prefabrication plant between Yard 3 and Yard 4. Then they were
brought to the vessel's hull one at a time and put in place. Wherever possible, welding, which could be learned relatively quickly, replaced the
skilled work of riveting. The result was record-breaking productivity,
much publicized by Kaiser and denounced as publicity-seeking by his rivals. In one of the most widely reported incidents, in late 1942, crews
assembled the Liberty ship SS *Robert E. Peary* in four days, fifteen hours,
and twenty-six minutes. Between 1941 and 1945, Kaiser produced ships
faster than any other builder. The 1,490 vessels manufactured in the company's Richmond and Portland/Vancouver yards included 821 Liberty
ships, 219 Victory ships, fifty small aircraft carriers, and a bevy of other
vessels. There were many other yards on both coasts—in fact there were
twelve others in the Bay Area, including the venerable Moore Shipbuilding Co. But on its own, Kaiser was responsible for 30 percent of U.S.
wartime shipping.[6]

It didn't take long for America to take notice. Henry Kaiser, a school
dropout and self-made upstate New Yorker, was hailed as "the master
Doer of the world" by one press agency. His success had not come easy:
In his youth, Kaiser had painstakingly opened a chain of photography
shops and had moved to the West Coast only as a result of an ultimatum
by his prospective father-in-law ("Make good or the marriage is off"). In
the 1920s, when he managed his own small road-construction outfit,
Kaiser himself, along with his wife and two kids, had lived out of his
car at times. Later, an alliance with Bechtel led to larger projects, and
Kaiser moved to better quarters. He spent increasing amounts of time in
Sacramento, where he honed his skills as a lobbyist. The bespectacled
and cherubic man's tool of choice was neither the rivet gun nor the
blowtorch, but the telephone, which he used to massage bureaucrats
and congressmen.

In the early 1930s, the Six Companies consortium won the bid to build Boulder Dam in an arid, remote area thirty miles south of Las Vegas. There, 3,000 workers toiled in 128-degree heat, exposed to explosives and a variety of other dangers and living in barracks-like dorms in a tightly controlled, liquor-free company town. Kaiser sweated it out as well—in an office in Washington, D.C., where he labored to keep the funding spigot flowing. As historian Kevin Starr has observed, Kaiser was anything but a field man. Instead, his genius consisted "in determining great projects, assembling teams, then handling the politics and finance." During an interview, *Inside U.S.A.* author John Gunther expressed astonishment when he learned that Kaiser had never even visited the completed Boulder or Grand Coulee dams. "I have no interest in a thing once it's done," Kaiser told him.[7]

One might expect such a nose-to-the-grindstone personality to be dull. But Kaiser was never uninteresting—and just to make sure of that, he often mythologized his past with little stories. Asked how as a man in his twenties he'd been able to fund his chain of photo stores, he explained how a stranger on the street had noticed Kaiser's forlorn appearance and responded by giving him the necessary money. In another tale, he described how, in a hurry to get to a meeting and win one of his early road-construction jobs, he'd risked life and limb by jumping from a moving train. And after Kaiser's employee health-care plan had become famous, he suggested that he had been motivated to launch it because his mother had died in his arms, unable to afford a doctor. Common to these stories is the idea that in a crisis, timing is all-important—along with a measure of compassion.

Richmond learned all about speed, especially with the sudden arrival of thousands of newcomers. Elected officials called their town "the wounded city," and the city manager penned an appeal for federal funds that he titled "An Avalanche Hits Richmond." So where was Kaiser's compassion? Why did he not do more to alleviate the catastrophe he'd loosed on the city?[8]

In time, he did. At first the parties turned to stopgap remedies for the housing crisis: The government urged citizens with empty rooms across the Bay Area to share space with war workers. Thousands responded, motivated by patriotism and the prospect of extra income. New roads linked Richmond with nearby communities where there might be lodging, and the government reopened old San Francisco–Oakland ferries. With federal assistance, the city even arranged to import a decommissioned New York City elevated train; it stretched sixteen miles between Oakland and Richmond and carried 11,000 commuters each day. Then the Federal Housing Authority funded such private developments as the seven hundred–unit Rollingwood homes in San Pablo and Brookfield Village in East Oakland. Here were prefabricated houses for the builders of prefabricated ships. But none of this sufficed. So in 1942 and 1943, Kaiser Shipyards and the Maritime Commission began constructing many two-story row houses within walking distance of the yards. Bearing such names as Harbor Gate and Richmond Terrace—and such unassuming appellations as Canal War Apartments and Terrace War Apartments—these cheap and standardized wood-frame structures sprawled across the harbor-front flatlands and came to house half of the shipyard's workforce. The projects were racially segregated. Altogether, the 30,000 new units included 6,000 small houses, and the worst of the housing crisis was over by 1944.[9]

More striking, Kaiser became a welfare-capitalism pioneer. He'd begun offering medical care to workers in the late 1930s during construction work at Grand Coulee Dam in Washington state. At Richmond, he deepened his commitment to such benefits—much needed given that a large number of employees had escaped military service only because of their serious physical disabilities. For 80 cents a week, Kaiser Shipyard workers could get private medical coverage for themselves and family members. Of the Richmond workers, 95 percent signed up. Kaiser also set up emergency medical stations in the yards under Dr. Sidney Garfield—who'd pioneered similar prepaid medical programs at the Los Angeles Aqueduct construction site and at Grand Coulee—and organized the nearby 175-bed Permanente field hospital, where the seriously injured could get treatment. (The mysterious "Permanente" comes from Permanente Creek in Cupertino, near which Kaiser Industries had a large cement plant.) Those in critical condition went to the Kaiser Hospital in Oakland. Such steps were forerunners of the Kaiser Permanente health plan that remains Henry Kaiser's preeminent legacy, today covering 8.6 million people in ten states.

At the Kaiser yards in Richmond and Portland, the company established twenty-four-hour-a-day child care centers funded by the Maritime Commission. Kaiser retained counselors to help with orientation, family problems, finances, and employee relations. Special counselors offered aid tailored to women, African Americans, Chinese, Native Americans—and teenagers, who were given special dispensation to work a restricted number of hours per day. A weekly Kaiser newspaper, *Fore 'N' Aft*, contained articles targeted to women and minorities. The company also organized a variety of sports teams and recreational events.

All of this was facilitated by organized labor's haughty abstention from such concerns. In the 1940s, Kaiser never made a move without a union contract—perhaps because of labor's clout within the Franklin Roosevelt administration. Earlier, during his dam-building years, Kaiser had not been a particular friend to unions, and at one point his supervisors had brought in goons to break a strike at Boulder Dam. But at Richmond, organized labor was a key player—and there, organized labor *was* the conservative Boilermakers union, by agreement with the federal War Labor Board. The Boilermakers opposed prefabrication but went along in exchange for a "closed shop," meaning employees were required to join up. Yet the Boilermakers made it quite clear that they had no interest in representing the newly arrived low-skill workers or in tending to their very evident needs. ("The bottom of the barrel was being scraped," the union said of the new workers, in one publication.) The newcomers were not like the native-born older union members: They were Okies, Arkies, and Texies. They were African American—numbering 10,000 in a town where there once had been only about 400 blacks. Perhaps worse in the eyes of the union, they were women, a group that constituted over a quarter of Kaiser's workers by 1944. The Boilermakers made special arrangements for blacks and women, establishing special "auxiliary locals" for the African Americans—they got to pay dues but had no business agent and no grievance procedure. The union amended its men-only constitution to allow women to join. And to make sure these newcomers had no ability to make trouble, the Boilermakers provided for direct control of certain locals by the national union.

Racial segregation was the rule for shipyard work. Although Henry Kaiser insisted on fair treatment for African Americans, management justified separating the races on the grounds that there would be fewer clashes that way. Whether such segregation helped or only made things worse, racial strife was certainly an issue, particularly if novelist Chester Himes's nightmarish treatment of life in the Los Angeles shipyards, *If He Hollers, Let Him Go*, is to be believed. Although Himes's gangs are segregated by race, his novel features ceaseless racial and sexual banter that occasionally bursts forth in violence. In Richmond, management concentrated African Americans in the difficult outdoor work. Women, on the other hand, worked alongside men and made up 40 percent of the welders. For the most part, supervisors were older white males.[10]

As of V-J Day, when Japan surrendered, Kaiser's shipyards had turned out $1.8 billion worth of ships. But war work had begun winding down a year earlier, and in 1945 employment fell to fewer than 35,000 workers from a high of nearly 100,000. Recruiters back in the early 1940s had not been altogether honest about postwar prospects—or much of anything else. They said workers would learn a trade, get high wages in a sunshiny area, and have employment for the duration of the war and likely thereafter, when the United States would turn to rebuilding its merchant marine fleet. (They also promised workers "pleasant homes at moderate rentals.") Instead, shipbuilding activities all but ceased by 1946. Kaiser closed its health-care facilities and child-care centers. What would happen to the migrant workers now?[11]

In a company survey conducted just before the end of the war, more than 60 percent of the immigrant workers said they wanted to stay in California when peace arrived—and 34 percent said they wanted to remain in Richmond. If that came true, postwar Richmond's population would be about double that of its prewar years. Assuming that the federal government would demolish the temporary blocks of row houses and that only one shipyard would remain open, city officialdom promised to build a community of worker homes in the former industrial areas. Rehabilitation would cost $6 million to $7 million, they said in an appeal to the federal government, and should include a new civic center, a library, firehouses, a hospital, and a police station.

Five years later, half of the town's population was still living in the temporary war housing, including three-fourths of the town's African-American population. The war workers, many unemployed now, had in fact stayed on—and, moreover, more immigrants had arrived, a quarter of whom were nonwhite and half of whom were veterans. Within the next few years, the town evicted thousands of these renters, particularly minorities and those with low income. It also razed hundreds of acres of the war housing, which was seen as crime- and poverty-infested. The area would not in fact become the site of new worker housing. Instead, the demolition opened up the lowlands for commercial development: In 1953, Harbor Gate, which had housed white workers, was among the last to fall, making way for a huge warehouse for the Safeway supermarket chain.

But even if the shipyards closed, continued military spending after the war helped to keep the Bay Area economy humming. New retail outlets offered employment—not equivalent employment, but jobs all the same—to the women who had once operated cranes or wielded welding torches. Many male shipyard workers turned to the docks and other industrial jobs. GI Bill financing helped many locate replacement housing in the burgeoning working-class suburbs.[12]

Kaiser Industries had a hand in constructing some of these postwar suburbs, notably Panorama City in Southern California's San Fernando Valley. The prefabrication techniques perfected in the shipyards were now turned to home-building, allowing two-bedroom, single-family structures to sell for as little as $9,100. The corporation included eighteen to twenty enterprises, including a steel mill at Fontana, fifty miles east of Los Angeles. But Kaiser's empire, it turned out, much depended on applying the man's personal magic. When Henry Kaiser died in 1967, most of his company's properties were sold off.[13]

Today, what most people remember when Henry Kaiser's name arises is the health-care plan, which in 1945 began enrolling thousands of members of the public at large. The value of that legacy is debatable in 2010, a year when the proper avenue to national health care is being much discussed. Immediately after the war, Kaiser Permanente was denounced by the American Medical Association as noxious socialized medicine. At roughly the same time, Kaiser himself was arguing against New

York Senator Robert Wagner's proposal for federal health insurance, asserting that his private-sector approach was preferable.[14] Over sixty years, it seems, the debate has hardly advanced at all.

Site X, the government called it at first. The advantages: a rural, middle-of-the-country location that allowed few prying eyes. Lots of hydroelectric power, plentiful water, a sizable labor pool, and loads of land available for under $50 an acre. Only 1,000 families would have to be evicted, according to preliminary studies.

In October 1942, the U.S. government went into federal court and filed a "declaration of takings" for 56,000 acres. Five months later, six architects from the New York firm of Skidmore, Owings and Merrill were handed train tickets in sealed envelopes and dispatched to the unknown destination, where they would scout out the turf. By mid-February, they had an initial plan for a town. Residents—small farmers, some of whose families had lived there for generations, and tenants—got as little as two weeks' notice that they were being ousted. Many came home to find eviction notices posted on their doors or nailed to a tree in the yard. As they moved out, often before the government purchase was completed, some crossed paths with the thousands of construction workers who were on their way to make the area into a city.

Site X, later known as Clinton Engineer District and ultimately as Oak Ridge, would be one of three supersecret locations central to the Manhattan Project, which produced America's first atomic bombs. (The name Oak Ridge, strictly speaking, applied only to the fourteen-square-mile residential area within the larger Clinton reservation.) The other locations were Hanford, Washington (also known as Site W), and Los Alamos, New Mexico (Site Y).

It was the U-235, produced in Tennessee, that in 1945 reduced Hiroshima, Japan, to a cinder, killing 140,000 people. Located twenty miles from Knoxville and only sixteen miles from the Tennessee Valley Authority's Norris Dam, the Clinton Engineer District was the largest of the three primary Manhattan Project facilities. Hanford, the second-largest, was the major source for plutonium, which was used in the somewhat different bomb that fell on Nagasaki. Los Alamos, even though it was the smallest facility, became the most well-known since it was where the renowned scientists led by J. Robert Oppenheimer worked at the best-equipped physics lab in the world.

In almost every sense, Oak Ridge was a company town. It was, of course, a community planned and owned by management—the U.S. government.

Among the great number of workers at Oak Ridge was a large pool of unskilled young women, many of whom were housed in dormitories—and so Oak Ridge harkened back to the model established at Lowell.

The labor needs of the Clinton works were massive, prompting massive residential construction. In 1943, the government estimated that 13,000 people would be required, but the project's demands kept growing. By 1945, around 75,000 worked in what had become the fifth-largest city in Tennessee. The federal government and its subcontractors built thousands of housing units, much as at Richmond, California. During one period, single-family houses were being erected in Oak Ridge at the rate of one every half-hour.

Oak Ridge was a closed community. The 59,000-acre reservation was surrounded by fences, with signs reading MILITARY RESERVATION, NO TRESPASSING posted every six hundred feet. Five lookout towers loomed above the perimeter, and guards carefully screened would-be entrants at each of seven gates. Even more elaborate fencing topped with a foot of barbed wire surrounded each of the plants within the reservation. A system of coded badges regulated entry, and there were a great many armed cops: 4,900 members of the Safety Forces, 740 military police, and 400 civilian police. Such precautions were elaborate, yes—but also reminiscent of the closed-community approach at mining towns in Colorado and Appalachia.

Also like mining towns, loss of employment meant immediate expulsion from Oak Ridge. This time the offense that might have you deposited outside the gates with all of your belongings was not mere union activity—it was a breach of Manhattan District security, perhaps only loose talk or a wrong word in a letter written to a relative. Spies and informants infiltrated every part of the culture at all Manhattan Project locations. Agents from an Intelligence and Security Division tracked rumors out of Oak Ridge across the globe, examined the press for any sign of leaks, and fingerprinted more than 300,000 people.

On the more positive side, Oak Ridge enjoyed federally financed schools, cheap medical coverage provided by doctors from prestigious university programs, and a range of recreational activities, from movies and skating rinks to folk dancing and a community theater.[15]

America's atom-bomb project had many fathers. In 1939, scientists Albert Einstein, Leo Szilard, and Eugene Wigner urged such an endeavor on President Roosevelt, arguing that the Nazi regime in Germany must certainly be pursuing such research and so the United States must as well. Other advocates included scientific-policy honchos Vannevar Bush, formerly of MIT, and James B. Conant, president of Harvard. Bush pushed and pushed, but governmental inertia got in the way, along with the fact that no one had yet proved that such a bomb could actually be made. Finally, in September 1942, Bush's argument that the military should take command of the fledgling effort prompted General William Styer to appoint Leslie R. Groves head of the Manhattan Project. The endeavor had found its sparkplug—a doer, not unlike Henry J. Kaiser or, for that matter, Nathan Appleton or Charles Cannon.

Groves was, in the words of one key subordinate, "the biggest sonovabitch I have ever worked for. He is most demanding and most critical. He is always a driver, never a praiser. He is abrasive and sarcastic. . . . He is the most egotistical man I know. He knows he is right and so sticks by his decision." Another friend observed: "Groves not only behaves as if he can walk on water, but as if he actually invented the substance."[16]

Another dumpling-shaped ball of fire, the forty-six-year-old Corps of Engineers brigadier general upbraided subordinates, disrespected officials, and dared to believe he understood the thinking of some of the most brilliant physicists of his day. The son of a Presbyterian army chaplain, Groves had left MIT in his junior year to enroll at West Point, where he graduated a year early at the head of his class. With his curly brown hair, 260 pounds of girth, and pencil-line moustache, he was hardly anyone's idea of an Achilles-like warrior-hero. But it was Groves who had overseen the building of the $83 million Pentagon and $10 billion worth of military construction. It would be Groves who would make J. Robert Oppenheimer the Manhattan Project's head of scientific research, despite that scientist's leftish background and relative lack of professional stature. And two days after he was named to lead the Manhattan Project, it would be Groves who began acquiring the Tennessee land that others had targeted but had been slow to grab.

It was an odd project, to say the least. To Groves, who had hoped to be assigned to a command in Europe or the Pacific, it looked like a demotion since the initial budget was a lot smaller than those of the projects he'd just supervised. Then there was the fact that the enterprise conjoined the military with a bevy of independent and unruly scientists. At first Groves wanted everyone commissioned into the Army, meaning strict security and following of orders. That notion ran up against another fundamental, the need to move quickly. Getting Army commissions for the scientists meant delay, and so the idea was abandoned. And of course the whole thing was an experiment—meaning that established scientific procedures, including collegial working conditions for the scientists, had to be observed.

The idea that nuclear fission could produce a bomb dated from German experiments in the late 1930s. Generating a powerful chain reaction from uranium atoms required the separation of its U-235 isotope from the predominant U-238. Experiments in university laboratories suggested several ways of doing this, but none had been employed on a large scale. And since time was of the essence, the project's scientific overlords determined to pursue several methods simultaneously.

Four processes would be employed in vast factories built in Tennessee. A "gaseous diffusion" method circulated uranium hexafluoride gas through porous barriers that parted the isotopes. An electromagnetic approach spun uranium atoms in large arcs through a magnetic field, allowing the separation since the isotopes took different paths. A "thermal diffusion" method employed tremendous heat to divide the isotopes. Finally, a reactor would produce small quantities of plutonium, a fissionable substance that doesn't occur in nature. This final process was pursued in Tennessee only as a pilot project: Plutonium was understood to be extremely toxic and therefore a separate facility was erected for its production in the desert wastes near Hanford, Washington.[17]

Shortly after his appointment, Groves and two subordinates traveled to Tennessee to inspect the site. They found little to complain about. The remote, seventeen-mile-by-seven-mile area was composed of a series of valleys extending from the lower reaches of the Cumberland Mountains and defined on the south by the Clinch River. The few roads that existed were all unpaved. Soon appraisers were sent out to each of the area's farms, where they catalogued and photographed crops and buildings and estimated worth. Thus began a process of intimidation: The appraisers sometimes referred to the overall area as the Kingston Demolition Range and even told occupants that they would have to get out, as bombs would shortly be falling on the area. Next came a second group of officials carrying take-it-or-leave-it offers and wielding orders of condemnation and eviction as bludgeons. By March 1943, the area had been cleared.[18]

Workers bulldozed and graded the location, employing methods that would have pleased the Wehrmacht: They eradicated trees and shrubs and turned rolling hillsides into a tabletop-like veld. That this may not have been the best approach quickly occurred to Groves's officers, who turned the town's design over to the innovative Boston architectural firm of Skidmore, Owings and Merrill. By July, the first 1,000 houses were standing, constructed of a material called Cemesto, made of low-cost fiberboard bonded with cement and asbestos. The government had previously used the cheap but presentable materials in various buildings, including a bomber plant in Baltimore.

The first structures included an administration building, fourteen dorms, three apartment buildings, and 3,000 Cemesto single-family homes. Three vast factories located some distance from the residential areas also appeared suddenly: Y-12, the electromagnetic works, consisted of 268 buildings including the electromagnetic "racetracks," chemistry labs, a foundry, and nineteen water-cooling towers. K-25, the gaseous diffusion plant, covered more than forty-two acres and was at the time the largest building on Earth. X-10, the plutonium-making "pile" plant, was relatively small by comparison.

America's foremost scientific corporations operated the plants. Kodak subsidiary Tennessee Eastman ran Y-12, Union Carbide operated K-25, and ultimately Monsanto ran X-10. General Electric, Allis-Chalmers, Bell Labs, and Chrysler also contributed. But actually getting the factories to produce proved tricky: Y-12 seemed ready to go in the fall of 1943, but numerous problems led to a shutdown and months of inactivity. Finally operative by the late spring of 1944, Y-12 generated enriched uranium very, very slowly. At K-25, the porous barriers didn't work well, and it was January 1945 before that plant produced anything. In despair, Grove and his officers turned to the thermal-diffusion method, which the Navy had been developing elsewhere. They began building the Oak Ridge thermal-diffusion plant, S-50, in the summer of 1944 and had it operating by September. The fissionable material that was ultimately used passed through all three facilities: Y-12 was fed somewhat enriched uranium that had already been processed at K-25 and S-50.[19]

Meanwhile, echoing the experience at Richmond, there was never enough housing for the growing workforce. A second phase of building beginning in the fall of 1943 anticipated a total population of 42,000, and a third phase begun in the spring of 1945 anticipated a total of 66,000. In fact, the peak population exceeded 75,000. As many as 20,000 commuted each day from housing outside the reservation.

As at, say, Sparrows Point, a hierarchical test was applied. High-ranking and skilled workers with families got the best single-family homes—of which there were 10,000. Other families found lodging in thousands of trailers. Unmarried workers might be stuck in dorms, barracks, or, at worst, in one of the 16,000 spaces in sixteen-by-sixteen "hutments," plywood cubes with hinged, unscreened windows that contained up to six beds and one stove for heat. The bathrooms and showers were in separate buildings. These hutments were segregated by race and sex, serving as lodging for, among others, 1,500 African-American construction workers. Embodying the project's racial segregation, a separate "Negro village" was planned but never constructed, leaving many black workers to fend for themselves.

The Skidmore, Owings and Merrill professionals had envisioned Oak Ridge as a model, picturesque community where design echoed American folk traditions, as at the nearby Tennessee Valley Authority town of Norris, Tennessee. However, in the end, Oak Ridge became another boomtown hodgepodge that ran from ranch houses to trailer parks and even hundreds of dilapidated farmhouses. A collection of slum villages included plywood houses on stilts with canvas roofs.

Complaints about housing assignments were common, both from individuals and from companies. Protesting the "acute" housing shortage,

Tennessee Eastman's operations officer threatened to cease recruitment of workers. "Oak Ridge remained like Topsy," recalled Oak Ridge's chief operating officer, District Engineer Kenneth D. Nichols. "It grew and grew throughout the war. We finished our last housing expansion three months after the Japanese surrender and a nursery school and gymnasium by Christmas, 1945." Despite such disarray, the spartan Groves considered the Oak Ridge housing a bit too cosseting.

Town construction ran to $101 million and included a water purification plant, two sewage-treatment plants, systems for water and utilities, and rail connections to the Southern and L&N railroads. There were two standard Army chapels, a high school and eight grammar schools, seven movie houses, and perhaps thirty stores in four retail areas, including thirteen supermarkets. There were also three hundred miles of paved roads, including a four-lane highway connecting the town with K-25.[20]

Who were the employees at Oak Ridge? Construction workers totaled around 100,000, or around half that number at any given time. Turnover for all workers was high thanks to the shortage and condition of the housing, the mediocre food served in grim cafeterias, and the bedlam that attended all daily affairs. Word of these limitations hampered hiring, as did the fact that recruiters could say nothing about the kind of work being done on the project.

Of the 40,000 employed in the nuclear plants, some number, including those operating the gaseous-diffusion operation, were scientists. There were mechanics to keep equipment running, electrical and chemical engineers, foremen, and a variety of operatives. Tennessee Eastman, which ran the electromagnetic facility, depended largely upon a group of unskilled employees, regularly referred to as "hillbilly girls." In the words of Manhattan District public relations officer George O. Robinson, they were "East Tennessee high school girls with not the faintest idea of what their jobs were about." Many of these young women sat in a control room, on stools spaced far enough apart to discourage communication, and for six days a week, ten hours a day, silently adjusted dials that controlled the electromagnetic "racetracks." Others robotically recorded the readings of gauges. Purposely misinformed about the actual product and punished if they asked questions or showed initiative, in Nichols's words they were like soldiers, trained either "to do or not to do—and not to reason why." Regardless of the method employed, production of U-235 was very, very slow, but Y-25's girls outdid the K-25 scientists in an early production race.

Some of the work at Oak Ridge was frightening and, whether employees knew it or not, dangerous. Those working near the 10,000-ton magnets found tools and keys disconcertingly jerked from their pockets and bobby pins pulled from their hair. Other workers at Y-12 had the job of removing tiny bits of uranium from the machinery—meaning exposure to perilous levels of radiation. Even leaky pipes at the gaseous diffusion plant were ominous harbingers of injury, but no one was offered the opportunity to refuse a hazardous assignment. Worse, doctors at the facility injected many unwitting employees with plutonium in an effort frighteningly similar to Nazi experiments. The scientists knew that exposure to radiation was risky but didn't know just how risky. Via the injections, they meant to find out.

An environment that was, if anything, even more restrictive than that in early Lowell enveloped the single women at Oak Ridge. Dormitory rules barred cooking in the rooms, consuming liquor, gambling, and receiving visits from members of the opposite sex. Moreover, along with all other residents of the nuclear town, they were regularly and insistently told not to discuss their work. At hiring, every worker had to sign a Declaration of Secrecy. Posters urging silence blanketed walls everywhere. "Compartmentalization" dictated that each worker knew only his or her own job and nothing about how it fitted into an overall scheme. Access to job sites was limited, with color-coded badges worn by all indicating just where within, say, K-25 the employee was allowed to go.

With the plants running seven days a week in three shifts around the clock, life could be a monotony of labor, sleep, and cafeteria meals. Nor was there any sense of participation in the larger win-the-war effort: Just compare Oak Ridge workers' experience of ignorance and enforced secrecy with the sense of celebration and contribution Dos Passos observed during the launching in the Pacific Coast shipyard. And since a great many supplies seemed to come into the area and nothing seemed to go out, local newspapers helped spread the idea that the project was an immense flop—and that notion must have taken a further toll on morale. As one War Department statement later acknowledged, "an atmosphere of unreality" reigned, "in which giant plants operated feverishly day and night to produce nothing that could be seen or touched."[21]

(In fact, beginning in March 1945, a crack team of heavily armed security operatives regularly transported the finished product—the volume of which was relatively small, of course—from Oak Ridge to Los Alamos. Arriving by car, the guards were handed cases containing U-235-filled nickel containers. Unimaginable as it may now seem, the team took the stuff by regular passenger train, first to Chicago and then on to New Mexico, where they were met by other couriers who made the final delivery to the Los Alamos lab.)[22]

In charge of the dorms and of town life in general was a subsidiary of Turner Construction Co. known as Roane-Anderson. Named for the two counties the Clinton Engineer District straddled, Roane-Anderson operated as landlord for all the housing, ran eight hundred public buses, handled such municipal functions as garbage collection and coal delivery, and provided police and fire departments. The company also managed the seventeen cafeterias that served 40,000 meals a day, a three hundred–bed hospital, a bank, and a post office, and it brought in two hundred private businesses including department stores, shoe shops, and grocery markets. Moreover, it was Roane-Anderson that enforced the various restrictions on residents' behavior.

Thus were met the basic requirements of life. But was there to be no civil society in Oak Ridge? In a town of strangers, what agency would provide for social life and group activities? A set of ersatz institutions emerged to take care of such things—citizens groups that were in fact run by the Manhattan District. A Recreation and Welfare Association, fronted by citizen-volunteers but organized and funded by Tennessee Eastman and other corporations, set up athletic teams, art classes, a dancing school, and a teen center. In addition, the association encouraged the hundred-odd organized groups including a Junior Chamber of Commerce, Boy and Girl Scouts, Kiwanis, and even a rabbit-breeders club. The association built five movie houses, four bowling alleys, snack shops, a miniature golf course, a library, and a riding academy. Oak Ridge even had a newspaper and a town council—although the former was just a work-hard-and-stay-silent propaganda sheet and the latter was a powerless "advisory" body.[23]

By 1945, the Manhattan Project had consumed $2 billion. The Oak Ridge plants had operated on a twenty-four-hour schedule, only barely generating sufficient enriched uranium to produce a test bomb plus one more. Was there any way, then, that the atomic weapon would not have been used on Japan?

A profound and surprisingly thoughtful debate took place in Washington over whether and just how the bomb might be used—and whether and how its terrible secret might be shared among nations. The dialogue involved such policymakers as Secretary of War Henry L. Stimson, Secretary of State–designate James F. Byrnes, Oppenheimer, General George Marshall, and, in absentia, physicists Leo Szilard and Niels Bohr. That discussion has been well described elsewhere, notably in Richard Rhodes's Pulitzer Prize–winning *The Making of the Atomic Bomb*, and need not be recapitulated here. But certainly the expenditure of time and treasure militated in favor of the bomb's use, further motivated by the uncertainty of what if any effect a mere demonstration of the bomb at an unpopulated site would have on the unpredictable and cornered government in Japan. The project's seeming success generated great excitement among even the most pacifistic of participants—and prompted a macabre interest in giving the thing a try. Stimson, for example, wrote in his diary after an Oak Ridge visit of having witnessed and participated in "the most wonderful and unique operation . . . the largest and most extraordinary scientific experiment in history." Although he was among the most ambivalent and conscience-wracked of the top Washington policymakers, Stimson clinically noted that "success is 99% assured, yet only by the first actual war trial of the weapon can the actual certainty be fixed."[24]

And so following the July 1945 test explosion at Alamogordo in New Mexico, the four-ton Little Boy was dropped on Hiroshima on August 6.

What had been wrought at Oak Ridge could now be revealed, both to the project's uninformed workers and to the public at large. As soon as they heard about Hiroshima, near hysteria seized the residents, and a New Year's Eve atmosphere complete with horns and whistles prevailed in the town. Public relations officer Robinson reported "a strange stirring in the community" followed by "great rejoicing." Abandoning their pledge of omertà, participants could now discuss what they had done and experience a bit of the pride known by U.S. war workers elsewhere. One Oak Ridge resident recalled that scientists "were running around town shouting, 'Uranium!' and 'atomic!' All these things they had never been able to say before, they were shouting out like dirty words."

The general public learned of the bomb and its production facilities in news reports that combined wonderment at the project's secrecy with a pride that the United States could produce such a device. One of the first mentions of Oak Ridge came in an August 7 *New York Times* article titled "Atom Bombs Made in 3 'Hidden' Cities." Adding to the gee-whiz factor were accompanying photos of the vast and mysterious K-25 and Hanford works.

Informed by Groves that the bomb drop "went with a tremendous bang," Oppenheimer reported feeling "reasonably good" about the effort, while Szilard wrote a friend that the use of the A-bomb was "one of the greatest blunders of history." Of course, the extent of the horrible destruction in Hiroshima was not appreciated by either Manhattan Project participants or the general American public—and really wouldn't be understood for several years, particularly given the reassuring picture painted by a U.S. commission sent in 1947 to take stock of the damage. To this day, the effects of the atomic explosions remain a subject of debate and denial.

The second bomb drop, at Nagasaki, prompted a less-celebratory reaction in Oak Ridge. One minister observed that attitudes shifted from "We did it!" to "What have we done?"[25]

Perhaps that spreading anxiety and guilt helps explain why so many Oak Ridge residents picked up and left shortly after the Japanese surrender. Within a few months, the town's population dropped by almost 10,000 and in less than a year, it was down by nearly 30,000. "Nobody knows what lies ahead for Oak Ridge," reported the *New Yorker*. "Some people, confident that the project will be made permanent, have started small flower gardens in front of their homes. Others, more dubious, have let the weeds grow tall."

The first official word that Oak Ridge operations would continue after the war came in September 1945. Some workers began for the first time to see themselves as long-term residents of the area. Trailer-park residents in particular began demanding better housing, and some of the worst structures were demolished.

Unionization became an issue. By request of the War Department, the National Labor Relations Board had declared a moratorium on union elections at Manhattan Project locations for the duration of the war. Groves in particular had wanted nothing to do with organized labor, which he saw as a threat to security and a source of hassles over jurisdiction and hiring. In 1946, though, the National Labor Relations Board oversaw elections that resulted in union representation at K-25 and X-10.

The military surrendered control of the project in 1947, to the civilian Atomic Energy Commission. Although employment fell and the population of Oak Ridge was down to 30,000 by 1950, the gaseous-diffusion plant continued operations until 1985, and the electromagnetic facility is still up and running.

It took until 1949 for the fences to come down and for Oak Ridge to be officially opened, with a ribbon-cutting ceremony, parades, and speeches. Roane-Anderson divested itself of town-management responsibilities over a period ending in 1952. And in 1959, the town was incorporated and adopted a city-manager/city-council form of government. X-10, the former plutonium pilot plant, became the Oak Ridge National Laboratory in 1948, serving as a source of radioactive isotopes used in medicine and biological research. Gradually opened to the public, the lab and the town's museum of science became tourist attractions, drawing more than 60,000 visitors a year during the 1950s and thousands more today. There are even little Oak Ridge souvenirs, some embossed with a cute version of the scary three-oval nuclear symbol.

Significant nuclear contamination took place at all of the Manhattan Project sites. Courts have ordered cleanups of toxic waste in both Oak Ridge and Hanford, but untold amounts of radiation were buried deep in the soil, discharged in local waterways, and released into the air. In 2000, the National Academy of Sciences declared that the Manhattan Project sites would pose risks to humans and the environment for tens or even hundreds of thousands of years to come. The previous year the government admitted that thousands of war workers had contracted cancer and other maladies as a result of exposure to radiation.[26]

For this and many other reasons, it seems safe to say that Oak Ridge can never be a normal American town. Six years after Hiroshima, a writer for the *New York Times Magazine* found that Oak Ridge citizens had divergent opinions about their heritage. One "veteran physicist" seemed to revel in the town's accomplishment, asserting that a gold rush–like "spirit of adventure" still prevailed. Meanwhile, the wife of Union Carbide's industrial relations manager reflected "a massive placidity," in the words of the writer. "We don't seem to mind the fact that we're sitting on an atomic bomb," she said. "During the war, we . . . couldn't have been more nervous. Now, we go from day to day and live with it."[27] Oak Ridge exhibited few signs that it was a unique place—its shopping district, for instance, reminded the writer of Levittown. Yet most citizens seemed unconcerned that the town might gradually lose its special identity.

Perhaps they understood that Oak Ridge would remain special given that weaponry will always be in demand. In 2003, Y-12 reopened after a period of suspension, with a mandate to produce warhead parts for MX missiles and to store weapons-grade uranium.[28] THE ATOMIC CITY WELCOMES YOU, reads a sign at the city's outskirts. DRIVE CAREFULLY.

CHAPTER 8

A World Transformed

Come let us travel into the future. What will we see? . . . A new world is constantly opening before us at an ever accelerating rate of progress. A greater world, a better world. A world which will always grow forward.

—From the sound track for General Motors'
1939 World's Fair exhibit, Futurama[1]

The 1939–1940 New York World's Fair purposely focused on the future—the grim present was better left unacknowledged. Key to making the event a reality were a group of New York businessmen including distillery executive Grover Whalen, who imagined that such an extravaganza might inspire the city and lift its people out of the Depression doldrums. Political leaders including Mayor Fiorello LaGuardia and Parks Commissioner Robert Moses accepted the concept and helped bring the fair into being.

In the fair's first year, 26 million people attended, and 50 million would go through the gates before the two-year run ended. Many corporations jumped at the exhibition as a means of pushing their products and their big ideas. RCA and General Electric showed off that new phenomenon, television. Inside the Heinz Dome, which was adorned with a giant "57" sign, staffers gave out free food and little pickle-shaped souvenir pins. Westinghouse put together a time capsule that would be buried at the Flushing Meadows site of the fair, not to be exhumed until 6939. Among the contents were copies of *Life* magazine, a pack of Camel cigarettes, and a message to the future from Albert Einstein.

At the Transportation Zone pavilion, a General Motors exhibit showed off the latest GM cars and Frigidaire appliances. But the real draw was GM's Futurama—a large diorama of an imagined United States of 1960, complete with miniature roads, towns, homes, and cities.

Futurama was by far the fair's most popular exhibit. After waiting in lines for up to two hours, visitors were seated in high-sided, upholstered chairs and treated to a simulated airplane ride over the three-dimensional display; an accompanying sound track described what they were seeing. The diorama offered glimpses of an ideal farm, an amusement park, a small village, a "thriving and prosperous steel town" with "hundreds of comfortable homes for workers" (U.S. Steel take note), a resort, a religious retreat, and a vast, futuristic metropolis. Conspicuously lacking: the sprawling suburbs that would meander across the real-life countryside beginning in the 1950s. But Futurama got one thing right: the important role highways would play in America's future.

Futurama's "great motorways" featured multiple lanes, exit loops, unvarying illumination, and radio controls for maintaining a proper distance between cars. The watchword of this "spectacular" traffic system: "safety, safety with increased speed," the sound track's languorous and godlike male voice intoned. Some of these features were never realized, but less high-tech highways became an ever more important and influential feature of American life as the twentieth century progressed.

The roads and motorcars meant an end to some residential company towns, as auto ownership freed workers from having to live within walking distance of their workplaces. Taking their place as corporate Edens alongside the company towns that did survive: corporate campuses accessible only by automobile. And Americans' increasing fondness for travel pointed the way to a new economic orientation to which many company towns adapted: tourism. Finally, by the final decades of the twentieth century, the automobile would make possible new corporate outposts that required few workers and were far away from population centers.

In the 1930s, the Bell Labs division of American Telephone & Telegraph began planning for a new Manhattan headquarters. The high-rise would cover four acres of prime New York real estate and house 5,600 of the research-and-development division's scientists and staffers. But by 1939, the plan had been discarded: Manhattan, it seems, was already plagued by "high living costs" and "urban noise and dirt." Staffers were said to be repelled by the hassles and costs associated with commuting. So instead, in 1944, Bell Labs relocated to a parklike campus on 250 acres near Summit, New Jersey, twenty-five miles from the city. Apparently, Bell Labs Chairman Dr. Frank B. Jewett had for years longed for more leafy surroundings.

Images of the New Jersey site show a complex of unthreatening, modern structures amid landscaped countryside. Indoors, a cafeteria, solarium, and employee lounge celebrate modernist aesthetics with "butternut woodwork," recessed lighting, and unfussy, upholstered furniture. Modular construction allows reconfiguration of laboratory spaces according to the needs of the moment.

Bell Labs was in the vanguard of the industrial-park and office-park movement that would not truly pick up speed until the 1960s, by which point the U.S. economy had begun an inexorable shift away from manufacturing and toward services and knowledge work. The first such parks—around New York, Chicago, and Kansas City—dated back to the turn of the century, but in 1940 there were fewer than thirty-five such developments. By the early 1970s, however, there were more than three hundred such industrial/office parks in California alone, and a large number in Florida, Georgia, Minnesota, Missouri, Texas, and Wisconsin.

Railroads had been prime movers of early industrial parks, encouraging flight from costly urban centers. But the acceleration of the trend was tied to more recent developments in transportation and communication—namely, truck deliveries via highways, automobile commuting, and the rise in computer applications. An increasing number of light-assembly operations found homes near airports.

Office-park pathbreakers included IBM and PepsiCo. In 1957, the computer company commissioned Finnish-born Eero Saarinen—an architect on his way to developing a world-class reputation in part due to his many company campuses—to design a scientific research center in Yorktown Heights, New York. The three-story, 770,000-square-foot building there would house 1,500 scientists in a fieldstone-and-glass structure that set a new standard for suburban offices. IBM was so pleased with the Yorktown facility that it decided to move its corporate headquarters out of Manhattan to Armonk, New York. Architects Skidmore, Owings and Merrill—the company that had arranged Oak Ridge—drew up plans for a 403,000-square-foot glass-and-concrete edifice, complete with two sculpture-filled courtyards on 420 acres. At the same time, Skidmore, Owings and Merrill created Connecticut campuses for Connecticut General Life and Emhart Manufacturing Co. Saarinen designed another complex for Bell Labs, at Holmdel, New Jersey, which opened in 1962.

PepsiCo followed IBM's lead, moving northward out of New York City. In 1958, the soft-drink giant bought a former polo club in Purchase, New York, and hired architect Edward Durell Stone to plan a prestigious headquarters complex that would consist of seven seemingly overlapping, three-story buildings on 112 acres. Native and exotic trees and grasses were as carefully chosen as the fifty celebrated works of sculpture by the likes of Alexander Calder, Henry Moore, and Isamu Noguchi.

Outside of the New York area, the flight from urban centers was perhaps even more pronounced. In the 1960s, more than thirty industrial parks representing seven hundred high-tech companies—Digital, General Electric, RCA, and Raytheon included—emerged along Route 128 near Boston. The Great Southwest Industrial Park, opened in 1967 on the outskirts of Atlanta, seems like a paradigm of the modern corporate campus. After passing through a ninety-foot-high abstract entry arch, employees and visitors traveled along wide, divided boulevards bearing such collegiate names as Bucknell and Colgate. Trees and shrubbery shared quadrangle space with modernist sculpture. Buildings housed regional distribution centers for Coca-Cola, Goodyear, Philco-Ford, and Stanley Home Products. Not far away, the Atlanta Executive Park, which opened in 1964, housed administrative rather than industrial activity. There, a central plaza, the Pantry in the Park, supplied office workers with a snack bar, copy service, and gift shop.[2]

Examining the emergence of corporate campuses and the exodus from New York City, urban sociologist William H. Whyte in 1988 noted that the new complexes had "little connection with their surroundings." He went on:

They are elements of a car culture. . . . Within the headquarters a range of services makes the outside unnecessary. These are particularly bountiful in outlying campuses. At Beneficial Management's corporate village in Peapack, New Jersey, a pleasant grouping of low buildings is arranged around a courtyard and bell tower. There are outdoors dining areas, dining rooms within, shops, health facilities; the garage is laid out so that one drives to an underground space and takes an elevator to within a few feet of his office.

An unabashed fan of the urban experience, Whyte concluded that corporate campuses were employee-unfriendly developments—isolated, accessible only via increasingly congested roadways, often both pharaonic and sprawling, with little functional use of vast open space and too few pathways for those who might simply like to take a walk. Some were fortresslike, as if intended to discourage visitors, he said. Most unforgivably, he found all of them inhospitable to the "unplanned, informal encounters" among people upon which both markets and spontaneous creativity depend. Ever hopeful, though, Whyte observed that the time-tested "idea of towns is gaining currency" as the campuses were found wanting. He seemed to forecast a return to sensible, small-community living and working.[3]

Corporate campuses have continued to sprout, but company towns are hardly things of the past: Hershey, Corning, Scotia, auto-production towns across Middle America, midwestern meatpacking towns, and even the Atomic City of Oak Ridge are still in business. Moreover, rather than supplanting company towns, corporate campuses reproduce much of company-town life, albeit with a postindustrial, white-collar twist, in places ranging from Federal Express's 500,000-square-foot Collierville, Tennessee, campus to the Mountain View, California, site of the Googleplex. The FedEx facility is home to 1,500 employees and features jogging trails, a library, a wellness center, and coffee bars on each floor of the four office buildings. Google famously offers its cosseted workers free gourmet meals (Indian or Latin American, if one likes), exercise facilities, and massages. Do employees need to get their pants dry cleaned or hair cut? There's a service right there. There are even "sleep pods" where employees can take soporific-music-induced naps. All of this may sound idyllic, until you realize that workers need never go home—or stop working.[4]

For a glimpse of the continuity with the past and the profound readjustments that mark the twentieth- and twenty-first-century American scene, one could hardly turn to a more appropriate place than Kohler, Wisconsin, a town of 2,000 souls fifty-five miles north of Milwaukee along the Lake Michigan shore. Search for that town on the Internet, and first thing, "Destination: Kohler" pops up, a Web page featuring dazzling photos of local fishing, golf, spas, and food-and-wine gatherings. Hotel packages are offered at the American Club and the Inn on Woodlake, with the former described as "the Midwest's only AAA Five Diamond Resort Hotel providing unique, luxurious décor that creates a singular experience room by room."

There's little on the Web site to identify the place as the hometown of plumbing-fixtures manufacturer Kohler Co.

The site does say that the American Club once provided housing, meals, and recreation to immigrant employees who could not afford their own homes. But it doesn't say much about the work of those immigrants. Instead, Web surfers are encouraged to book a room in the club's Carriage House, visit the Kohler Waters Spa—where now there's no immigrant immiseration in sight. The late-October Kohler Wine & Food Experience is touted as offering brushes with celebrity chefs and sips of vintage plonk. The Memorial Day Kohler Festival of Beer, it suggests, is an opportunity to sample Wisconsin microbrewery products, not to mention the Blackwolf Run Beer Cup Golf Tournament. Clicking on the "Kohler: At Home" link brings the first hint that, oh, all of this is connected somehow with the toilet-and-tub maker.[5]

Life was not always like this in Kohler Village.

In the 1910s, Walter J. Kohler—head of the eponymous company founded in the 1870s to sell retrofitted "hog scalders" as bathtubs to a swelling immigrant population—decided his firm had outgrown its Sheboygan home. Like many others observed in this account, Kohler and his architect, W. C. Weeks, toured industrial garden villages in Europe. Then, upon returning, he engaged landscape architects from the Olmsted firm—who had also designed Vandergrift, Pennsylvania—along with engineers and town planners. The executive acquired a tract of land at the southwest edge of Sheboygan and in 1912 began to build the new burg that would be known as Kohler Village. The result was a picturesque settlement of winding streets, parks, and brick and frame houses amid plentiful greenery. A separate outfit, the Kohler Improvement Co., sold the completed houses to employees with the understanding that the company retained rights to buy them back if they were ever put on the market. As in Vandergrift, Pennsylvania, restrictive covenants limited the uses of these properties, including barring "immoral" enterprises and taverns.

For itself, the Kohler family erected a mansion called Riverbend, located not far from the company offices and foundry and adjacent to the Sheboygan River. Proud of its Austrian heritage, the family had long been at the center of Sheboygan cultural, social, and political life. In the 1890s, company founder John M. Kohler held several public offices including the mayoralty—he was endorsed by the *Sheboygan Telegram*, which cited his efforts in building the town's harbor and in local charity. His four sons were active in politics and various cultural institutions, with one son, Walter Sr. (founder of Kohler Village), and a grandson, Walter Jr., both serving as governors of Wisconsin.

By the mid-1930s, Kohler Village consisted of the company's 191-acre works—including a headquarters, foundry, ceramics plant, engine-making plant, and design center—along with 450 houses, half occupied by company officials and office workers and half by production workers. These residents composed less than 10 percent of Kohler's total workforce, but their experience had a big impact on company-employee relations. The American Club, which included a dormitory and eating hall, accommodated unmarried plant workers. Kohler Co. also financed fine schools and a large public auditorium. The village was governed by an elected board, which was nevertheless easily moved to rubber-stamp all company proposals.

Moreover, company employees benefited from Kohler corporate-welfare measures, including group life insurance, a pension plan, and banquets for the many recently naturalized U.S. citizens among the workforce.

Into the 1920s, wages of Kohler's 4,000 workers were higher than those at other area employers.

But as the Depression set in, labor relations deteriorated. Layoffs were concentrated among those who did not live in the model village. Those who continued working saw dramatic cuts in hours, and the wages of village residents were often garnished to pay home mortgages held by the company-affiliated Kohler Building and Loan Association. Checks issued for two weeks' work were for as little as 85 cents. Although the company continued to see itself as a generous, empathetic employer, Kohler workers decided they needed union representation, and turned to the American Federation of Labor (AFL), forming Federal Labor Union No. 18545. Thus began a thirty-year struggle for union recognition, marked by two violent strikes.

Initially, the company responded by forming a company union, the Kohler Workers Association (KWA), which it openly supplied with equipment and manpower. In July 1934, following a few bouts of unproductive negotiating with management, the AFL union went out on strike. Actions and rhetoric escalated quickly, with the union turning to mass picketing involving up to 4,000 people at the plant and management refusing to bargain with "law violators." Kohler Village employed 1,000 "special deputies" and armed them with machine guns, rifles, tear gas, and clubs. Only ten days after the strike began, a confrontation between these deputies and pickets led to rioting and violence in which forty-nine strikers were shot, most in the back, and two were killed. *The Nation* opined that the labor conflict signified "the rise and fall of America's most widely advertised venture in industrial paternalism." The issue quoted the testimony of federal mediator Father J. W. Maguire: "I have been in many strikes, but I never saw such needless and ruthless killing by supporters of the law. . . . You don't have to shoot people in the back when they are running away!"

Later that year, the National Labor Relations Board held a union-representation election, with both strikers and nonstrikers being allowed to vote. The result was a victory for the company union, KWA. That organization ran a campaign that utilized both petty bribery—cigarettes, candy, and sandwiches were distributed on the shop floor—and intimidation, with supervisors instructing workers to vote for KWA. Picketing by Local 18545 continued at the plant until 1941, when the company agreed to a contract with KWA so it might win more war contracts from the government.

In fact, the company's antiunion attitude remained, and another vicious strike broke out in 1954. Over the years, substandard pay and hazardous working conditions had prompted a change in the KWA, which became more militant and in 1952 affiliated with the United Auto Workers/CIO. It negotiated one contract with the company, but then Kohler dug in its heels. As the strike date approached, the company again adopted a siege mentality: Guards armed with shotguns, tear gas, and revolvers moved into the plant. The company also hired two private-detective agencies to spy on union supporters—and also, it later emerged, on National Labor Relations Board investigators. Kohler reopened its factory, utilizing a workforce of those who crossed picket lines and of new employees, and it made no effort to bargain with the union. For its part, the UAW once again employed mass picketing and demonstrations, and ultimately sponsored a nationwide boycott of Kohler products.

Despite numerous efforts at conciliation involving various elected officials, clergy, and others, the strike stretched on for eight years. In 1957, a U.S. Senate committee investigated what had become the country's longest-running labor dispute. Before that committee and elsewhere, company officials were open about their thinking. Chief counsel Lyman Conger—balding, thin, and bespectacled, the very picture of a tightwad—said he believed that the union was "trying to overthrow all industry, not just the Kohler company, but all industry." Herbert V. Kohler, who was now the company's president, accused the union of promoting "class hatred" and serving "the Marxian doctrine."

Over the years, the company consistently accused "outsiders" of stirring up the labor discontent. In response to the union boycott, Herbert Kohler maintained a busy schedule of speaking to business groups across the country. Before a Salt Lake City audience, the portly, Teutonic executive maintained that UAW President Walter Reuther was "a Moscow-trained socialist." (Reuther was in fact a staunch anticommunist.) Kohler offered many complaints about the union, especially union "violence." But the true sticking point seemed to be what he saw as the union's attempt to usurp management rights in such matters as shop rules, merit pay, subcontracting of work, and working hours.[6]

The walkout finally ended thanks to the 1960 intervention of the National Labor Relations Board, which ruled it an "unfair labor practice strike" and said that by law all strikers must be restored to their jobs. The U.S. Supreme Court ultimately upheld that ruling, and in 1965 the company agreed to pay $4.5 million in back wages and pension money to settle all unfair labor practice charges. Several one-year contracts were subsequently negotiated with the UAW.[7]

So, what happened over subsequent years to turn Kohler Village from a maelstrom of class warfare into a bliss-inducing locus of heated-rock massages and gourmet food?

I tried to ask, but the company said its current CEO was unavailable for comment. It could just be that the change was motivated by golf—and, perhaps, modern marketing.

By the early 1970s, the older generation of Kohler corporate leaders was gone from the scene. Herbert V. Kohler Sr. had died in 1969, and in 1972, thirty-three-year-old Herbert V. Kohler Jr. became company chairman and chief executive. In time, Junior would establish a reputation as a world-class golf nut. He would develop four primo golf courses in Wisconsin and purchase two shrines, the Duke's Course and the Old Course Hotel, in the birthplace and mecca of the sport, St. Andrews, Scotland. In 2006, the *Wall Street Journal* would call such endeavors "vanity projects," suggesting that they made no economic sense. In addition to Herb Kohler, other "golf-bewitched billionaires," according to the *Journal*, included Reebok International founder Paul Fireman and investor Charles Schwab, each of whom had constructed on the choicest bits of real estate, golf links that were for duffers the ne plus ultra.

But another line of argument, promoted in the same publication, suggested that such courses were simply the shrewdest kind of marketing. Along with such brands as Viking stove and Cuisinart kitchen appliances, Kohler had chosen to generate a greater awareness of its brands via oases aimed at tourists. Just as Viking had constructed a posh hotel near its Mississippi headquarters—complete with a mud-bath- and massage-ready spa—Kohler's St. Andrews and Wisconsin hotels and golf courses were "a very big part of its image," in the terms of a company spokeswoman. The Old Course Hotel—no landmark-status restrictions there, it seems—would soon sport Kohler faucets and bathroom fixtures, Ann Sacks tiles (another company-owned brand), and Baker Furniture (ditto). In the Wisconsin town, one could tour the factory and the company Design Center, and then repair to the links to get in at least nine holes, all in advance of happy hour.[8]

If Kohler Co.'s unusual grab-bag of enterprises—resorts, bath fixtures, furniture, small engines, and generators—strikes some as weird . . . well, no matter. Kohler is virtually a privately held company, thanks to a 1998 arrangement that placed control of voting shares in a family-owned trust and issued nonvoting stock to other shareholders.[9]

Moreover, the evolution of the company and its town represents not so much a repudiation of America's industrial past as an adjustment to modern economic realities. The trend of deindustrialization is well-advanced in the United States, having first been described in the late 1970s. Americans now live in a postindustrial society, where industrial work has come to seem a bit quaint, even campy. Kohler factory tours are handled by old-timers demonstrating hallowed verities—as when a quality-control inspector strikes finished toilets with a mallet, seeking that crystal-goblet-like sound that ensures it to be free of defects.

That same adjustment to modern economics can be found in many other places. In Hershey, Pennsylvania, there are no tours of the chocolate-making plant (tourists might bring germs in with them, it seems). But visitors can still take a twelve-minute ride through a simulated chocolate factory—Hershey's Chocolate World—and absorb just how those chocolate Kisses and Hershey bars are made. Once that excursion is at an end, there is—after a store where visitors are welcome to buy as much candy as they'd like—HersheyPark, the 110-acre Disneyland-like playground that offers rides, live entertainment, and "photo opps with HERSHEY'S Product Characters." There's an eleven-acre zoo, botanical gardens, four golf courses, and more. Hershey also bridges the gap between fun sites and more education-oriented locations: The Hershey Museum offers a glimpse of the company's history, and Hershey Community Archives provide scholars with a range of historical materials including photographs, diaries, and oral-history interviews with company veterans.[10]

Lowell, Massachusetts, may be the apotheosis of the historic company town as educational experience. The Lowell National Historical Park, operated by the U.S. National Park Service, gives visitors a glimpse of cotton-mill labor: In a weave room in the former Boott Cotton Mills, workers show off operating looms. As protection against the shattering noise, guests are handed earplugs as they enter the area. A nearby boardinghouse exhibit demonstrates what it was like to be a Lowell mill girl in the 1840s—what they ate, where they slept, and how they spent their working lives and free time. There's also a working water wheel/turbine and boat tours on the canals and river. The national park features numerous music and arts festivals, youth programs, a day camp, and a summer music series with such performers as Los Lobos and Hot Tuna. The New England Quilt Museum has its own quilt festival. The American Textile History Museum spotlights the art, science, and history of textiles. And there are numerous scholarly and historical enterprises on the fringes of the national park, including the Center for Lowell History and the Tsongas Industrial History Center, which offers resources to public schools.

As a good stopover point that's more than halfway between New York City and Niagara Falls, Corning, New York, welcomes thousands of tourists each year. The world-class Corning Museum of Glass features stunning art-glass displays, glassblowing demonstrations, historical exhibits on how the company came to make such products as Corningware and fiberglass, and workshops in which kids get to construct their own vitreous souvenirs. On downtown Market Street a short ride away, there's the Gaffer District with various shops, restaurants, and outdoor concerts including seasonal harvest and tree-lighting festivals. The town also is home to the Rockwell Museum of Western Art and a Ladies Professional Golf Association tournament, and it's just a hop to the Finger Lakes wineries and Watkins Glen car racing.

Not even remote coal towns are exempt from makeovers for the tourist trade. In Colorado, where miners once exchanged rifle fire with vigilantes and militiamen, skiers now schuss down the slopes. Crested Butte, once home to silver and coal mines, features a resort with sixteen ski lifts capable of handling more than 20,000 people per hour. There are 121 trails, a superpipe for snowboard daredevils, a kids' park, and a variety of jumps and intermediate runs. Vacation home developments have surged in the Purgatoire Valley near Trinidad, site of the 1913 mass labor march that preceded the events in Ludlow.

And perhaps the most unlikely tourist traps of all exist at the former Manhattan Project towns of Oak Ridge, Tennessee, and Hanford, Washington, where visitors are allowed to examine no-longer-used bomb-making facilities, now designated as National Historic Landmarks. In Oak Ridge, visitors get to view Y-12 and K-25, and at X-10 they see an actual graphite reactor and its control room. The Museum of Science and Energy features "atom-smasher" demonstrations. Hanford, with its five "cocooned" nuclear reactors and radioactive-waste deposits, is one of the most toxic sites on the planet. Nevertheless, the Energy Department conducts tours there of the B Reactor, described by the *New York Times* as a "three-story square of iron, steel and Masonite housed in a block of graphite." Visitors get to inspect the control room as the tour guide explains why the remote site was chosen for the Manhattan Project and how plutonium was produced. After the tour, Hanford visitors can take in the splendors of the adjacent Columbia River and consider the abundant flora and fauna in the surrounding Hanford Reach National Monument. Once again, the area sports wineries and golf courses to complement its warm climate.[11]

One final—for now—development merits observation: the burgeoning of remote outposts of new high-tech industries. Among these are Google's data centers across the U.S., including its Project 02 on the Columbia River in Oregon, and the solar-energy installations in the Southwestern deserts. But can these be anything like company "towns" if the residents are primarily machines tended by a few humans?

Every one of Google's data centers costs the company around $600 million, but only two hundred human attendants are necessary to mind the generally fail-safe equipment. The huge center near The Dalles, Oregon, consists of three mammoth, low-slung buildings on thirty acres, housing tens of thousands of inexpensive processors and disks. All this computing power generates lots of heat—and so large rooftop cooling systems are necessary. Also within the fenced perimeter are an administration building, an electrical substation, and a "transient employee dormitory building."

As negotiations to make arrangements proceeded during 2005, Google insisted upon secrecy to keep competitors Microsoft and Yahoo in the dark, making local officials sign confidentiality agreements. But when Google went public with its $1.87 million land purchase that year, the natives waxed enthusiastic about the millions of dollars in investment they saw forthcoming, along with the fifty to one hundred jobs that would be created, each paying an average of $60,000. Fifty to one hundred jobs from deep-pocketed Google—that's all? In the United States today, people take what they can get.

A big draw for Google: plentiful and cheap electricity, supplied by Bonneville Power's hydroelectric and nuclear-power facilities. Google negotiated a guarantee of the electricity along with tax exemptions and a city-built fiber-optic network. Manpower was not a major concern.[12]

Google is not alone in building such installations. Microsoft and Yahoo also have data centers in the Columbia River region, near Quincy, Washington. Moreover, data centers are sprouting across the globe—in Siberia and Ireland (Microsoft) and in China (AT&T). For all of these companies, the main attraction is cheap power.[13]

Solar-energy outfits are also on the edge of a building boom, particularly in such remote areas as the deserts of the American Southwest where sunlight is plentiful. Solar-thermal company Stirling Energy Systems has numerous projects afoot, including plans to build the "world's largest solar energy generating plant" on 6,500 acres in California's Imperial Valley desert. The facility would include 30,000 solar-energy concentrators—each one composed of a mirrored dish forty feet in diameter, an engine that's driven by the heat from the dish, and an electric generator powered by the engine. Far from a pipe dream, the company already has agreements to supply power to San Diego Gas & Electric and Southern California Edison. A different technology—perhaps the one most familiar to most Americans—uses photovoltaic panels. Largely associated with private-home-rooftop applications, SunPower Corp. and OptiSolar are now employing the panels in large projects, including two big plants announced in 2008, both in San Luis Obispo County, California.[14]

With twenty-five states so far having mandated a greater use of "green power"—California now requires that 33 percent of its electricity come from renewable sources by 2020—solar, wind, and wave technologies could play a big role in the country's energy future, provided the companies can get costs low enough to compete with coal-fired plants.[15]

Green-energy promoters like to say that renewable-energy plants generate lots of jobs: The American Wind Industry Association, for example, announced that its companies had more workers than in all of coal mining during 2008, about 85,000. Even if one accepts these figures—and many dispute them or challenge their significance—these are largely construction and manufacturing jobs, not long-term maintenance positions. In Arizona, a 280-megawatt solar project was announced in 2008 by Arizona Public Service and Spanish company Abengoa Solar. The job payoff for what Abengoa claims will be "the largest solar power plant in the world": 1,500 in construction and only 88 permanent jobs at the Gila Bend site, sixty miles southwest of Phoenix. That same year, Aspen Environmental Group, a Sacramento-based consultancy, estimated that if geothermal and wind installations were substituted for a coal-fired plant that Sierra Pacific Power proposed to build in Nevada, five times more jobs would be created. Translation: 500 to 750 green jobs, at most.[16]

Whether new installations are operated by Google, Microsoft, or one of the renewable-energy companies, none seems likely to compare to the company towns built in past decades, either in size or importance. From textiles in New England and the Piedmont region to steel and a variety of industries in the Midwest, extractive operations across the country, and shipbuilding on the coasts, over the decades American companies erected industrial powerhouses supported by their own towns, large and small. These burgs were the scenes of high drama: empire-building, urban landscaping, labor strife, abject misery, upward mobility, and often urban decay. By comparison, such new-economy operations seem the settings for a more modest version of human theater. They might best be thought of as something like lighthouses—out-of-the-way but necessary installations, attended by minders who have no aversion to solitude.

Of the country's growing industries—which also include medicine and energy—tourism seems the most likely to become the mainstay of established and burgeoning company towns. It is an industry notoriously prone to starts and fits, as tourism-dependent lands from the Caribbean to Africa can attest. But then nothing in the American experience has been particularly predictable. Just consider the sturdy brick edifices in Lowell—built to last many lifetimes and now abandoned, like the great pyramids, to the fickle vicissitudes of history.

CONCLUSION

A Tale of Two Cities

History . . . must speak, not merely of the setting up there of factories and spindles, but of the wise and prudent foresight, so characteristic of the New England character; which in the beginning made provision for religious worship, schools, a hospital for the sick, and established a system of management, well calculated to preserve the morals of the people there to be gathered.

—Letter of Merrimack Manufacturing Co. Treasurer
F. B. Crowninshield and others to Lowell, Massachusetts,
cofounder Nathan Appleton, 1858[1]

In a land of plenty, every corporate would-be town-builder confronted questions of scarcity: Where could one best locate the appropriate raw materials along with the power and talent to fuel, conceptualize, and extract or manufacture a product? Often, raw materials proved to be the primary concern. The Boston Associates chose East Chelmsford, Massachusetts, for its water power—and then over the next hundred-plus years, managers at Lowell struggled with the question of manpower. Milton Hershey selected a home base in rural Pennsylvania for its dairy farms and upright labor force; his product, chocolate, seemed to practically sell itself as the country grew up, and with few exceptions, employees seemed to find contentment in the well-appointed town of Hershey. Coal and copper barons, oil magnates, and timber kings had little choice over location—they had to locate where the limited resources existed and hope either via carrot or stick to induce working people to follow. The creators of the Manhattan Project, too, were restricted in their choice of location: Electricity and isolation were their key considerations.

So, with some regularity, managers of company-town-domiciled businesses faced a conundrum: What human-relations formula would serve them best? What combination of policies toward their workers and the surrounding community would lead to the most productive outcome? No matter their outlook—utopian paternalist or exploitative despot—managers and their companies were constrained in how they could treat their employees not only by their own outlooks but by the market. Remember, too, that very few companies lived at either end of the spectrum. Rather, all companies are some mix of utopia and exploitationville—and their direction is often set by both economic and strategic considerations.

Managers have inclined toward utopian, or at least more benevolent, policies when they faced some of the following:

- A labor shortage, as in early Lowell. When necessary workers are rare, it makes sense to treat them well.
- A need to retain a skilled labor force. Among others, this applies to the fabric- and woodworkers at Pullman, Corning Glass Works' professional glassblowers, and the carefully screened and painstakingly trained employees at the U.S.-residing Japanese auto companies.
- Fat margins, or at least a high level of profitability. Why not share the bounty, which in some cases must seem like a gift from above? Milton Hershey shrewdly cast aside caramel-making for chocolates, but no one could have foreseen the success he went on to enjoy. Other highly successful and generous employers included shipbuilder Henry J. Kaiser, oil baron Frank Phillips, and the Murphy clan who managed Pacific Lumber and Scotia, California, for ninety years.
- A remote location—where it was difficult to get and keep workers— or at least location within a small town where the corporation wished to cultivate a sense of community. Here again, Pacific Lumber is representative of an employer stuck in an out-of-the-way outpost. Maytag seemed to find it desirable to cultivate a sense of community within Newton, Iowa. The same was true, for per-

haps fifty years, for Geo. A. Hormel and its hometown of Austin, Minnesota..

- A desire for positive public relations. Starting in the 1910s, American companies became increasingly aware that good feelings radiating from a blessed hometown could help them sell products. Pullman, Hershey, Corning, Phillips, Maytag, Hormel, and even the Rockefellers' Colorado Fuel and Iron worked at community relations as public relations.

- A liberal or progressive national political climate. This consideration is related to public relations. To take a contemporary example, in the 1990s, Wal-Mart was unflinchingly stingy toward its employees, shirking on overtime pay and offering few benefits. After the turn of the twenty-first century, the company seemed nonplussed to discover that the public no longer found its everyday low prices to be sufficient—and it started making small changes in employee relations. Similar circumstances affected the Rockefeller coal operations during what became known as the Progressive Era and Harlan County coal operators during Franklin Roosevelt's New Deal. Finally, since they first came here in the 1980s, Japanese automakers with U.S. operations have been keenly aware that they must work hard to be perceived as good neighbors rather than as interlopers who are stealing away American jobs and wealth.

On the other hand, executives have cared less about progressive relations with communities and employees when the following conditions applied:

- A need for only unskilled workers, and a supply of such labor is available. Coal operators and steelmakers sometimes had to scramble to recruit workers, but despite punishing conditions on the job, the employers generally found a way to fill openings. Immigration from Europe helped supply Appalachian mines, Pennsylvania and Illinois steel mills, and textile mills in the Northeast. Carolina textile mills drew a supply of willing workers from the "cracker proletariat" that was being forced to abandon subsistence agriculture. Today's midwestern meatpacking concerns experience huge labor turnover thanks to considerable workplace dangers and miserable pay—but their labor-force ranks draw a steady infusion of new-comers from Latin America and Asia, with less-than-salubrious results for towns across Iowa, Nebraska, Kansas, and southern Minnesota.

- Margins are perceived to be low—or the future competitive situation is uncertain. Appalachian coal operators said they had no choice but to squeeze their workers: They had to absorb higher freight rates than did mines in the Midwest. Copper miner Phelps Dodge regularly bemoaned the huge swings in copper prices, along with the lower pay at competitors in South America. Textile companies north and south regularly pointed toward the lower wages being paid by rival companies, and U.S. meatpackers justified their brutal wage cuts of the late twentieth century on the cutthroat competitive situation.

- Their products are "commodity" wares—where public relations, branding, advertising, and so forth have little impact on sales. Few consumers directly purchase steel or very much coal, so such producers' reputation for good or evil had little impact on the bottom line. Except for a few branded products, the source of much of the meat that is sold in supermarkets is a mystery to purchasers. That was also true for the yards of textiles that companies once marketed with little regard for brand names.

- Production at a remote location. Yes, it can go either way, as the Appalachian coal barons demonstrated: A company can get workers to come from far away and keep them from leaving via various strategems. As I speculated earlier, the filthy and dangerous work of coal mining may have been enough to get coal operators to feel that they must treat workers as near prisoners rather than as valued assets. If the location is remote, who's to notice if workers and communities are treated poorly?

- A conservative national political climate prevails. Pullman's tough policies toward his workers were backed by President Grover Cleveland, if not always by local Illinois politicians. Carnegie Steel and U.S. Steel long found support for their harsh labor-and-community policies from big-business-oriented federal administrations. Meatpackers including Hormel shifted away from "utopian" labor relations once the laissez-faire Reagan administration seemed to give them permission with its rhetoric and its firing of federal air-traffic controllers in a labor dispute.

That said, a measure of managerial discretion always exists.

Pacific Lumber, for example, adopted self-described "paternalistic" policies despite that company's low-skilled workforce. It doesn't take a rocket scientist to make a Hershey bar or a Maytag washer. And almost all of Henry J. Kaiser's shipyard workers were low-skilled.

It is hard to deny that, for example, the mistreatment of coal miners by Colorado Fuel and Iron or the high-handedness exhibited by U.S. Steel toward its steelworkers had a lot to do with management's elitist, even hostile, attitude toward them. "I can hire half of the working class to shoot the other half," steel man Henry Clay Frick famously boasted before the bloody 1892 strike and shootout in Homestead, Pennsylvania. U.S. Steel's competitive situation steadily worsened over the course of the twentieth century—but long before this became clear, the corporation insisted that it meant to do little to develop Gary, Indiana. U.S. Steel could have done more for the town, but it very openly and publicly opted for a hands-off policy.

The changed competitive situation facing Lowell's Boston Associates and Hormel led these companies to dramatically revise their human-relations policies. But Corning Inc., too, has seen its bottom line hammered—and through thick and thin, that company has largely maintained a consistent, progressive posture toward the town of Corning and its employees.

The bottom line: American conservatives and many businessmen have long maintained that all problems can be solved via the free market and private enterprise. But only one of the strains of business thinking that we've discussed here recognizes that many social problems are also problems that business has a proper role in addressing. Only if business recognizes the existence of this "utopian" tradition of business practice and continues to develop it can the free-market-solves-all-woes argument be supported.

This is more than a suggestion that everyone "be nice." It is an argument that companies need to recognize, where employees are concerned, one of the fundamentals of markets—the necessity of fair dealing, good behavior, and trust. Economists often speak of these elements as a prerequisite for the development of relationships between buyers and sellers, and between enterprise and investors. Who would buy anything from a company, or invest in it, if people thought it produced shoddy or dangerous merchandise? The same mutual respect should characterize relations between companies and their employees and hometowns, without whose input and support little gets done.

Nor must one be a closet socialist to agree with such sentiments. In his well-known essay "The Social Responsibility of Business Is to Increase Its Profits," conservative economist Milton Friedman railed against the notion that an executive should use corporate resources for social purposes, which he said necessarily implied "that he is to act in some way that is not in the interest of his employers." The very idea: squandering the stockholders' money! But even Friedman admitted that "it may well be in the long run interest of a corporation that is a major employer in a small community to devote resources to providing amenities to that community or to improving its government." Such "hypocritical window dressing," he admitted, could have "worthwhile effects." I don't regard such doings as necessarily hypocritical—and neither did the benevolent paternalists at Hershey, Corning, Kaiser's shipyards, or Pacific Lumber.[2]

There are contemporary stirrings in this direction. "Social entrepreneurship" has become a hot trend in business-education circles. For example, in 1998, faculty at Harvard Business School and a select group of corporate executives began an effort to get corporations to address social needs, from public education to inner-city job creation. Harvard's Initiative on Social Enterprise sponsors forums on corporate social responsibility and offers fellowships to recent Harvard B-school graduates who are launching enterprises "with a central focus on creating social value." The Harvard effort is global in orientation, favoring Third World betterment (Milton Friedman would howl), but it also encourages involvement with domestic projects such as early-childhood literacy programs. Faculty member Rosabeth Moss Kanter describes the thinking behind the initiative, along with the benevolent efforts of many U.S. companies, in her recent book, *SuperCorp: How Vanguard Companies Create Innovation, Profits, Growth, and Social Good.*[3]

The *Stanford Social Innovation Review*, published by that university's business school, considers the same matters as the Harvard project. Recent articles probe corporate philanthropy, nonprofits management, "responsible" investing, and developing-world concerns. Along with the San Francisco–based Tides Foundation, the *Review* sponsors a yearly Momentum conference, where social entrepreneurs and philanthropists connect and discuss issues. The Wharton School at the University of Pennsylvania also sponsors conferences and courses on social entrepreneurship.[4]

Additionally, former Microsoft chairman Bill Gates made headlines in 2008 with a call for "creative capitalism" to help solve the world's problems. The suggestion was hotly debated online and ultimately in the pages of a book, *Creative Capitalism*, compiled by journalist Michael Kinsley. Observing a similar impulse, numerous companies are often cited for their social contributions, including Southwest Airlines, Costco, and Google. These corporations, in the words of Harvard Business School professor Nancy F. Koehn, "meet the needs of a broader set of stakeholders than shareholders."[5]

Such contemporary projects, though, take little recognition of the historical record, which shows a long tradition of business social experimentation and efforts at social betterment. Business utopias of the past and present have not always succeeded—many, in fact, were colossal failures. But particularly in these recession years, when the temptation is to bear down ever harder on those who have managed to keep their jobs, there should be a greater recognition of this strain in U.S. culture and civilization. Today's social-enterprise champions could do worse than to reflect upon the diverse experience of America's company towns.

ACKNOWLEDGMENTS

This book is the product of many years' experience and reflection. As a native Tennessean, I have long been acquainted with Oak Ridge, the daunting atomic city in the far eastern part of the state. In the 1970s, I lived in Massachusetts and became familiar with the imposing brick mills and decaying tenements of such factory towns as Lowell, Lawrence, Fall River, and Adams, Massachusetts, and Manchester, New Hampshire.

In the 1980s, I traveled to the Carolinas, Alabama, Georgia, and Virginia on numerous occasions—to such places as Roanoke Rapids and Kannapolis, North Carolina; Darlington, South Carolina; Columbus, Georgia; Galax, Virginia; and Cordova, Alabama, as a member of the staff of the Amalgamated Clothing and Textile Workers Union. But it was later in that decade that a company town—and company-town culture—made its greatest impression on me, in Austin, Minnesota. I spent many weeks there as a member of a consultancy that worked with labor organizations, and I traveled with Hormel union local members to Dubuque, Ottumwa, and Sioux City, Iowa; Fremont, Nebraska; Dakota City, South Dakota; and other meatpacking towns. It was also during that time that headlines trumpeted traumatic industrial events in such locales as Watsonville, California; Morenci, Arizona; Mahwah, New Jersey; and Flint, Michigan.

Over the decades, I also passed through Gary, Indiana; Dearborn, Michigan; Hershey, Pennsylvania; Amana, Iowa; Pawtucket and Woonsocket, Rhode Island; and Corning, New York. And I became aware that there existed no general history of the company town in America. This book is an effort to right that situation.

The list of friends and colleagues from whom I learned about such places is long. It includes Tom Herriman, Sandra Cate, Bob Gumpert, Gretchen Donart, Victoria Williams, Ed Allen, Ray Rogers, Jim Guyette, Peter Winkels, Carole and Jim Apold, Merrill Evans, Peter Rachleff, and Dick Blin.

Onetime *BusinessWeek* colleague Christopher Farrell and former Rhodes College history professor James Lanier read the manuscript and made very useful suggestions. Any errors or omissions in the book are, of course, my fault alone. My agent James Levine was an early believer in the project and immediately made useful suggestions for additions. My editor, Tim Sullivan, was ever helpful with ideas and is probably due extra remuneration for his ready encouragement and emotional support during dark moments of that unhappy year, 2009. Other Basic Books stalwarts who provided invaluable service include publisher John Sherer, publicity director Michele Jacob, marketing director Rick Joyce, and Internet marketing chief Peter Costanzo, who provided advice and technical expertise in support of my halting efforts in the digital realm. And finally, none of this would have been possible without my loving and ever-responsive wife and soul mate, Emily M. Bass.

NOTES

Introduction

1. William F. Nolan, *Hammett: A Life at the Edge* (New York: Congdon & Weed, 1983), pp. 13, 75–77; Melvyn Dubofsky, *We Shall Be All: A History of the IWW* (New York: Quadrangle Books, 1969), pp. 186–187; Dorothy Gallagher, *All the Right Enemies: The Life and Murder of Carlo Tresca* (New Brunswick, NJ: Rutgers University Press, 1988), p. 65.

2. Dashiell Hammett, *Red Harvest*, in *The Novels of Dashiell Hammett* (New York: Alfred A. Knopf, 1965), p. 3.

3. Ron Chernow, *Titan: The Life of John D. Rockefeller, Sr.* (New York: Random House, 1998), pp. 378–379.

4. John Gunther, *Inside U.S.A.* (New York: New Press, 1997), pp. 166–172. Originally published in 1946.

5. John Markoff and Saul Hansell, "Hiding in Plain Sight, Google Seeks More Power," *New York Times*, June 14, 2006.

6. Housing statistic in Stuart D. Brandes, *American Welfare Capitalism 1889–1940* (Chicago: University of Chicago Press, 1976), p. 38.

Chapter 1: A City on a Hill

1. Henry David Thoreau, "A Week on the Concord and Merrimack Rivers," in *Walden and Other Writings of Henry David Thoreau*, ed. Brooks Atkinson (New York: Modern Library, 1937), pp. 340–341. Originally published in 1839.

2. E. J. Hobsbawm, *Industry and Empire* (Harmondsworth, England: Penguin Books, 1968), p. 56.

3. Gary Kulik, Roger Parks, and Theodore Z. Penn, eds., *The New England Mill Village, 1790–1860* (Cambridge and London: MIT Press, 1982), p. xxiii.

4. Kulik et al., *The New England Mill Village*, pp. xxiv–xxv; Thomas Dublin, *Women at Work: The Transformation of Work and Community in Lowell, Massachusetts, 1826–1860* (New York: Columbia University Press, 1979), pp. 15–16.

5. Robert F. Dalzell Jr., *Enterprising Elite: The Boston Associates and the World They Made* (Cambridge, MA: Harvard University Press, 1987), p. 12.

6. Friedrich Engels, *The Condition of the Working Class in England* (London: Panther Books, 1969), pp. 80–96. Originally written in 1844.

7. Hobsbawm, *Industry and Empire*, p. 56.

8. Barbara Freese, *Coal: A Human History* (Cambridge, MA: Perseus Publishing, 2003), p. 81.

9. Kulik et al., *The New England Mill Village*, pp. xxv–xxxi.

10. Ibid., p. xxvi; Thomas Dublin, *Lowell: The Story of an Industrial City* (Washington, DC: Department of the Interior, 1992), pp. 21–32; Dalzell, *Enterprising Elite*, p. 6.

11. Nathan Appleton, *Introduction of the Power Loom and Origin of Lowell* (Lowell, MA: B. H. Penhallow, 1858), pp. 1–14.

12. Ibid., p. 12–14; Dalzell, *Enterprising Elite*, pp. 38–44; *Correspondence Between Nathan Appleton and John A. Lowell in Relation to the Early History of the City of Lowell* (Boston: Eastburn's Press, 1848), pp. 5–11, 18.

13. Ron Chernow, *Alexander Hamilton* (New York: Penguin Press, 2004), pp. 370–374, 386–388.

14. Richard C. Wade, *The Urban Frontier: Pioneer Life in Early Pittsburgh, Cincinnati, Lexington, Louisville, and St. Louis* (Chicago: University of Chicago Press, 1959), pp. 21, 190–195; Sam Bass Warner Jr., *The Urban Wilderness: A History of the American City* (Berkeley: University of California Press, 1972), pp. 70–71.

15. Harriet H. Robinson, *Loom and Spindle or Life Among the Early Mill Girls* (New York: T. Y. Crowell, 1898), p. 5.

16. Appleton, *Introduction of the Power Loom and Origin of Lowell*, pp. 23–25, 32; Joseph Lipchitz, "The Golden Age," in *Cotton Was King: A History of Lowell, Massachusetts*, ed. Arthur L. Eno (Somersworth, NH: New Hampshire Publishing Co., 1976), pp. 84–86; John Coolidge, *Mill and Mansion: A Study of Architecture and Society in Lowell, Massachusetts, 1820–1865* (New York: Columbia University Press, 1942), pp. 28, 183; Coolidge notes that, unfortunately, only a few quotes remain from Boott's diary, which is now lost.

17. Appleton, *Introduction of the Power Loom and Origin of Lowell*, pp. 28–31; Dublin, *Women at Work*, pp. 20–22, 61–62, 133–134; Dublin, *Lowell*, pp. 36–39; Dalzell, *Enterprising Elite*, pp. 49–50; Coolidge, *Mill and Mansion*, pp. 32–62; Michel Chevalier, *Society, Manners, and Politics in the United States: Being a Series of Letters on North America* (Boston: Weeks, Jordan & Co., 1839), pp. 128–129; Robinson, *Loom and Spindle*, pp. 8–9.

18. Appleton, *Introduction of the Power Loom and Origin of Lowell*, p. 16; Chevalier, *Society, Manners, and Politics in the United States*, pp. 133–142; Charles Dickens, *Amer-

ican Notes (London and New York: Cassell & Co., n.d.), pp. 55–58; *The Lowell Offering*, ed. Benita Eisler (New York: W. W. Norton & Co., 1977), pp. 82, 161–162; Harriet Martineau, *Society in America*, vol. 2 (New York: Saunders and Otley, 1837), pp. 57–58.

19. For a discussion of nineteenth-century women's role as civilizing agents, see William R. Taylor, *Cavalier and Yankee: The Old South and American National Character* (New York: Harper & Row, 1969), pp. 118–122; Nancy Zaroulis, "Daughters of Freemen," in *Cotton Was King*, pp. 107–108; Norman Ware, *The Industrial Worker, 1840–1860: The Reaction of American Industrial Society to the Advance of the Industrial Revolution* (Chicago: Quadrangle Books, 1964), pp. 72–74, 107–110.

20. Dublin, *Women at Work*, pp. 35–40, 80; Dublin, *Lowell*, p. 40–50.

21. Ware, *The Industrial Worker*, pp. 74–78, 84, 148; Kulik et al., *The New England Mill Village*, p. 265.

22. Dublin, *Women at Work*, pp. 86–107.

23. Ibid., pp.108–123; Ware, *The Industrial Worker*, p. 88. In 1842, the *Offering* was taken over by the *Lowell Courier*, which was controlled by the corporations. When revived in 1847 as the *New England Offering*, it was purely an organ of company propaganda.

24. Ware, *The Industrial Worker*, pp. 102–106, 149–151; Dublin, *Women at Work*, pp. 135–144.

25. Dalzell, *Enterprising Elite*, pp. 51, 69–81, 225; Dublin, *Lowell*, p. 67; Ware, *The Industrial Worker*, pp. 105, 152; Fidelia O. Brown, "Decline and Fall: The End of the Dream," in *Cotton Was King*, pp. 143–144; Manchester, New Hampshire, planned and developed in 1837, was modeled on Lowell, and originally used a workforce of unmarried Yankee women living in boardinghouses. In the final decades of the century, the separate corporations there were merged into the Amoskeag Co., which for a time was proprietor of the world's largest textile factory. See Tamara K. Hareven and Randolph Langenbach, *Amoskeag: Life and Work in an American Factory-City* (New York: Pantheon, 1978).

26. Brown, "Decline and Fall," pp. 142, 145–155; Dublin, *Lowell*, pp. 65–77.

27. Coolidge, *Mill and Mansion*, 2nd ed., p. vii; Louis Adamic, *My America, 1928–1938* (New York: DaCapo Press, 1976), pp. 263–278.

28. Dublin, *Lowell*, pp. 82–89; Brown, "Decline and Fall," p. 155.

29. Jack Kerouac, *The Town and the City* (New York: Harcourt Brace & Co., 1950), p. 46.

30. Coolidge, *Mill and Mansion*, 1942 ed., p. 113.

Chapter 2: Utopia

1. Stanley Buder, *Pullman: An Experiment in Industrial Order and Community Planning, 1880–1930* (New York: Oxford University Press, 1967), p. 4; Sir Peter Hall, *Cities in Civilization* (New York: Pantheon Books, 1998), pp. 746–747. New York

population figures are complicated by the fact that the city was growing physically as well, absorbing Brooklyn, Queens, and Richmond in 1898. For consistency's sake, the figures given are for the boroughs of Manhattan and the Bronx only.

2. Strong reprinted in *Popular Culture and Industrialism 1865–1890*, ed. Henry Nash Smith (Garden City, NY: Anchor Books, 1967), p. 173; Howe reprinted in *The Progressive Years*, ed. Otis Pease (New York: George Braziller, 1962), pp. 25–57.

3. Philip S. Foner, *The Great Labor Uprising of 1877* (New York: Monad Press, 1977), pp. 8–9; American Social History Project, *Who Built America*, vol. 2 (New York: Pantheon, 1992), pp. xxiv–xxviii.

4. Buder, *Pullman*, p. 35.

5. William O. Stoddard, *Men of Business* (New York: Charles Scribner's Sons, 1893), pp. 248–249; Buder, *Pullman*, pp. 4–6.

6. Buder, *Pullman*, pp. 8–11; Carroll R. Harding, *George M. Pullman and the Pullman Company* (New York: Newcomen Society, 1951), pp. 9–14; Louis Menand, *The Metaphysical Club: A Story of Ideas in America* (New York: Farrar, Straus & Giroux, 2001), pp. 289–290.

7. Buder, *Pullman*, pp. 42–43; Menand, *The Metaphysical Club*, pp. 289–316. In 1894, a New York newspaper reprinted a letter from Pullman to "a prominent resident of Chicago," amplifying the magnate's belief that the town had had a positive effect upon its workers. "You lay much stress on the fact that there has been no destruction of property at Pullman [during the strike]. . . . May not, perhaps, some credit be given to the administration of the company, which prohibits drinking saloons and provides various sources of elevation of character?" *New York Sun*, July 5, 1894, reprinted in *The Strike at Pullman: Statements of President George M. Pullman and Second Vice-President T. H. Wickes Before the U.S. Strike Commission* (Washington, DC: Government Printing Office, 1895), p. 28.

8. Buder, *Pullman*, pp. 49–74; Richard T. Ely, "Pullman: A Social Study," *Harper's New Monthly Magazine*, 1884–1885, pp. 458–461.

9. Ely, "Pullman: A Social Study," p. 457.

10. Harding, *George M. Pullman and the Pullman Company*, p. 25. In his statement before the U.S. Strike Commission, Pullman repeatedly insisted that the company had two businesses, railroad-car production and real estate, and that "the renting of the dwellings and the employment of workmen at Pullman are in no way tied together." See *The Strike at Pullman*, p. 28.

11. Edward Chase Kirkland, *Dream & Thought in the Business Community, 1860–1900* (Chicago: Quadrangle Books, 1964), pp. 19–23, 154–155. Others in the business community agreed with Pullman's approach, holding the factory and town to be "exemplifications of practical philanthropy based upon business sagacity." *Iron Age*, July 12, 1894, quoted in Sven Beckert, *The Monied Metropolis: New York City and the Consolidation of the American Bourgeoisie, 1850–1896* (Cambridge: Cambridge University Press, 2001), p. 446, note 117.

12. Buder, *Pullman*, pp. 97–103; Ely, "Pullman: A Social Study," pp. 460, 465.

13. Reprinted as an addendum in *The Strike at Pullman*, p. 27; also U.S. Strike Commission, *Report on the Chicago Strike of June–July 1894*, Senate Executive Document No. 7, 53rd Congress, 3rd Session (Washington, DC: Government Printing Office, 1895), p. 530.

14. Buder, *Pullman*, pp. 129–199; American Social History Project, *Who Built America*, pp. 141–143.

15. James Chace, *1912: Wilson, Roosevelt, Taft & Debs—the Election That Changed the Country* (New York: Simon & Schuster, 2004), pp. 74–82.

16. Buder, *Pullman*, pp. 210–215; Menand, *The Metaphysical Club*, p. 316.

17. Arthur E. Morgan, *Edward Bellamy* (New York: Columbia University Press, 1944), pp. 6–47, 101–119; Sylvia E. Bowman, *The Year 2000: A Critical Biography of Edward Bellamy* (New York: Bookman Associates, 1958), pp. 15–43; Edward Bellamy, *Looking Backward: 2000–1887* (New York: Penguin Books, 1982), pp. 65, 111.

18. Bowman, *The Year 2000*, pp. 43–44; Bellamy, *Looking Backward*, pp. 176–178.

19. Bowman, *The Year 2000*, pp. 122–148.

20. Michael D'Antonio, *Hershey: Milton S. Hershey's Extraordinary Life of Wealth, Empire, and Utopian Dreams* (New York: Simon & Schuster, 2006), pp. 50–51; Carol Off, *Bitter Chocolate: The Dark Side of the World's Most Seductive Sweet* (New York: New Press, 2006), pp. 76–80.

21. Hershey Co. Web site at www.hersheypa.com/town_of_hershey/history; D'Antonio, *Hershey*, pp. 63–71, 88–96; Joel Glenn Brenner, *The Emperors of Chocolate: Inside the Secret World of Hershey and Mars* (New York: Random House, 1999), pp. 75–88.

22. A brief account of British model company towns, from Cadbury's Bourneville to soap baron William Lever's Port Sunlight, may be found in John Micklethwait and Adrian Wooldridge, *The Company: A Short History of a Revolutionary Idea* (New York: Modern Library, 2003), p. 86. Both of these towns, along with chocolatier Joseph Rowntree's New Earswick, aimed at a preindustrial aesthetic. Port Sunlight even contained replicas of famous Tudor and Elizabethan buildings.

23. D'Antonio, *Hershey*, pp. 84–87, 100–105, 115–118, 123–140; Off, *Bitter Chocolate*, pp. 74–80; Brenner, *The Emperors of Chocolate*, pp. 106–117, 132–135.

24. Hershey Co. Web site; D'Antonio, *Hershey*, pp. 199–219.

25. Wikipedia entry on Hersheypark at http://en.wikipedia.org/wiki/Hersheypark.

26. Brenner, *The Emperors of Chocolate*, pp. 262–274.

27. Mark Twain, *Roughing It*, vol. 2, (New York and London: Harper & Brothers Publishers, 1871), p. 131.

28. James Allen, *The Company Town in the American West* (Norman: University of Oklahoma Press, 1966), pp. 13–29; "Step into New England at Port Gamble National Historic Landmark," *Seattle Times*, February 26, 2009.

29. Wikipedia entry on Pacific Lumber at http://en.wikipedia.org/wiki/Pacific _Lumber_Company; Humboldt Redwoods State Park history at www.humboldt

redwoods.org/park_history; David Harris, *The Last Stand: The War Between Wall Street and Main Street Over California's Ancient Redwoods* (New York: Times Books, 1995), pp. 16–19.

30. Wikipedia entry on Pacific Lumber; Hugh Wilkerson and John van der Zee, *Life in the Peace Zone: An American Company Town* (New York: Macmillan, 1971), pp. 15–21, 45–46, 50, 53, 92, 99, 150–152; Harris, *The Last Stand*, pp. 10–15; Gaye LeBaron, "Remembering Scotia, the Last of the Company Towns," *Santa Rosa Press Democrat*, October 12, 2008.

31. Harris, *The Last Stand*, p. 19; "Pacific Lumber Offer Is Begun By Maxxam," *Wall Street Journal*, October 2, 1985, p. 8; "Maxxam Group Plans to Double Redwood Harvest," *Wall Street Journal*, July 3, 1986, p. 27; "Suit on Takeover of PL Tied to Drexel Case," *Wall Street Journal*, October 24, 1988, p. B12; James B. Stewart, "Scenes from a Scandal: The Secret World of Michael Milken and Ivan Boesky," *Wall Street Journal*, October 2, 1991, p. B1; Ned Daly, "Ravaging the Redwood: Charles Hurwitz, Michael Milken and the Costs of Greed," Multinational Monitor Web site, www.multinationalmonitor.org/hyper/issues/1994/09/mm0994_07.html. On the benefits of Wall Street takeovers, see for example Steven M. Davidoff, "Wall Street's Deal Factory Hits the Reset Button," *New York Times*, September 17, 2009. Natural disasters have been a recurring feature of Scotia's history, with 1955 and 1964 floods of the Eel River that each time threatened to destroy the town. See Wilkerson and van der Zee, *Life in the Peace Zone*, pp. 62–63, 141–147; "California, Oregon Damage Near $1 Billion from Floods that Claimed About 40 Lives," *Wall Street Journal*, December 29, 1964, p. 4.

32. Wikipedia entry on Headwaters Forest Preserve at http://en.wikipedia.org/wiki/Headwaters_Forest; Humboldt Redwood Co. Web site, www.hrcllc.com; LeBaron, "Remembering Scotia," *Santa Rosa Press Democrat*, October 12, 2008; "Declaring Victory, Tree-Sitters Leave Redwoods," Associated Press, September 24, 2008; Josh Harkinson, "Out of the Woods," *Mother Jones*, November/December 2008, pp. 62–64; Heidi Walters, "For Sale: Scotia Inn," *North Coast Journal*, May 14, 2009.

33. Davis Dyer and Daniel Gross, *The Generations of Corning: The Life and Times of a Global Corporation* (Oxford and New York: Oxford University Press, 2001), pp. 47–59; Thomas P. Dimitroff and Lois S. Janes, *History of the Corning-Painted Post Area: 200 Years in Painted Post Country* (Corning, NY: Corning Area Bicentennial Committee, 1977), pp. 53–60, 85–96, 117–129; cut-glass wares of the Hawkes and Hoare companies are on display at the Corning Museum of Glass.

34. Dimitroff and Janes, *History of the Corning-Painted Post Area*, pp. 147–149.

35. Dyer and Gross, *The Generations of Corning*, pp. 77–103, 117–118; Dimitroff and Janes, *History of the Corning-Painted Post Area*, p. 137–139.

36. Dyer and Gross, *The Generations of Corning*, pp. 138–156, 165–168; Dimitroff and Janes, *History of the Corning-Painted Post Area*, pp. 223–233.

37. Dyer and Gross, *The Generations of Corning*, pp.195–196, 204–205, 213–214, 221–222; Dimitroff and Janes, *History of the Corning-Painted Post Area*, pp. 253, 273.

38. Dyer and Gross, *The Generations of Corning*, pp. 103, 236, 243–264, 271–278, 289–296; Dimitroff and Janes, *History of the Corning-Painted Post Area*, pp. 295–297; Brian Howard, "Corning Incorporated," *American Biotechnology Laboratory*, October 2005.

39. Dyer and Gross, *The Generations of Corning*, pp. 312–316, 411, 452.

40. Dyer and Gross, *The Generations of Corning*, pp. 335, 353–367, 380; Ann Harrington, "The Scion in Winter," *Fortune*, November 18, 2002, p. 129.

41. Dyer and Gross, *The Generations of Corning*, pp. 380, 394–396; Stephanie N. Mehta, "Cooking Up Hope for Corning," *Fortune*, May 3, 2003, p. 158; William C. Symonds, "Corning: Back from the Brink," *Business Week*, October 18, 2004; Michael Mandel, "Corning: Lessons from the Boom and Bust," *Business Week* On-line, May 4, 2009.

42. Interview with Corning Enterprises President G. Thomas Tranter Jr., June 12, 2009; interview with former Corning chairman James R. Houghton, June 16, 2009.

43. Jean Strouse, *Morgan: American Financier* (New York: Random House, 1999), pp. 582–589.

44. Margaret Crawford, "The New Company Town," *Perspecta 30: Settlement Patterns* (Cambridge, MA: MIT Press, 1999), pp. 49–54.

45. Margaret Crawford, "Bertram Goodhue, Walter Douglas and Tyrone, New Mexico," *Journal of Architectural Education*, Summer 1989, www.jstor.org/pss/1425018; also see www.ghosttowns.com/states/nm/tyrone.html.

46. Wikipedia entry, http://en.wikipedia.org/wiki/Atco,_Georgia.

47. Wikipedia entry at http://en.wikipedia.org/wiki/Alcoa,_Tennessee.

48. "Portal 31: Kentucky's First Exhibition Coal Mine," www.portal31.org; also www.coaleducation.org/coalhistory/coaltowns/lynch.htm.

49. Crawford, "The New Company Town," pp. 55–56.

Chapter 3: Exploitationville

1. Herbert G. Gutman, "Two Lockouts in Pennsylvania, 1873–1874," in *Work, Culture and Society in Industrializing America* (New York: Vintage Books, 1976), pp. 326–343.

2. Ronald D. Eller, *Miners, Millhands, and Mountaineers: Industrialization of the Appalachian South, 1880–1970* (Knoxville: University of Tennessee Press, 1982), pp. 182–186; Helene Smith, *Export: A Patch of Tapestry Out of Coal Country America* (Greensburg, PA: McDonald/Sward Publishing Co., 1986), pp. 104–105; Crandall A. Shifflett, *Coal Towns: Life, Work, and Culture in Company Towns of Southern Appalachia, 1880–1960* (Knoxville: University of Tennessee Press, 1991), p. 146. Nor were towns necessarily better outside of the South. In his autobiography, former miner

John Brophy describes the town of Nanty Glo, Pennsylvania, as "a grimy huddle in the narrow valley of Black Lick Creek overshadowed by slag piles and the hills of the Alleghenies." John Brophy, *A Miner's Life* (Madison: University of Wisconsin Press, 1964), p. 111.

3. Eller, *Miners, Millhands, and Mountaineers*, pp. 208–216; Shifflett, *Coal Towns*, pp. 117–118; Stuart D. Brandes, *American Welfare Capitalism, 1880–1940* (Chicago: University of Chicago Press, 1976), p. 3; John W. Hevener, *Which Side Are You On? The Harlan County Coal Miners, 1931–1939* (Urbana: University of Illinois Press, 1978), p. 18.

4. Archie Green, *Only a Miner: Studies in Recorded Coal-Mining Songs* (Urbana: University of Illinois Press, 1972), pp. 156–166.

5. American Social History Project, *Who Built America: Working People & the Nation's Economy, Politics, Culture & Society* (New York: Pantheon Books, 1992), p. 211.

6. Shifflett, *Coal Towns*, p. 50.

7. Barbara Freese, *Coal: A Human History* (Cambridge, MA: Perseus Publishing, 2003), pp. 132–134; Kevin Kenny, *Making Sense of the Molly Maguires* (New York: Oxford University Press, 1998), pp. 48–62, 117–119, 131–284, and passim; Sir Arthur Conan Doyle, *The Valley of Fear*, in *Sherlock Holmes: The Complete Novels and Stories*, vol. 2 (New York: Bantam Books, 1986), p. 219.

8. Wikipedia entry for Battle of Blair Mountain, http://en.wikipedia.org/wiki/Battle_of_Blair_Mountain.

9. Jim Garland, "Biography" included in album liner notes of Sarah Ogan Gunning, *The Silver Dagger*, Rounder Records 0051, 1976.

10. Freese, *Coal*, pp. 106–110, 119–122; Wikipedia entry on Schuylkill Canal, http://en.wikipedia.org/wiki/Schuylkill_canal#Competition_with_the_railroad.

11. Freese, *Coal*, pp. 105, 137; Shifflett, *Coal Towns*, pp. xi, 27; Howard Zinn, "The Colorado Coal Strike, 1914–1914," in *Three Strikes: Miners, Musicians, Salesgirls, and the Fighting Spirit of Labor's Last Century* (Boston: Beacon Press, 2001), pp. 8–9.

12. Eller, *Miners, Millhands, and Mountaineers*, pp. 56–69.

13. Ibid., pp. 65, 71; Shifflett, *Coal Towns*, pp. 29–30.

14. Shifflett, *Coal Towns*, pp. 29–33.

15. Eller, *Miners, Millhands, and Mountaineers*, pp. 130–133; Shifflett, *Coal Towns*, p. 35.

16. Eller, *Miners, Millhands, and Mountaineers*, pp. 134–136, 143–145.

17. Ibid., p. 190; Memories of Widen and Dille, West Virginia, at www.appalachiacoal.com/Widen,%20West%20Virginia,%20Appalachian%20coal%20camp.html (as of February 8, 2010).

18. Shifflett, *Coal Towns*, pp. 59–64.

19. Thomas G. Andrews, *Killing for Coal: America's Deadliest Labor War* (Cambridge, MA: Harvard University Press, 2008), pp. 179–232; Priscilla Long, "The 1913 Colorado Fuel and Iron Strike, With Reflections on the Cause of Coal-Strike

Violence," in *The United Mine Workers of America: A Model of Industrial Solidarity?* ed. John H. M. Laslett (University Park: Pennsylvania State University Press, 1990), pp. 347–349.

20. Harry M. Caudill, *Night Comes to the Cumberlands: A Biography of a Depressed Area* (Boston: Little, Brown & Co., 1963), p. 93; Eller, *Miners, Millhands, and Mountaineers*, pp. 145–148.

21. Caudill, *Night Comes to the Cumberlands*, pp. 107–109, 112–115; quote is on p. 115.

22. Ibid., pp. 145–146.

23. Ibid., pp. 325, 343–344.

24. Caudill interview with *Mother Earth News* at www.motherearthnews.com/Nature-Community/1975–07–01/The-Plowboy-Interview-Harry-Caudill.aspx.

25. Green, *Only a Miner*, pp. 281–312; Merle Travis, *Folk Songs of the Hills*, Capitol 48001.

26. Although Eller (*Miners, Millhands, and Mountaineers*, p. 188) argues that some company stores exploited workers by charging "all the market would bear," Shifflett (*Coal Towns*, pp. 183–184) argues that debt peonage was in fact rare in the towns he investigated, including Stonega, Virginia. As to the entrapment aspect of scrip, Shifflett asserts that after 1900, Virginia and West Virginia miners received 50 percent to 70 percent of their earnings in cash. Moreover, says Shifflett, the existence of the railroads meant miners were not isolated and that company stores faced increasing competition from out-of-town retailers. See also Price V. Fishback, "Did Coal Miners 'Owe Their Souls to the Company Store'? Theory and Evidence from the Early 1900s," *Journal of Economic History* 46 (December 1986): 1011–1029; Price V. Fishback, *Soft Coal, Hard Choices: The Economic Welfare of Bituminous Coal Miners 1890–1930* (New York: Oxford University Press, 1992); and James Allen, *The Company Town in the American West* (Norman: University of Oklahoma Press, 1966), pp. 128–137.

27. Caudill, *Night Comes to the Cumberlands*, pp. 114, 190; Brandes, *American Welfare Capitalism*, p. 45; Brophy, *A Miner's Life*, pp. 35, 47, 51, and passim.

28. Shifflett, *Coal Towns*, pp. 176–180; the photo of the Lynch store may be found at www.portal31.org/images/bigstore.jpg; Andrews, *Killing for Coal*, pp. 217–221.

29. Caudill, *Night Comes to the Cumberlands*, pp. 98–108; Shifflett, *Coal Towns*, pp. 68–80; Eller, *Miners, Millhands, and Mountaineers*, p. 197.

30. Eller, *Miners, Millhands, and Mountaineers*, p. 176.

31. Caudill, *Night Comes to the Cumberlands*, p. 110; Shifflett, *Coal Towns*, pp. 85–92; Brophy, *A Miner's Life*, pp. 43–45; David Montgomery, *The Fall of the House of Labor: The Workplace, the State, and American Labor Activism, 1865–1925* (Cambridge and New York: Cambridge University Press, 1987), p. 333.

32. Caudill, *Night Comes to the Cumberlands*, pp. 118–121; Shifflett, *Coal Towns*, pp. 103–106; EH.Net entry on workers' compensation at http://eh.net/encyclopedia/article/fishback.workers.compensation.

33. Caudill, *Night Comes to the Cumberlands*, pp. 142–143; Shifflett, *Coal Towns*, pp. 108–109.

34. John H. M. Laslett, "A Model of Industrial Solidarity? Interpreting the UMWA's First Hundred Years, 1890–1990," in *The United Mine Workers of America*, pp. 1–2; Green, *Only a Miner*, p. 166.

35. Freese, *Coal*, pp. 137–141; Caudill, *Night Comes to the Cumberlands*, p. 133; Shifflett, *Coal Towns*, p. 30.

36. Montgomery, *The Fall of the House of Labor*, pp. 343–351; Andrews, *Killing for Coal*, pp. 233–286; Zinn, "The Colorado Coal Strike," pp. 20–52; Long, "The 1913 Colorado Fuel and Iron Strike," pp. 347–359.

37. Ron Chernow, *Titan: The Life of John D. Rockefeller, Sr.* (New York: Random House, 1998), pp. 579–589; Brandes, *American Welfare Capitalism*, pp. 125–126; Montgomery, *The Fall of the House of Labor*, pp. 348–351.

38. Chernow, *Titan*, p. 590; Brandes, *American Welfare Capitalism*, pp. 127–137; Montgomery, *The Fall of the House of Labor*, p. 355; Irving Bernstein, *The Lean Years: A History of the American Worker, 1920–1933* (Boston: Houghton Mifflin Co., 1960), p. 168–171; Hevener, *Which Side Are You On?* pp. 144–145.

39. David Brody, "The Rise and Decline of Welfare Capitalism," *Workers in Industrial America: Essays on the 20th Century Struggle* (New York: Oxford University Press, 1980), pp. 48–81.

40. Bernstein, *The Lean Years*, pp. 162–163; Andrews, *Killing for Coal*, pp. 287–288; Montgomery, *The Fall of the House of Labor*, pp. 395–399, 407–409; Laslett, *The United Mine Workers of America*, p. 19.

41. Bernstein, *The Lean Years*, pp. 360–366, 377–384; Shifflett, *Coal Towns*, pp. 117–118; Eller, *Miners, Millhands, and Mountaineers*, pp. 155–158.

42. Bernstein, *The Lean Years*, pp. 385–390.

43. Irving Bernstein, *Turbulent Years: A History of the American Worker 1933–1941* (Boston: Houghton Mifflin Co., 1970), pp. 30–45, 61; Alan J. Singer, "'Something of a Man': John L. Lewis, the UMWA, and the CIO, 1919–1943," in *The United Mine Workers of America*, pp. 117–119.

44. Hevener, *Which Side Are You On?* pp. 4, 16–17, 22, 102–103, 129–146; testimony of Harlan County Sheriff J. H. Blair in *Harlan Miners Speak*, ed. Theodore Dreiser et al. (New York: Harcourt, Brace & Co., 1932), pp. 234–237.

45. Hevener, *Which Side Are You On?* pp. 181–182.

46. Robert Glass Cleland, *A History of Phelps Dodge, 1834–1950* (New York: Alfred A. Knopf, 1952), pp. 21–137, 161–188, 248–253; John Collins Rudolf, "Talk of the Town: Is Copper Up Today?" *New York Times*, November 28, 2008; James Allen, *The Company Town in the American West* (Norman: University of Oklahoma Press, 1966), pp. 11–12, 42–46, 103; Jonathan D. Rosenblum, *Copper Crucible: How the Arizona Miners' Strike of 1983 Recast Labor-Management Relations in America* (Ithaca, NY: ILR Press, 1995), pp. 3–6, 15–39.

47. Leland M. Roth, "Company Towns in the Western United States," in *The Company Town: Architecture and Society in the Early Industrial Age*, ed. John S. Garner (New York: Oxford University Press, 1992), pp. 180–184; Phelps Dodge company history at www.answers.com/topic/phelps-dodge-corp; Allen, *The Company Town in the American West*, pp. x, 128–137; Rosenblum, *Copper Crucible*, pp. 40–44.

48. Rosenblum, *Copper Crucible*, pp. 52–139; Jonathan Rosenblum, "The Dismal Precedent that Gave Us Caterpillar," *Wall Street Journal*, April 16, 1992; Robert S. Greenberger, "Striking Back: More Firms Get Tough and Keep Operating In Spite of Walkouts," *Wall Street Journal*, October 11, 1983.

49. Rosenblum, *Copper Crucible*, pp. 171–196; Allanna Sullivan, "Union Decertification Possible This Week at Phelps Dodge Operations in Arizona," *Wall Street Journal*, January 28, 1985.

50. Allanna Sullivan and John Valentine, "U.S. Copper Industry Is Ill and Getting Sicker," *Wall Street Journal*, June 18, 1985; Phelps Dodge company history at www.answers.com/topic/phelps-dodge-corp; Don Lee, "A Copper Town Digs Out: China's Hunger for the Metal Pushes Up Its Price and Invigorates a U.S. Mining Community," *Los Angeles Times*, April 13, 2004; Andrew Ross Sorkin and Ian Austin, "Smaller Rival in Agreement to Acquire Copper Giant," *New York Times*, November 20, 2006; Henny Sender, "Heat of a Copper Deal: Why Lower Prices May Have Sealed the Fate of Phelps Dodge," *Wall Street Journal*, January 25, 2007; Freeport-McMoRan 2008 Annual Report, p. 30; "Major Layoffs at Morenci Mine," Associated Press, January 10, 2009.

Chapter 4: A Southern Principality

1. Lois McDonald, *Southern Mill Hills* (New York: Hillman, 1928), p. 44, quoted in Irving Bernstein, *The Lean Years: A History of the American Worker, 1920–1933* (Cambridge, MA: Riverside Press, 1960), p. 7.

2. "Kannapolis: Still Feeling Change at Cannon," *Raleigh News & Observer*, September 1, 1985; Mildred Gwin Andrews, *The Men and the Mills: A History of the Southern Textile Industry* (Macon, GA: Mercer University Press, 1987), p. 98; Cynthia D. Anderson, *The Social Consequences of Economic Restructuring in the Textile Industry: Change in a Southern Mill Village* (New York and London: Garland Publishing, 2000), pp. 57–69; "Powerful C.A. Cannon Rules Kannapolis, N.C., But He Faces Challenge," *Wall Street Journal*, April 29, 1969; Jacquelyn Dowd Hall et al., *Like a Family: The Making of a Southern Cotton Mill World* (Chapel Hill: University of North Carolina Press, 1987), pp. 188–194.

3. Helen Arthur-Cornett, *Remembering Kannapolis: Tales From Towel City* (Charleston, SC: History Press, 2006), p. 36; *Kannapolis: A Pictorial History* (Kannapolis: City of Kannapolis, 2008), pp. 18–19; "Cannon II," *Fortune*, November 1933, pp. 55, 140–141; Anderson, *The Social Consequences*, p. 57.

4. Fieldcrest-Cannon Inc. company history at www.fundinguniverse.com/company -histories/Fieldcrest-Cannon-Inc-Company-History.html; Arthur-Cornett, *Remembering Kannapolis*, pp. 13–26; Andrews, *The Men and the Mills*, pp. 25–28, 249; "Cannon II," p. 141.

5. Fieldcrest-Cannon Inc. company history; Arthur-Cornett, *Remembering Kannapolis*, pp. 36–38; Andrews, *The Men and the Mills*, p. 81; "Cannon II," p. 141.

6. *Kannapolis: A Pictorial History*, pp. 24–81.

7. C. Vann Woodward, *Origins of the New South, 1877–1913* (Baton Rouge: Louisiana State University Press, 1951), pp. 107–134; David L. Carlton, *Mill and Town in South Carolina, 1880–1920* (Baton Rouge: Louisiana State University Press, 1982), pp. 13–32; Broadus Mitchell, *The Rise of Cotton Mills in the South* (Baltimore: Johns Hopkins University Press, 1921), pp. 106–112, 122–125; Andrews, *The Men and the Mills*, pp. 2–3.

8. Woodward, *Origins of the New South*, pp. 131–132.

9. Carlton, *Mill and Town in South Carolina*, p. 40.

10. Ibid., p. 132.

11. Hall et al., *Like a Family*, pp. 114, 379, note 1. At the height of the coal boom of the 1920s, only 79 percent of West Virginia coal miners and only 64 percent of eastern Kentucky and Virginia miners lived in company towns, according to a congressional study quoted by Hall: U.S. Congress, Senate, *Woman and Child Wage-Earners*, 1: 520, 523.

12. Hall et al., *Like a Family*, pp. 115–120.

13. W. J. Cash, *The Mind of the South* (New York: Alfred A. Knopf, 1941), p. 205.

14. Harriet L. Herring, *Passing of the Mill Village: Revolution in a Southern Institution* (Chapel Hill: University of North Carolina Press, 1949), p. 26; Andrews, *The Men and the Mills*, p. 195. Hall offers a slightly higher figure: Drawing upon a congressional study, she says rents in 1908 averaged $3.57 per month, roughly 6 percent of workers' total monthly expenditures. See p. 126.

15. Valerie Quinney, "Farm to Mill: The First Generation," in *Working Lives: The Southern Exposure History of Labor in the South*, ed. Marc S. Miller (New York: Pantheon, 1974), pp. 5–7.

16. Joel Williamson, *The Crucible of Race: Black-White Relations in the American South Since Emancipation* (New York: Oxford University Press, 1984), pp. 432–433. W. J. Cash notes that child labor was the norm: "At six, at seven, at eight years, by ten at the latest, the little boys and girls of the mill families went regularly to work." *The Mind of the South*, p. 203.

17. Hall et al., *Like a Family*, p. 130.

18. Anderson, *The Social Consequences*, p. 58–59; according to Hall et al., by 1910 most urban mills had converted to cheaper and more dependable electric power, but small-town and rural mills lagged behind. In the Carolinas, 75 percent of mills still ran on water or steam. *Like a Family*, p. 48.

19. Anderson, *The Social Consequences*, pp. 61–62; Andrews, *The Men and the Mills*, p. 99; "Cannon I," *Fortune*, November 1933, p. 50.

20. Arthur-Cornett, *Remembering Kannapolis*, p. 41.

21. James A. Hodges, *New Deal Labor Policy and the Southern Cotton Textile Industry, 1933–1941* (Knoxville: University of Tennessee Press, 1986), p. 31.

22. Hodges, *New Deal Labor Policy*, pp. 29–30.

23. Andrews, *The Men and the Mills*, p. 80; Hall et al., *Like a Family*, pp. 105–106, 186–194; Anderson, *The Social Consequences*, p. 60.

24. Hall et al., *Like a Family*, pp. 197–219.

25. Jeremy Brecher, *Strike!* (Greenwich, CT: Fawcett Publications, 1972), pp. 210–211; Hodges, *New Deal Labor Policy*, p. 49; Hall et al., *Like a Family*, pp. 290–294, 325, 329–332, 342; Arthur-Cornett, *Remembering Kannapolis*, pp. 45–47.

26. Brecher, *Strike!* pp. 212–217.

27. Ibid., pp. 218–219; Hall et al., *Like a Family*, pp. 349–354.

28. Edward Levinson, *Labor on the March* (Ithaca, NY: ILR Press, 1938), pp. 239–240.

29. Margaret Crawford, *Building the Workingman's Paradise: The Design of American Company Towns* (London and New York: Verso, 1995), p. 194.

30. Herring, *Passing of the Mill Village*, pp. 8–11; Andrews, *The Men and the Mills*, pp. 197–199.

31. "Cannon II," *Fortune*, November 1933, p. 141. The same issue of *Fortune* (pp. 131–134), however, reported that Charles Cannon, who also served as a director of the Federal Reserve branch in Charlotte and on the board of New York Life Insurance, was "the foremost figure in textiles" and that Cannon Mills "is the most secure if not the greatest textile company in the South."

32. Arthur-Cornett, *Remembering Kannapolis*, p. 115; Anderson, *The Social Consequences*, p. 64; *Wall Street Journal*, April 29, 1969.

33. *Wall Street Journal*, April 5, 1971.

34. *Wall Street Journal*, April 29, 1969; Andrews, *The Men and the Mills*, p. 249; *Kannapolis: A Pictorial History*, pp. 146–147.

35. *Wall Street Journal*, June 7, 1956; October 8, 1956; April 29, 1966. The *Journal* commented that, with four wage increases in less than two years, Cannon generally led the way in wages, and other textile companies followed that lead.

36. *Wall Street Journal*, November 22, 1974; July 24, 1974. Further votes failed in the 1980s and 1990s, before the textile union's successor, UNITE, was victorious in 1999, becoming the bargaining representative for Pillowtex.

37. Andrews, *The Men and the Mills*, pp. 250–252, 287; Arthur-Cornett, *Remembering Kannapolis*, p. 91; Anderson, *The Social Consequences*, p. 69; Fieldcrest-Cannon Corp. and Pillowtex company history, www.fundinguniverse.com/company-histories/Fieldcrest-Cannon-Inc-Company-History.html.

38. *Kannapolis: A Pictorial History*, pp. 247–248, 275.

Chapter 5: The Magic City

1. Robert Lewis, *Chicago Made: Factory Networks in the Industrial Metropolis* (Chicago: University of Chicago Press, 2008), pp. 48–49; Margaret Crawford, *Building the Workingman's Paradise: The Design of American Company Towns* (London: Verso, 1995), pp. 43–44; the steel man's quote appears in David Brody, *Steelworkers in America: The Nonunion Era* (New York: Harper & Row, 1969), p. 88; Eugene J. Buffington, "Making Cities for Workingmen," *Harper's Weekly*, May 8, 1909, p. 15; Graham Romeyn Taylor, *Satellite Cities: A Study of Industrial Suburbs* (New York: D. Appleton & Co., 1915), p. 165. Taylor's book grew out of an article first published in *The Survey*. The magazine ran several pieces on steel towns as follow-ups to the Pittsburgh Survey, a social-scientific investigation of conditions in that town initiated by the Charity Organization Society of the City of New York and backed financially by the Russell Sage Foundation.

2. Ida M. Tarbell, *The Life of Elbert H. Gary: A Story of Steel* (New York: D. Appleton & Co., 1925), pp. 28–113, 150; Jean Strouse, *Morgan: American Financier* (New York: Random House, 1999), pp. 397–404, 445–447; Kenneth Warren, *Big Steel: The First Century of the United States Steel Corporation* (Pittsburgh: University of Pittsburgh Press, 2001), pp. 109–111.

3. Taylor, *Satellite Cities*, p. 10; Isaac James Quillen, *Industrial City: A History of Gary Indiana to 1929* (New York: Garland Publishing, 1986), p. 175.

4. William Serrin, *Homestead: The Glory and Tragedy of an American Steel Town* (New York: Times Books, 1992), pp. 33–36; Crawford, *Building the Workingman's Paradise*, pp. 68–69.

5. Tom Bell, *Out of This Furnace* (Pittsburgh: University of Pittsburgh Press, 1976), pp. 122–123.

6. Paul Krause, *The Battle for Homestead 1880–1892* (Pittsburgh: University of Pittsburgh Press, 1992), pp.12–43; Serrin, *Homestead*, pp. 66–95.

7. Anne E. Mosher, *Capital's Utopia: Vandergrift, Pennsylvania 1855–1916* (Baltimore: Johns Hopkins University Press, 2004), pp. 64–95, 113–123.

8. Buffington, "Making Cities for Workingmen," p.16.

9. Mosher, *Capital's Utopia*, pp. 110–112, 141–149; Brody, *Steelworkers in America*, pp. 67, 173–174.

10. Buffington, "Making Cities for Workingmen," p. 15; Raymond A. Mohl and Neil Betten, *Steel City: Urban and Ethnic Patterns in Gary, Indiana, 1906–1950* (New York and London: Holmes & Meier, 1986), pp. 12–14; Taylor, *Satellite Cities*, pp. 169–171, 188–189.

11. Mohl and Betten, *Steel City*, pp. 15–23; Taylor, *Satellite Cities*, pp. 17, 184–195, 207; James B. Lane, *City of the Century: A History of Gary, Indiana* (Bloomington: Indiana University Press, 1978), pp. 43–44; Buffington, "Making Cities for Workingmen," p. 17; Quillen, *Industrial City*, pp. 98–102, 117–119, 125–128, 145.

12. Lane, *City of the Century*, pp. 44–45, 47; Brody, *Steelworkers in America*, note, p. 124.

13. Taylor, *Satellite Cities*, pp. 165–166, 217–229; Quillen, pp. 152–163; advertisement reproduced in Crawford, *Building the Workingman's Paradise*, p. 44.

14. Taylor, *Satellite Cities*, pp. 237–243, 248–251.

15. Brody, *Steelworkers in America*, p. 112; Irving Bernstein, *Turbulent Years: A History of the American Worker, 1933–1941* (Boston: Houghton Mifflin Co., 1971), p. 475.

16. Mark Reutter, *Sparrows Point: Making Steel—the Rise and Ruin of American Industrial Might* (New York: Summit Books, 1988), pp. 10, 22–34, 41–79, 87–115, 140–154; Brody, *Steelworkers in America*, pp. 208–213.

17. Stuart D. Brandes, *American Welfare Capitalism 1880–1940* (Chicago: University of Chicago Press, 1976), pp. 28–29, 77.

18. Brody, *Steelworkers in America*, pp. 25, 89, 154; Brandes, *American Welfare Capitalism*, p. 83; Reutter, *Sparrows Point*, pp. 140–142.

19. Brody, *Steelworkers in America*, pp. 86, 96–111, 149, 162–177.

20. Ibid., pp. 69, 75, 184, 197, 201; Quillen, *Industrial City*, p. 266.

21. Brody, *Steelworkers in America*, pp. 191–193, 208–213, 226–229; Quillen, *Industrial City*, pp. 271–272.

22. Mohl and Betten, *Steel City*, pp. 31–42; Brody, *Steelworkers in America*, pp. 252, 258–262; Harvey O'Connor, *Steel-Dictator* (New York: John Day Co., 1935), pp. 102–103; Serrin, *Homestead*, pp. 149–156.

23. Quillen, *Industrial City*, pp. 388–395; Edward Greer, *Big Steel: Black Politics and Corporate Power in Gary, Indiana* (New York and London: Monthly Review Press, 1979), pp. 81–82.

24. Brody, *Steelworkers in America*, pp. 270–274; O'Connor, *Steel-Dictator*, pp. 105–114.

25. Mohl and Betten, *Steel City*, pp. 6, 28; Brody, *Steelworkers in America*, pp. 266–267; Quillen, *Industrial City*, pp. 375–418.

26. Quillen, *Industrial City*, pp. 172, 462–489; Greer, *Big Steel: Black Politics and Corporate Power*, pp. 69, 83.

27. Warren, *Big Steel*, pp. 145–160, 166–167; O'Connor, *Steel-Dictator*, pp. 220–224; Bernstein, *Turbulent Years*, pp. 458–474.

28. Warren, *Big Steel*, pp. 193–195, 223; Reutter, *Sparrows Point*, p. 397.

29. Greer, *Big Steel: Black Politics and Corporate Power*, pp. 86–88, 138; Serrin, *Homestead*, pp. 219–222; Mohl and Betten, *Steel City*, pp. 55–70. On Gary's innovative public education program see Randolph Bourne, *The Gary Schools* (Boston: Houghton Mifflin Co., 1916).

30. Sandra L. Barnes, *The Cost of Being Poor: A Comparative Study of Life in Poor Neighborhoods in Gary, Indiana* (Albany: State University of New York Press, 2005), p. 41; "Dead End Streets," *The Guardian*, August 27, 1996, p. 22; Monica Davey,

"City's Bad Luck Takes Another Spin," *New York Times*, November 30, 2003, p. 1; "Blueprint: Gary Indiana," *Wall Street Journal*, May 7, 2008, p. C12; U.S. Steel 2007 Annual Report and Form 10-K at www.uss.com/corp/proxy/documents/2007-annual -report.pdf.

31. Warren, *Big Steel*, pp. xvii, 1–2.

Chapter 6: On the Road to the Consumer Economy

1. Edward Chase Kirkland, *Industry Comes of Age* (Chicago: Quadrangle Books, 1967), p. 271; Lawrence B. Glickman, ed., *Consumer Society in American History* (Ithaca, NY: Cornell University Press, 1999), p. 3; Robert S. Lynd and Helen Merrell Lynd, *Middletown: A Study in Contemporary American Culture* (New York: Harcourt, Brace & Co., 1929), pp. 81, 153; Lizabeth Cohen, "Encountering Mass Culture at the Grassroots: the Experience of Chicago Workers in the 1920s," in Glickman, *Consumer Society in American History*, pp. 147–148.

2. Simon N. Patten, *The New Basis of Civilization* (London: Macmillan Co., 1907), pp. 14–16.

3. Lizabeth Cohen, *A Consumers' Republic: The Politics of Mass Consumption in Postwar America* (New York: Random House, 2003), p. 195 and passim.

4. Daniel Yergin, *The Prize: The Epic Quest for Oil, Money & Power* (New York: Free Press, 1991), pp. 66–79; Mody C. Boatright and William A. Owens, *Tales from the Derrick Floor: A People's History of the Oil Industry* (Lincoln: University of Nebraska Press, 1970), pp. 60–62; Diana Davids Olien and Roger M. Olien, *Oil in Texas: The Gusher Age, 1895–1945* (Austin: University of Texas Press, 2002), pp. 57–67, 84; Roger M. Olien and Diana Davids Olien, *Oil Booms: Social Change in Five Texas Towns* (Lincoln: University of Nebraska Press, 1982), pp. 6–9, 22–25, 45.

5. Robert M. Olien and Diana Davids Olien, *Life In the Oil Fields* (Austin: Texas Monthly Press, 1986), pp. 2–6, 108–122; Olien and Olien, *Oil in Texas*, pp. 118–122, 138–147, 206; Olien and Olien, *Oil Booms*, pp. 46–48, 133–139.

6. Olien and Olien, *Oil in Texas*, pp. 88–91, 145.

7. Michael Wallis, *Oil Man: The Story of Frank Phillips and the Birth of Phillips Petroleum* (New York: Doubleday, 1988), pp. 27, 47–48, 61–76, 103, 161.

8. Ibid., pp. 90, 123–135, 184–191, 222–253, 295, 388, 439–443.

9. Joe Williams, *Bartlesville: Remembrances of Times Past, Reflections of Today* (Bartlesville, Oklahoma: TRW Reda Pump Division, 1978); "Pickens Is Target of Numerous Barbs in Oklahoma Town," *Wall Street Journal*, December 12, 1984, p. 1; Francis C. Brown III, "Dear Mr. Pickens: Please Send Me Lots of Money, (Signed) A Pen Pal," *Wall Street Journal*, July 25, 1985, p. 1; Caleb Solomon, "Lingering Oil Shock: Takeover Raids Leave Phillips Employees Fearing New Assaults," *Wall Street Journal*, February 1, 1989, p. 1; Dawn Blalock, "Phillips Petroleum, Long Buried in Debt, Frees Itself," *Wall Street Journal*, April 15, 1996, p. B3; Thaddeus Herrick, "Big-

ger is Better for Mulva, ConocoPhillips's First CEO," *Wall Street Journal*, November 21, 2001, p. B6; Alexei Barrionuevo and John R. Wilke, "Conoco-Phillips Merger to Get FTC's Approval," *Wall Street Journal*, August 30, 2002, p. A2; Ben Casselman and Angel Gonzales, "Corporate News: Oil Industry Strives to Limit Its Layoffs," *Wall Street Journal*, March 9, 2009, p. B3; Bartlesville, Oklahoma, Web site, www .bartlesville.com/business/category.php?cat=1059; company museum Web site, www .phillips66museum.com/index.htm.

10. Ron Chernow, *Titan: The Life of John D. Rockefeller, Sr.* (New York: Random House, 1998), pp. 430, 556.

11. Richard S. Tedlow, *Giants of Enterprise: Seven Business Innovators and the Empires They Built* (New York: HarperBusiness, 2001), pp. 119–176.

12. Irving Bernstein, *The Lean Years: A History of the American Worker 1920–1933* (Boston: Houghton Mifflin Co., 1960), pp. 432–434; Douglas Brinkley, *Wheels for the World: Henry Ford, His Company, and a Century of Progress* (New York: Viking, 2003), pp. 390–392.

13. Irving Bernstein, *Turbulent Years: A History of the American Worker 1933–1941* (Boston: Houghton Mifflin Co., 1971), pp. 519–520; Brinkley, *Wheels for the World*, pp. 276–279.

14. Brinkley, *Wheels for the World*, p. 442; John Gunther, *Inside U.S.A.* (New York: New Press, 1997), pp. 417–418; Howard P. Segal, *Recasting the Machine Age: Henry Ford's Village Industries* (Amherst: University of Massachusetts Press, 2005), pp. 6–59, 122.

15. Tom Krisher, "U.S. Automakers Lose Majority of U.S. Market," Associated Press, August 1, 2007.

16. David Gelsanliter, *Jump Start: Japan Comes to the Heartland* (New York: Farrar Straus & Giroux, 1990), pp. 4–11, 58, 94–95, 157, 185, and passim; Paulo Prada and Dan Fitzpatrick, "South Could Gain as Detroit Struggles," *Wall Street Journal*, November 20, 2008, p. B1; "A Tale of Two Industries," *Wall Street Journal*, November 22, 2005; David Welch, "Why Toyota Is Afraid of Being Number One," *BusinessWeek*, March 5, 2007.

17. David Welch and David Kiley, "The Tough Road Ahead for GM and Chrysler," *BusinessWeek*, May 27, 2009; Ed Wallace, "Viewpoint: The U.S. Auto Industry in 2012," *BusinessWeek*, June 23, 2009.

18. Robert Hoover and John Hoover, *An American Quality Legend: How Maytag Saved Our Moms, Vexed the Competition, and Presaged America's Quality Revolution* (New York: McGraw-Hill, 1993), pp. 62–156, 176–201.

19. Robert Johnson, "Iowa Villages' Tourism Boom Brings Questionable Progress," *Wall Street Journal*, May 8, 1984, p. 37; Joseph T. Hallinan, "Maytag Will Buy Amana Appliances for $325 Million," *Wall Street Journal*, June 6, 2001, p. B6; Carl Quintanilla, "So, Who's Dull? Maytag's Top Officer, Expected to Do Little, Surprises His Board," *Wall Street Journal*, June 23, 1998, p. A1; Richard Gibson, "Maytag Faces

Big Settlement Payments," *Wall Street Journal*, December 29, 2004, p. 1; "Maytag Corp.: Restructuring Plan Includes Cutting 20% of Work Force," *Wall Street Journal*, June 7, 2004, p. B4; "Maytag Corp: Shareholders Approve the Sale of Company to Whirlpool," *Wall Street Journal*, December 23, 2005, p. B4; "Maytag Closing Means More Than Loss of Jobs," Associated Press, June 26, 2006.

20. Michael J. McCarthy, "Town Fears Being Hung Out to Dry by Maytag Sale," *Wall Street Journal*, May 27, 2005, p. C1; "Don't Worry, Newton Won't Be a Washout," *Wall Street Journal*, June 13, 2005, p. A9; Jessica Lowe, "After Maytag's Departure, Good Fortune Blows Newton's Way," *Newton Daily News*, April 27, 2009, www.newtondailynews.com/articles/2009/04/27/r_tfbftxd7tpcfdcuctlv1ow; Jessica Lowe, "President Unveils Energy Plan During Newton Visit," *Newton Daily News*, April 23, 2009, www.newtondailynews.com/articles/2009/04/23/75398989.

21. Cheri Register, *Packinghouse Daughter: A Memoir* (New York: HarperCollins, 2001), pp. 30–31.

22. Wilson J. Warren, *Tied to the Great Packing Machine* (Iowa City: University of Iowa Press, 2007), pp. 7–21, 63.

23. Hardy Green, *On Strike at Hormel: The Struggle for a Democratic Labor Movement* (Philadelphia: Temple University Press, 1990), especially pp. 6–8, 35–41; Fred H. Blum, *Toward a Democratic Work Process: The Hormel-Packinghouse Workers' Experiment* (New York: Harper & Brothers Publishers, 1953), pp. 57–61.

24. Richard Dougherty, *In Quest of Quality: Hormel's First 75 Years* (Austin, MN: Geo. A. Hormel & Co., 1966), pp. 35–37, 64–82, 119–141.

25. Blum, *Toward a Democratic Work Process*, pp. 4–13; Larry Englemann, "'We Were the Poor People'—The Hormel Strike of 1933," *Labor History* 15 (Fall 1974): 490–493, 508–510; Peter Rachleff, *Hard-Pressed in the Heartland: The Hormel Strike and the Future of the Labor Movement* (Boston: South End Press, 1993), pp. 29–35; David Brody, *The Butcher Workmen: A Study of Unionization* (Cambridge, MA: Harvard University Press, 1964), p. 161.

26. Blum, *Toward a Democratic Work Process*, pp. 16–61, 126–160; Warren, *Tied to the Great Packing Machine*, pp. 83–85 and passim; Dougherty, *In Quest of Quality*, pp. 158–159, 179, 302–303; Green, *On Strike at Hormel*, pp. 38, 323, note 35.

27. Warren, *Tied to the Great Packing Machine*, pp. 24–28, 41–45, 68–71; Deborah Fink, *Cutting Into the Meatpacking Line: Workers and Change in the Rural Midwest* (Chapel Hill: University of North Carolina Press, 1998), pp. 135–136; Michael J. Broadway, "From City to Countryside: Recent Changes in the Structure and Location of the Meat-and-Fish Processing Industries," in *Any Way You Cut It: Meat Processing and Small-Town America*, ed. Donald D. Stull, Michael J. Broadway, and David Griffith (Lawrence: University Press of Kansas, 1995), pp. 19–22; Donald D. Stull and Michael J. Broadway, "Killing Them Softly: Work in Meatpacking Plants and What It Does to Workers," in *Any Way You Cut It*, pp. 64–70; "Meatpacking in the U.S.: Still a 'Jungle' Out There?" Public Broadcasting System program *NOW*, week of De-

cember 15, 2006, www.pbs.org/now/shows/250/meat-packing.html; Dennis Farney, "A Town in Iowa Finds Big New Packing Plant Destroys Its Old Calm," *Wall Street Journal*, April 3, 1990.

28. Julia Preston, "Child Labor Charges Are Sought Against Kosher Meat Plant in Iowa," *New York Times*, August 6, 2008, p. A15; Thomas Frank, "Captives of the Meatpacking Archipelago," *Wall Street Journal*, August 6, 2008; Julia Preston, "After Raid, Federal Charges for Ex-C.E.O. at Meatpacker," *New York Times*, October 31, 2008.

Chapter 7: The Instant Cities of the Good War

1. The Census Bureau quote appears in Marilynn S. Johnson, *The Second Gold Rush: Oakland and the East Bay in World War II* (Berkeley: University of California Press, 1993), p. 2; the armed forces number appears in George Q. Flynn, *The Mess in Washington: Manpower Mobilization in World War II* (Westport, CT: Greenwood Press, 1979), p. 190; American Social History Project, *Who Built America*, vol. 2 (New York: Pantheon Books, 1992), pp. 445–446; Richard Polenberg, *War and Society: The United States, 1941–1945* (Philadelphia and New York: J. B. Lippincott Co., 1972), pp. 11–20, 140.

2. John Dos Passos, *State of the Nation* (Boston: Houghton Mifflin Co., 1944), pp. 92–94, 301–302.

3. "Richmond Took a Beating," *Fortune*, February 1945, pp. 262–264; Kevin Starr, *Embattled Dreams: California in War and Peace, 1940–1950* (Oxford and New York: Oxford University Press, 2002), pp. 146–147; Mark S. Foster, *Henry J. Kaiser: Builder in the American West* (Austin: University of Texas Press, 1989), pp. 69–71.

4. Foster, *Henry J. Kaiser*, pp. 72–73; Johnson, *The Second Gold Rush*, pp. 83–86, 124, 147–148; "Richmond Took a Beating," p. 267.

5. Joseph Fabry, *Swing Shift: Building the Liberty Ships* (San Francisco: Strawberry Hill Press, 1982), p. 16; William Martin Camp, *Skip to My Lou* (Garden City, NY: Doubleday, Doran & Co, 1945), p. 343.

6. Starr, *Embattled Dreams*, pp. 146–147; Foster, *Henry J. Kaiser*, pp. 82–88; Johnson, *The Second Gold Rush*, pp. 62–65.

7. Foster, *Henry J. Kaiser*, pp. 6–64, 114–117; Starr, *Embattled Dreams*, p. 145; John Gunther, *Inside U.S.A.* (New York: New Press, 1997), p. 69.

8. Foster, *Henry J. Kaiser*, pp. 13, 15–17, 35; "Richmond Took a Beating," p. 265.

9. Johnson, *The Second Gold Rush*, pp. 87–101; "Richmond Took a Beating," pp. 262–264; Foster, *Henry J. Kaiser*, p. 73.

10. Foster, *Henry J. Kaiser*, pp. 56–57, 73; Johnson, *The Second Gold Rush*, pp. 34, 46–79, 124; Chester Himes, *If He Hollers Let Him Go* (New York: Da Capo Press, 1945).

11. Gunther, *Inside U.S.A.*, p. 71; Johnson, *The Second Gold Rush*, pp. 39, 198–200;

12. "Richmond Took a Beating," p. 268; Johnson, *The Second Gold Rush*, pp. 199–223.

13. Kevin Starr, *Golden Dreams: California in an Age of Abundance, 1950–1963* (Oxford and New York: Oxford University Press, 2009), pp. 11–12.

14. Foster, *Henry J. Kaiser*, pp. 216–218; Kaiser Permanente's own account of its history can be found at http://xnet.kp.org/newscenter/aboutkp/historyofkp.html.

15. Charles W. Johnson and Charles O. Jackson, *City Behind a Fence: Oak Ridge, Tennessee, 1942–1946* (Knoxville: University of Tennessee Press, 1981), pp. xix–xx, 8–28, 41, 139; Peter Bacon Hales, *Atomic Spaces: Living on the Manhattan Project* (Urbana: University of Illinois Press, 1997), pp. 128–129, 176–180; George O. Robinson, *The Oak Ridge Story* (Kingsport, TN: Southern Publishers, 1950), pp. 45, 49, 68–70.

16. Richard Rhodes, *The Making of the Atomic Bomb* (New York: Simon & Schuster, 1986), pp. 312–315; quotes regarding Groves are from Major General K. D. Nichols, *The Road to Trinity* (New York: William Morrow & Co., 1987), p. 108, and Johnson and Jackson, *City Behind a Fence*, p. 4.

17. William Lawren, *The General and the Bomb: A Biography of General Leslie R. Groves, Director of the Manhattan Project* (New York: Dodd, Mead & Co., 1988), pp. 43–60; Rhodes, *The Making of the Atomic Bomb*, pp. 407, 424–426, 454, 487; Stephen M. Younger, *The Bomb: A New History* (New York: Ecco, 2009), pp. 14–15, 21–22; Hales, *Atomic Spaces*, p. 134; Robinson, *The Oak Ridge Story*, pp. 44–45.

18. Hales, *Atomic Spaces*, pp. 50–57, 60; Robinson, *The Oak Ridge Story*, pp. 22–25.

19. Rhodes, *The Making of the Atomic Bomb*, pp. 490–494, 547; Robinson, *The Oak Ridge Story*, p. 48; Johnson and Jackson, *City Behind a Fence*, pp. 8–10, 21–23; Nichols, *The Road to Trinity*, p. 149; Stephane Groueff, *Manhattan Project: The Untold Story of the Making of the Atomic Bomb* (Boston: Little, Brown, 1967), pp. 239–244, 313–337.

20. Johnson and Jackson, *City Behind a Fence*, pp. 21–23, 32, 52, 87–79, 111; Robinson, *The Oak Ridge Story*, pp. 48–49; Hales, *Atomic Spaces*, pp. 81–90, 109–113; Nichols, *The Road to Trinity*, 58–59, 124–128, 159.

21. Johnson and Jackson, *City Behind a Fence*, p. 28; Robinson, *The Oak Ridge Story*, pp. 45, 70; Hales, *Atomic Spaces*, pp. 176–177, 218–221; Nichols, *The Road to Trinity*, p. 131; Russell B. Olwell, *At Work in the Atomic City: A Labor and Social History of Oak Ridge, Tennessee* (Knoxville: University of Tennessee Press, 2004), pp. 42–61; Jay Walz, "Atom Bombs Made in 3 Hidden 'Cities,'" *New York Times*, August 7, 1945, p. 1.

22. Groueff, *Manhattan Project*, p. 346.

23. Johnson and Jackson, *City Behind a Fence*, pp. 65–77; Robinson, *The Oak Ridge Story*, pp. 52–53, 94–96; Hales, *Atomic Spaces*, pp. 226–238; Lawren, *The General and the Bomb*, p. 154.

24. Rhodes describes the debate over the bomb's use in *The Making of the Atomic Bomb*, pp. 617–649; Stimson's diary is quoted in Nichols, *The Road to Trinity*, p. 165.

25. Robinson, *The Oak Ridge Story*, pp. 106–107; "Atom Bombs Made in 3 Hidden 'Cities'"; Olwell, *At Work in the Atomic City*, p. 67; Rhodes, *The Making of the Atomic Bomb*, pp. 734–735; Hales, *Atomic Spaces*, pp. 356–359.

26. Johnson and Jackson, *City Behind a Fence*, pp. 167, 185, 204–205; Robinson, *The Oak Ridge Story*, pp. 49, 101, 128–129; Olwell, *At Work in the Atomic City*, pp. 70–71, 100, 131; Daniel Lang, "The Atomic City," *New Yorker*, September 29, 1945; "Stopover at Oak Ridge: Atomic City Attracts Increasing Number of Drivers on Cross-Country Tours," *New York Times*, October 14, 1951; "Nuclear Sites May Be Toxic in Perpetuity, Report Finds," *New York Times*, August 8, 2000, p. A16; "Work on Weapons Affected Health, Government Says," *New York Times*, July 15, 1999, p. A12; William Yardley, "No More Bomb-Making, but Work Aplenty," *New York Times*, September 11, 2008; Oak Ridge National Laboratory Web site, www.ornl.gov; Wikipedia entry for Oak Ridge, Tennessee, http://en.wikipedia.org/wiki/Oak _Ridge,_Tennessee.

27. Gilbert Millstein, "No Atomic Jitters in the Atomic Capital," *New York Times Magazine*, November 25, 1951.

28. "National Briefing South: Tennessee: Nuclear Weapons Plant to Reopen," *New York Times*, March 15, 2003.

Chapter 8: A World Transformed

1. Futurama sound track and film at www.youtube.com/watch?v=74cO9X4 NMb4.

2. Joel Garreau, *Edge City: Life on the New Frontier* (New York: Doubleday, 1991), p. 26; Don Graf, *Convenience for Research: Buildings for the Bell Telephone Laboratory Inc., Murray Hill, New Jersey* (New York: Voorhees, Walker, Foley and Smith, Architects and Engineers, 1944); Jeremy Bernstein, *Three Degrees Above Zero: Bell Labs in the Information Age* (New York: Charles Scribner's Sons, 1984), pp. viii, 7–9, 173; David W. Dunlap, "The Office as Architectural Touchstone," *New York Times*, March 2, 2008; Truman A. Hartshorn, "Industrial/Office Parks: A New Look For the City," *Journal of Geography* 62 (March 1973): 33.

3. William H. Whyte, *City: Rediscovering the Center* (New York: Doubleday, 1988), pp. 290–306, 341.

4. FedEx's facility is described in Barbara E. Hampton, "Why Corporate Campuses Make Sense in All Economic Conditions," *Site Selection* (January 2002): 49.

5. "Destination: Kohler" Web site, www.destinationkohler.com/hotel/tac/tac _index.html.

6. Walter H. Uphoff, *Kohler on Strike: Thirty Years of Conflict* (Boston: Beacon Press, 1966), pp. 3–28, 35–95, 124–158, 201, 257–316, and passim; "Labor Notes:

What Is News" and Gunnar Mickelson, "The Kohler Myth Dies," *The Nation*, August 15, 1934; "Kohler's Paternalism Policy Fails to Head Off Labor Trouble," *Business-Week*, May 24, 1952; for an example of Herbert Kohler's public statements see the widely circulated *Can a Free Economy Tolerate Union Violence? An Address Given by Herbert V. Kohler, President of Kohler Co., Given Before the Economic Club of Detroit, February 25, 1957* (Kohler, WI: Kohler Co., n.d.).

7. "Kohler Appeals NLRB Order to Reinstate Most Strikers; Union Asks More Rehiring," *Wall Street Journal*, August 29, 1960; "Kohler, Union Agree on First Pact Since Strike Began in 1954," *Wall Street Journal*, October 1, 1962; "Kohler's 11-Year Dispute with UAW Terminated by Pay, Pension Accord," *Wall Street Journal*, December 20, 1965.

8. "Grandson of Founder of Kohler Co. Named Its Chairman and Chief," *Wall Street Journal*, June 30, 1972; "Golf Journal: The Way a Golf Trip Ought to Be," *Wall Street Journal*, July 8, 2006; "Golf Journal: The Vanity Project for Golf Fanatics," *Wall Street Journal*, August 19, 2006; "How Much Is That Faucet in the Honeymoon Suite? Kohler, Cuisinart, Viking Step Up Marketing Efforts Via Company-Owned Resorts," *Wall Street Journal*, December 27, 2005; "Kohler Seeks to Expand His Course-Building Horizons," *Milwaukee Journal Sentinel*, July 4, 2007.

9. Scott Kilman, "Family Squabble Brews at Kohler Over Control," *Wall Street Journal*, March 23, 1998; John H. Christy and Shlomo Reifman, "The Importance of Being Private," *Forbes*, November 29, 2004.

10. See Barry Bluestone and Bennett Harrison, *The Deindustrialization of America: Plant Closings, Community Abandonment, and the Dismantling of Basic Industry* (New York: Basic Books, 1982); "Travel: Vacation Paradise on a Factory Floor," *Wall Street Journal*, July 7, 1995; Hershey information is available at the company's Web site, www.hersheys.com/discover/museum.asp

11. A good description of Oak Ridge sights may be found at http://physics -history.suite101.com/article.cfm/tour_the_secret_city_of_oak_ridge; Jeff Schlegel, "Unspoiled Nature in Shadow of Nuclear Site," *New York Times*, September 4, 2009.

12. A blueprint of the Google installation accompanies Ginger Strand, "Keyword: Evil," *Harper's Magazine*, March 2008; John Foley, "Google's Data Center Strategy Revealed . . . At the Rotary Club," *Information Week's Google Weblog*, November 30, 2007, www.informationweek.com/blog/main/archives/2007/11/googles_data_ce.html; Randall Stross, *Planet Google: One Company's Audacious Plan to Organize Everything We Know* (New York: Free Press, 2008), pp. 55–59; Kathy Gray, "Port Deal with Google to Create Jobs," *The Dalles Chronicle*, February 16, 2005; John Markoff and Saul Hansell, "Hiding in Plain Sight, Google Seeks More Power," *New York Times*, June 8, 2006. In addition to The Dalles facility, other Google data centers are near Lenoir, North Carolina; Goose Creek, South Carolina; Pryor, Oklahoma; and Council Bluffs, Iowa.

13. Peter Burrows, "Servers as High as an Elephant's Eye," *BusinessWeek*, June 12, 2006; Strand, "Keyword: Evil."

14. Press release at www.stirlingenergy.com/pdf/2008-06-30.pdf; www.bright sourceenergy.com; Matthew L. Wald, "Two Large Solar Power Plants Are Planned in California," *New York Times*, August 15, 2008.

15. Kate Galbraith, "Schwarzenegger Orders Increase in Renewable Energy Use," *New York Times*, September 16, 2009; John Carey, "Solar's Day in the Sun," *BusinessWeek*, October 15, 2007.

16. http://greenwombat.blogs.fortune.cnn.com/2009/01/28/wind-jobs-outstrip -the-coal-industry; Rebecca Smith, "Where the Jobs Are: As the Renewable-power Industry Takes Off, So Does the Demand for Green-Collar Workers," *Wall Street Journal*, March 24, 2008; Abengoa's Web site is at www.abengoasolar.com/corp/web/ en/abengoa_solar_ist/our_projects/arizona/index.

Conclusion: A Tale of Two Cities

1. Printed as preface to Nathan Appleton, *Introduction of the Power Loom and Origin of Lowell* (Lowell, MA: B. H. Penhallow, 1858).

2. Milton Friedman, "The Social Responsibility of Business Is to Increase Its Profits," *New York Times Magazine*, September 13, 1970.

3. Rosabeth Moss Kanter, *SuperCorp: How Vanguard Companies Create Innovation, Profits, Growth, and Social Good* (New York: Crown Business, 2009).

4. The Stanford journal may be found online at www.ssireview.org; the Momentum conferences are described at www.momentumconference.org/index.php?id=1159; Wharton's social-entrepreneurship efforts are described at http://www.wharton.upenn .edu/social/centers-initiatives.cfm

5. Michael Kinsley, ed., *Creative Capitalism: A Conversation with Bill Gates, Warren Buffett, and Other Business Leaders* (New York: Simon & Schuster, 2009); Nancy F. Koehn, "The Time Is Right for Creative Capitalism," Harvard Business School Web site at http://hbswk.hbs.edu/item/5988.html.

PHOTO CREDITS

1 Pollard Memorial Library, Lowell, Massachusetts
2 Center for Lowell History
3 Chicago History Museum
4 New York Public Library
5 Hershey Community Archives
6 Hershey Community Archives
7 Hardy Green
8 Ben Shahn, U.S. Library of Congress
9 Lewis Hine, New York Public Library
10 Frank Leslie's Illustrated Newspaper
11 Hinson History Room, Kannapolis Branch, Cabarrus County Public Library
12 Hinson History Room, Kannapolis Branch, Cabarrus County Public Library
13 Hinson History Room, Kannapolis Branch, Cabarrus County Public Library
14 Lewis Hine, New York Public Library
15 New York Public Library
16 Calumet Regional Archives, Indiana University Northwest
17 Bartlesville Area History Museum
18 Bartlesville Area History Museum
19 Kaiser Permanente Heritage Archive
20 Ann Rosener, U.S. Office of War Information
21 New York Public Library
22 Ed Wescott, National Archives and Records Administration
23 Postcard produced by Standard Souvenirs & Novelties Inc., Knoxville, Tennessee

INDEX